NEW JOY

Response to a Changing World

GITTY STOLIK

PRAISE FOR NEW JOY

New Joy adds new insights to the discussion about Simcha. I recommend this book to anyone looking for direction and tools to enhance the simcha in their life. Simcha is the key to, not only personal redemption, but also global Redemption through Moshiach.

Rabbi Shloma Majeski, educator and author of the popular book *The Chassidic Approach to Joy*

In reading *New Joy*, one feels that it is truly possible to live with Simcha. Not only does the author show us the importance of joy in our lives but more so, she demonstrates how to implement it. I strongly urge this book as necessary reading as a lifeline for spiritual and material success.

Rabbi Chaim Dalfin, prolific author and mentor

First published 2018

Copyright © 2018 by Gitty Stolik

All rights reserved

ISBN: 978-1-56871-622-0

Published by
Targum Publishers
Shlomo ben Yosef 131a/1
Jerusalem 9380581
editor@targumpublishers.com
www.targumpublishers.com

Distributed by
Ktav Publishers & Distributors Inc.
527 Empire Blvd.
Brooklyn, NY 11225-3121
Tel: 718-972-5449, 201-963-9524
Fax: 718-972-6307, 201-963-0102
www.ktav.com

Jacket and cover design by Batsheva Lubin
Book layout by Rashi Marcus

Printed in Israel

Dedicated to my grandchildren who are making our world a more joyful place. May we be joy-filled role models for them as grandparents are meant to be.

TABLE OF CONTENTS

Section I. Who Knows Joy?

Section II. What is Joy? Prisms of Joy

Section III. How to? The Joy Production Center

Section IV. Why? The Jewish Joy Imperative

Section V. It's Jewish to be Joyous

Section VI. The Payoffs

Section VII. Spanning History

INTRODUCTION

Every book begins with a first page. This book begins with a single page – on a wall. Many years ago, one of my sons had brought home a simple black-and-white enlarged-text printout featuring a most exciting and revolutionary statement excerpted from a talk of the Lubavitcher Rebbe, Rabbi Menachem Mendel Schneerson:

> "We've done everything we can to bring Moshiach – including plenty of Tehillim (Psalms). There's one thing we haven't tried yet, and now is the time to try it: A specific kind of joy – pure joy. That will bring Moshiach!"[1]

The excerpt finished with these tantalizing words: "Go ahead, **try it and you'll see!**"

That bold quote about pure, unqualified joy as the new, futuristic way of life just had to hang on the "Happy Wall" in my dinette. The printout was placed right next to the "Recipe for a Happy Home" where it remained for several years until it became tattered. Rather than dispose of it, I reverently tucked it away in my file cabinet. Every time I open the drawer to file my humdrum statements and bills, the joyous potential of that page beams its joy out at me.

I didn't start writing this book then, but the seeds were sown. It wasn't until years later, when I experienced a revealing moment about the powers of humor, laughter and joy, that I was hooked on sharing the potency of joy in our times (as described in my first book *It's Okay to Laugh, Seriously*).

Admittedly, I began this project with a superficial and modest perception about the concept of joy, but my research into the rich resources of our wise Rabbis, who know more about joy than I ever imagined, added layers of depth. If Joy is Divine, then scholars who delve into the Divine worlds through Kabbalah and Chassidus are closest to intuiting its source. I say "intuiting" because the essence and source of Divine joy is beyond our grasp.

A topic like joy, I discovered, prompts a great deal of soul-searching, and it propelled me to explore not only my own inner self but also to engage the people who crossed my path. My Shabbos guests were prime targets, the perfect captive audience for my existential, investigative questions. "You chose a difficult topic!" one guest commented. She was right, but I was too invested to let anything stop me!

In particular I was exploring the mystery of "pure joy," the phrase used by the Lubavitcher Rebbe – *"Pure joy...will bring Moshiach!"* and it lured me deeper and deeper.

I followed joy all the way up to the Heavens, and I came to understand that its source is shrouded in the deepest recesses of G-dliness. The deeper we go, the simpler and purer joy becomes. The Essence of G-d (*Atzmus*) is simple (*pashut*). However, G d's simple Oneness is far from simple for us humans to apprehend! As I worked my way through complex descriptions of Supernal Pleasure and its intricate relationship with Supernal Joy, I felt that I was trespassing in worlds beyond my ken. With a mere word I could, G-d forbid, misrepresent the truth that was there. In perusing these esoteric sources I often felt like an elephant learning Chumash.

Ah, we were getting so serious. A little humor expands the mind. The sage Rabba would preface his lectures with humor to open his students' minds to receive his teachings. In my first book, we explored the depth and breadth of laughter and humor, and we laughed our way through it. Now that we are loosened up, we are ready to receive, to delve into the stunning depth and breadth of deeply-rooted joy, and to sample its pure delight. Laughter and humor are the appetizers. Joy is the main dish.

A Journey and a Destination

I saw a sign in a travel agent's window that read: *"Joy is not a destination. It is a journey."* It is indeed an epic journey – the longest, most interesting, and most turbulent journey ever travelled. Mankind was created in a state of joy and bliss, and will end it in a state of greater joy, in a world illuminated with everlasting joy. So, joy is a journey *and* a destination.

It's a journey from "joy to shining joy," but yet an ultra-serious one. There are so many detours – the forty-year sojourn in the desert was just the first of many to come. So many potholes, so many traffic jams. We seem to be stuck in one for a long time. Trapped in galus (exile). Beset by terrorism, illness, pandemics. Crime. Breakdown of morality. Global warming.

We're stuck. Who will break these galus walls? Will it just "happen"?

We actually can impact the walls of galus. Revolutionary discoveries in the world of physics and science demonstrate the power we wield. Observership has become an accepted concept in quantum mechanics: By consciously observing something we determine its state.[2]

We, the people, make things happen in this universe of ours.

We can impact our reality by the way we regard it. Our very thoughts make a difference. The observership concept breathes new life into our role as "partners in creation" and into the pivotal role of man-power (just when we thought we were losing it to computers). We can speed things up! We are co-creators of reality.

> *"On the verse, 'Zion – there are none who seek her out,'[3] our Sages comment: "This indicated that one should seek her out," implying that we must demand the Redemption. Similarly, we must seek out joy, including the ultimate joy, the joy of the Redemption. We must demand that G-d grant us the consummate joy of the Era of the Redemption."[4]*

Rabbis from all sectors have made it clear that today we are so close to Moshiach that we can hear his footsteps.[5] The secular world, too, seems to be picking up the vibes and signals: "We're upending the natural order and embracing new realities," proclaimed the editor of a contemporary periodical. The world as we know it is coming to an end. Admittedly, I thought that the world was coming to an end many a time, like when the taxi to the airport didn't show, the caterer was late, my wallet went missing, or an engagement broke off – but it didn't. The world as we know it *is* coming to an end – but not the good parts. Only the parts we don't need. The misery. The illness. The strife.

In the pages of this book, I've collected particles of many kinds of joy. The atoms of joy were analyzed under the microscopic lens of Torah enlightened by Chassidus and Kabbalah and tested in the laboratory of life, all so we can fill our lives with millions of molecules of joy, and thus help make change happen.

Since I embarked on compiling this book, I suddenly started to see joy everywhere. I was becoming hyper-aware of the threads of joy woven throughout my life. My daily prayers, the Tehillim, were all suddenly shouting messages of joy. Careful listening uncovered boundless joy-messages in my daily life. A snatch of conversation on the way home from shul, a recorded message on an answering machine, a comment by a co-worker, all offered pathways to joy.

ACKNOWLEDGMENTS

couldn't have unraveled the depth and layers described in Torah, Chassidic and esoteric sources by myself. My husband and sons were priceless assets, as I probed and questioned and challenged. I thank them for taking time from their many responsibilities to share their stores of knowledge and help make sense of intricate and profound concepts. They have helped enrich this book far beyond its humble beginnings. A separate thank you is due to my sons- and daughters-in-law for being sounding boards when I needed a second opinion on delicate choices of expression.

Thanks to my wonderful family who is always ready with some joy and laughter, much needed to keep the fires of enthusiasm burning. My family generously offered to provide me with my own "laughtop" to do my book, as there was too much traffic on our one computer.

My advisors were many and I am grateful to each of them. Rabbi Shmuel Bluming, Rabbi Daniel Kahn, Rabbi Gershon Schusterman and Professor Shimon Silman for their knowledgeable input to ensure content integrity. Mrs. Sara Balkany, a simcha champion, was always there to offer a word of encouragement when needed. Chaya'le Gourarie another simcha champ, provided a wise suggestion that enhanced the book immeasurably during its fledgling phase. My manuscript went through two editing phases. Chaya Rivkah Zwolinski, Mimi Hecht, Lisa Mitchell, Chanie Banishewitz,

Yocheved Lerner, and Mushky Sandhaus ushered it through phase one, each leaving her imprint on various pages of the book. And then, G-d sent me a wonderful copy editor, Sharon Lite. She edited the book from page one to the finish line with expertise, sensitivity, and unflagging enthusiasm and patience. Her scientific editing background was a plus for my occasional science forays.

I especially wish to express my most profound admiration and appreciation to my husband Rabbi Eli Stolik, the resident scholar, my most invaluable resource, may he be well. It is a blessing to have someone close by who can answer questions and locate sources, and who knows if the ideas make sense, Torah-wise and life-wise. I write, and he "knows."

Above all, my parents and the one grandparent I knew were real-life models who palpably evinced Divine joy. I knew joy intimately through them. I, too, wanted that fullness and richness of life; my first encounter with my grandfather enticed me with the delight of fully-articulated joy. My parents and grandfather authenticated that joy when they continued to live joyously regardless of challenges. Probably, davka because there were challenges. If not for them, this book would not be. From them I learned to:

> Be Happy – Because I have so much to be grateful for.
> Be Happy – Even when there are zssminmany reasons not to be.
> Be Happy – Because I'm a Jew.

I pray to G-d that whatever I write does not deviate from the truth and through it I do my small part to help lead us forward to our final joyous destination.

In compiling the material for this book, I have reaped a wonderful by-product. I have deepened my own capacity for joy and formed new and better pathways of thinking. If only for that, this huge project has already proven its worth. I am grateful to the One Above for guiding me through the process. Joy is transformative. Take my word for it, transformation is enticing, and enticing things should be shared.

Section I:

Who Knows Joy?

People ask me, "What got you started on joy?" and I ask myself the same question. All my life I knew that there was a better way to live than just muddling through life. Someday I would learn to sail serenely over the bumps of life, smile my way through its negative spaces and avoid being swallowed by its black holes of self-absorption. Someday, I would master the art of heart-expanding, joyous living.

Doesn't everyone share the same ambition? Isn't attraction to joy universal?

Maybe it was a result of the fancy quotes and plaques about joy that I got as gifts or mementos, which I duly pinned on my wall or slipped into my wallet. Happy walls and wallets have a way of getting under your skin and affecting you subliminally.

Doesn't everyone have their own collection of treasured quotes? And wouldn't everyone be likewise affected? So, what motivated me to dedicate countless hours writing and promoting joy?

Perhaps my captivation with joy can be traced back to a childhood memory...

1

Glimpse of a Joy-Genius
How I Know Joy – My Joy Roots

"Gitele," called the distinguished man with the snow-white beard, as he looked up from the large Gemara resting on the dining room table. I was sprawled on the couch, engrossed in a reading assignment.

"Yes, Zeide?" I jumped up, ready and eager to do his bidding.

I was thirteen years old when I first met my grandfather, Zeide Bentzion, a devout Belzer chassid. Although I was just getting to know him, my heart was brimming with love for this dignified, endearing man. His demeanor exuded a sense of positivity, a perpetual hint of a laugh brewing.

He had made the journey from Israel for his first grandchild's wedding together with the choson (groom) and the choson's family. What a lucky break that this wedding would be taking place on our side of the world. My father's immediate family all lived together in Bnei Brak, and I would be meeting them for the first time. We happily squeezed over to accommodate the wedding party of five in our cozy Brooklyn apartment.

Did he need a cup of tea? Did he want me to find him a specific sefer (book), or send a message to someone? I'd noticed that, except for the occasional break to eat or take a nap, my grandfather learned Torah constantly. Why this sudden interruption from his studies?

"Gitele, my dear child, look up and see – we are sitting in this room and we are warm and dry. There are no leaks; it is not raining in, thank G-d."

If he had told me the ceiling was about to fall in, I couldn't have been more surprised.

Up until that day, I found happiness in things like friends, good food and fun activities. It never occurred to my adolescent mind that I should take time to be appreciative and happy simply because things were running the way they should.

That one statement opened a new window in my formative weltanschauung, my outlook. It unfurled a new roadmap for life, a sense that we are never really excused from happiness because no matter what happens, we can always find gratitude in the many things that are going the way we want.

My zeide's life was by no means easy. He lost three wives, a set of twins, and buried several stillborn babies. But nothing could destroy my zeide's commitment to serving G-d with joy. On the contrary, when the chips were down, his joy seemed to go up.

> Sometimes, when we are down, G-d sends someone our way who seems to be in a more pitiable state than we are. Then we think, "I am so blessed!" Not that we're building our happiness on someone's misery, but the encounter serves as a reminder of our many blessings.
>
> Alternately our spirits lift when we regain the use of a gift after we'd lost it, such as feeling good about a functioning washing machine after it was repaired.
>
> My grandfather was happy over regular daily occurrences. He did not have to look at someone more miserable than himself. He did not have to regain a lost gift. He just looked at the ceiling.
>
> He gave me a lifetime gift: He turned "nothing special's going on" into "something special is always going on."

I will always remember my grandfather's display of joy at that first grandchild's wedding, when he clambered onto a table during the dancing. Family members and guests tried to stop him. He was, after all, in his seventies at the time, but he ignored them. They had good reason to be concerned, the way he stomped on that table. He was not a light-footed dancer.

It was an amazing sight. No, it was not his dancing skills that astounded me. It was his welling over of simcha and exhilaration such as I had never seen. He was literally drunk with delight. The glee spilled out from within, accompanied by a lilting ripple of laughter elevating in pitch as if he were exulting over winning a multi-million-dollar lottery, or hearing that the war was over. But it was not mashkeh he was high on. He was simply intoxicated with joyous gratitude.

Six years later, he came to America again for my own wedding. Now, a day before my wedding and in that same living-dining room where he had previously set me straight about life, he cradled my cheeks in his worn hands, adorned with painful cracks – souvenirs of the raw Siberian winters that had reappeared in New York's wintry weather. He chortled, "Gitele, Gitele!" accompanied by his trademark exulting laugh. It was raw joy (and I thought only grief could be raw). I marveled again at how this man translated life. It was a wordless life lesson.

And once again, to my amazement and delight, at almost eighty years of age, he climbed up onto one of those shaky round tables to dance and stomp out his ecstasy and gratitude. I'm told that he did so at every grandchild's wedding until he passed away, well into his nineties.

I never had to read about joy to discover what it was. The table-dancing scene was more eloquent than a thousand words.

My zeide, as I remember, was a whiz at mental math. More importantly, he was a whiz at the math of life. He did his calculations differently than most others. His losses did not diminish his daily joy. On the contrary, every deduction was balanced with an addition. Every tragedy that brought him into the negative zone provided that much more proof that joyous occasions are rare treasures and should be cherished, and that every breathing moment should be exploited.

People who suffer losses in their lives often schlep their emotional baggage wherever they go. When they finally have an occasion to rejoice, they let their heavy history subtract from their current joy. The person who remains is a chastened remnant of his original self. The difficult times have taken their toll.

A joy-genius realizes that the more difficult good things are to come by, the more we can relish every gift we get.

Here and there we find these veritable joy-geniuses who seem to have drunk from the fountain of eternal joy. Wouldn't it be wonderful if we all could respond to life's curve balls as my grandfather did?

Genius is defined as the ability to entertain two contradictory truths, as joy and grief, at the same time. *Gadlus hamochin* is "a mind capable of integrating even opposing concepts."[6] My zeide suffered and grieved like anyone else when tragedy struck, but he was able to clear a space in his mind and heart and move decisively and proactively back to a joyous setting.

> *I think I've spotted a joy-genius in the making: Four-year-old Rivkah was old enough to be articulate but young enough to enjoy some mischief. Caught in the act with Mommy's make-up all over her face, she brightly pointed out to her mother, "Baruch Hashem (thank G-d) it's not on my neck!" (She is a fifth-generation granddaughter of Zeide Bentzion.)*

In contrast:

> *A client called her financial planner each time the market dipped, moaning about the sorry, sagging state of her invest-ments. "Look at the market!" the panicked investor would hiss. Her financial planner told her, "Look, I don't mind that you call me when the market's down, as long as you also call me when your statements record a period of growth."*

We are programmed to look for what's wrong and react to it, rather than what's right. Would you react differently from this client? Which of the two stories best illustrates your typical response?

> A great joy-genius strategy is developing the art of seeing how the situation is better than it might have been.
>
> ☹ What a lousy cold!
>
> ☺ Lucky I didn't get the cold last week when I was flying.
>
> ☹ Oh, it's raining.
>
> ☺ Thank G-d it's not pouring.
>
> ☹ It's pouring!
>
> ☺ Lucky it's not snowing; at least we can get around.
>
> ☹ Oww, I have a boo-boo!
>
> ☺ Tsk...tsk...I know, it hurts... Lucky you don't have two boo-boos! (I hope I remember, when a dozen eggs break all over my floor, to cheerfully declare, "Lucky it wasn't two dozen!")

I wonder...did my grandfather get up one day and make a willful decision to live this way? Psychologists are divided over whether genius is innate or acquired. If it is innate, why couldn't I have inherited that wonderful gene from my zeide? Instead, I wasted energy feeling sorry for myself over real or imagined deprivation. I didn't handle it very gracefully when my neatly laid out plans for the day, or for my life, were disrupted. I fretted and fussed over issues that, in retrospect, were petty. And I'm still a work in progress. Aren't we all?

...And the Rest of Us: The In-Between'ers

Most of us are not joy-geniuses, but neither are we perpetual pessimists. We are somewhere in the middle of the joy continuum – we are not always soaring and we are not always sinking. We form a "middle class" of joyous living. You and I, and most people reading this book, probably fall into this category. We may be essentially happy people with occasional ups and downs, coasting along in neutral (*same-old...*), maybe a bit jaded. Hardly as vitally alive as those unique joy-geniuses who warm us to our very toes when we meet them.

We middle-class joy'ers have our issues. We need more time to regroup from life's punches. We firmly resolve that we will be strong and that we will surf through life from now on – until the next wave comes and washes our resolution away.

For many of us, joy seems to be based on preconditions. Most of us will recognize ourselves in this more typical "middle class" as we "if" and sniff our way through life.

"*If* I could just find the right (or any) job, I would be the happiest person."

"*If* that deal came through, I would be happy forever."

"*If* only the scale would register three pounds less, I would jump for joy."

"Those kids...*if* they would only stop fighting, it would make my day.

"*If* my son got accepted into that class, it would put me on a high."

"*If* only those noisy neighbors would move out."

"*If* you would call me just once during the day to check on me, you know what a lift that would give me!"

"*If* only I could be married to the right person (who would surely call me during the day)."

If only I could live life brimming with joy!

Whatever joy is left after the *if onlys* inflict their damage, the "*what if*" worriers can finish off. *What if* the child is late...the husband didn't call...I'm laid off... The fear of what might happen robs a great deal of the enjoyment right out of our lives.

"If only" our happiness would flow steadily like an escalator that keeps moving upward evenly and serenely. We of the "middle class" often feel like we're attempting to go up the down escalator. We keep climbing, but we're barely keeping even.

Joy-geniuses and middle-class joy'ers each enjoy an intimate relationship with joy. We either have it or we want it!

The Galus Guarantee

It's easier to be happy when you don't have any problems. But – who doesn't have problems?

We run from the doctor's office because of that new back pain, to the lawyer's office for legal advice for that sticky situation we're dealing with. We make a stop at the bank to hold the checks, and then to the mechanic, again, for that lemon of a car.

The problem with problems is that they create another problem: a negative climate that interferes with our ability to live a full and expansive life. And these problems of assorted weights and sizes define our lives. Those problems are designed and orchestrated to last as long as the galus does – I call it *the Galus Guarantee*. It's not all bad, but a jumble of good and bad stuff.

☺ Sarah was so excited to share her good news with her husband. The day she received confirmation of her second pregnancy was also the day that ☹ her husband received his MS diagnosis.[7]

☺ Michael and Aliza were on a grand tour in Europe, a landmark anniversary trip. ☹ Aliza tripped on the cobblestones and broke a leg. She was in a foreign country, with a foreign language. That was not the "trip" she had in mind.

☺ It was a beautiful bar-mitzvah. Berel and Batya were so proud of their son's performance and a wonderful time was had by all. ☹ They came home to find that their home had been burglarized.

Not everything has a bad ending, of course. Nasty surprises can have surprisingly happy endings.

☹ Tehila had to move out of her apartment by the end of the month, but her new place would not be available until the next morning. She loaded her personal belongings into her car and went to sleep at a friend's house. All of her clothing was stolen from her car trunk during the night. ☺ On the very same date, exactly one year later, she got engaged.

That's life. A tug-of-war between hope and despair, celebration and frustration, moments of jubilation followed by disasters unforeseen. We don't even notice how we bob back and forth between the conflicting emotions. We're too busy trying to keep a neuro-signal ahead of anxiety, stress, worries, and fears. What will our crowning achievement of life be? "He lived...because he was afraid to die." "She was a person of remarkable caliber; she survived – excelled! – in stress for eighty years."

> Since Adam and Chava ate from the forbidden fruit, the Good and the Bad became mixed. When we focus on the good, we give it ascendancy. Joy expresses that focus.

Joy is our rescue boat. A smattering of joy provides a lifeline to hang on to and help us pull through. That little bit of joy keeps us afloat. We won't necessarily soar, but we won't sink.

That's the way it's been until now. Don't you think it's time for a change?

2

The Joy We Know

The Strengths and Flaws of Our Current Joy System

What needs to change?

There are just "a few" imperfections in our contemporary world that are waiting to be resolved. But there is one that has been around for so long that we have stopped noticing its limitations:

Joy – as we know it now. Galus joy.

Joy is both the easiest and hardest attainment. Easy, because people crave it and are inherently attracted to it. Hard, because joy is not stable and enduring.

There are things that just "go." The sun rises daily in the east and sets in the west. Ocean waves break reliably and unceasingly. Birds migrate south for the winter with unerring accuracy.

Joy is the all-important fuel of life. The "thing" about joy – it doesn't just "go." Short-term triggers help, but as their name implies, they have short-term duration.

We turn to joyous stimuli to help regroup from life's miseries or to overcome general malaise. Joy is the analgesic that temporarily alleviates emotional angst.

"Oww, my joy-level is sinking! Quick, two laughter and humor tablets needed."

But joy is more than an antidote to distress and despair. The origin of joy is a lofty one. *Oz v'chedva bimkomo* – strength and joy are in His place.[8] The source of joy is simply Divine! (It does feel Divine, doesn't it, when we are so happy at a special event, or at a celebration close to our heart, that we are euphoric?) That's why joy has a radiance and is so attracting; it beckons because of its source. There's strength in joy. Joy has an unlimited G-dly quality to it. It is transcendent and powerful. It can break through limitations; it is not constrained by in-your-face realities.

Joy is Divine. Sounds good...and sounds right! So we want lots of it, and we want it all the time.

Wouldn't it be nice if that radiant joy consistently powered our everyday life? Instead, it's here today, gone tomorrow. Why can't joy get comfortable and stay a while? Why is joy so difficult to sustain?

It's the Galus Guarantee...

No matter how exciting the moment, eventually the feeling dissipates, the novelty of the moment wears off or something happens to intrude. My feet are "killing" me; the taxi didn't show up; the kids are grouchy. Slowly but surely, we are nudged into our everyday routine. Though we don't mean to, we often allow the little annoyances, the daily "potholes" of life to deflate our buoyancy.

The Galus Guarantee:
Joys will be diffused by oys.
Highs are bound to fade.

Galus joy: Difficult to secure and sustain

Let's follow an event where everything was going right: A festive trailer, playing infectiously lively music, was once driving slowly down our street on the festival of Purim. A team of costumed musicians was dancing on the flatbed with animated gusto. To our delight, they parked right in front of our house. All our neighbors were out, snapping pictures and videotaping the scene. Everyone was grinning from ear to ear. If this wasn't pure delight, what was? After a while, everyone went back into their houses. Sometime later, as I heard the music still blaring outdoors I began to worry that it may interfere with the babies' sleep.

Even the delight of delightfulness dribbles out! That is one of joy's imperfections – the highs fizzle out even when everything is good! Depreciation is inevitable in the galus landscape. You may have experienced variations of the following appreciation/depreciation "slides":

☺ For people in Canada, snow is not exciting, but for a family in Jerusalem it is a dream event. One day the dream event happened – it snowed! Motty and his friends had a blast with that magic white fluff. And then, another snowfall!

☹ This time, Motty wrinkled his nose when he opened the shutters. The weather was interfering with the plans he had made with his friends. *It's human nature. The fizzle-out phenomenon is inevitable.*

☺ You got married to the best guy that walked the earth. The list of his good qualities filled an entire page.

☹ Ten years later, all you see are his faults. You are hard-pressed to remember even one good quality. *The shrinkage of gratitude is subtle.*

☺ Two healthy feet don't normally excite me but regaining the use of my feet after a lengthy mobility impairment made me want to dance with joy. It really did feel as if I had gained something new.

☹ But then...I forgot about it. *We don't mean to be ungrateful, but appreciation feeds on renewal, like the novelty of the sun that emerges after several days of rain, or the restoration of one's wellbeing after being "under the weather."*

☺ Try eating your favorite dish for breakfast, lunch and dinner for days in a row.

☹ Your taste buds would acclimate and your passion for chocolate chip cookies would fade into oblivion (along with the other myriad blessings we take for granted.) *A constant delight just isn't delightful.*[9]

In the spiritual domain as well, joy is not on automatic cruise. Woven into the eternality and joy associated with Torah and mitzvahs are counterpoints of declining interest, ebbing zeal, fading passion. There are many mitzvahs that are constantly repeated, such as the daily blessings over food and prayers. We are charged to do the mitzvahs with joy, and yet the joy seems to be a brook that dries up a little here and there. There's a need to constantly refresh by continual learning. That's why we review and reignite our excitement in advance of each holiday.

If only we could hold on to joy and never let it go. But these joy embers must be stoked in order for us to live joyously the way G-d would like to see us. We don't want to be caught performing His commandments in the unenthusiastic way we write a check for a parking violation.

Almost all of the good things around us are programmed to depreciate and deplete.

I just emptied the hampers and they're filling up again. Speaking of filling up, is it lunchtime already? I'm hungry... and it's getting late, I must get supper started... Uh-oh, we're out of potatoes... Maybe I should write up my shopping list before I forget... Are there any pens around here that work?

Did you ever think what we'd do without all this busy-ness? Those distractions are G-d looking out for our happiness – don't you know busier people are happier?

Joy-genius tip: We're happy when we do what we love. Or – we could love what we're doing. It's what's in the mind that matters. We can view folding laundry as a drudgery or think loving thoughts of the people whose laundry we are folding.[10]

The shopping list: Laundry detergent/ potatoes/ pens / food!

And I just checked the cabinet... *I think my joy needs replenishing.*

What a wonderful place this world would be if we had "joy stations" where we could "fill up" every time we run low. Actually, we do, in a way. It's heartening to know that we have protectzia – "connections" – up there. Joy is, after all, Divine. This may come as a surprise to many. It reminds me of this mountain story:

> Many daring and persistent mountain climbers had tried to scale a steep and rugged mountain but none could make it to the top. After many perilous climbs and failures, one determined mountain climber finally made it. When he got to the top, he encountered a young boy playing. "How did you get here, little boy?" he asked in amazement. "I was born here."

Like the little boy on the mountain, "we were born there." We are all organically equipped with joy. We don't actually need to climb tall, faraway mountains. Our connection is not dependent on an external pipeline – we don't even need to drive to a joy station. As Jews, we are born with innate gifts. We are endowed from birth with love, awe, and joy, inherited from our forefathers and packaged within our souls. But we do have to unwrap it and avail ourselves of it.

This might be the Jewish version of a Peanuts dialogue.

> "Are you happy?"
> "No."
> "Are you sad?"
> "No, I'm normal."
> "Well, the good news is, your normal default is joy!"

If we have full-time access to a joy tank, why is it still so difficult to sustain joy day after day, through bad mood days and bad news days? Because it's not on automatic refill. (The good news is, though, we *do* control the valve. Future chapters expand on this.)

It's all planned by G-d, Who engineered every aspect of our existence with the utmost ingenuity. He built joy depleters into our world system. He rigged human nature to shrink our excitement.

And He added some science to the mix – let's call it the "gravity principle."

The Ups and Downs of The Gravity Principle

Gravity is that wonderful force that keeps us rooted to the ground rather than floating about. When it comes to our moods, on the other hand, the "gravity principle" works against us. Downs flow naturally. Ups are harder and more arduous. (Now why couldn't G-d have made it work the other way?)

This too is Divine, because...downs make you look up.

Notice how effortless it is to lose your good humor. Notice how long it takes to recover it. Sliding down takes no time. Climbing back up needs some laughter tracks, a comedy show, a new outfit, plus a gourmet meal to round it all out.

Down is always easier, as this smart little boy figured out. *"Moish, why aren't you sharing your scooter with your little brother?" "I am, Mom, half and half. I use it on the way down the hill, and he has it on the way up the hill."*

Ups and downs are part of our reality. It's comforting to know that the "ups" that follow the "downs" are more empowering even than the smooth uninterrupted journeys.

The light that follows the darkness shines brighter than it did before the darkness fell.

And, let's give ourselves some credit. We're an amazingly resilient species. We refuse to go under. We smile and grin our way through life's grimmest moments. We recover from blows and learn to laugh again. As a people, we have been doing an admirable job.

We're great mountain climbers. And I see the peak. Do you? We're practically there.

We look forward to living with the fullness of life... How appealing that sounds. But what is "fullness" of life? Is our ultimate objective only the fulfillment of our own needs?

There must be more to life than pre-occupation with our personal miseries and joys! Even if we achieve our own happiness, we will not be truly happy while everyone around us is unhappy.

Only when we have a happy world will we finally be at peace.

We are ready for an expansion of perspective, a "fuller" glimpse from the peak. Let's think big. Larger than our own immediate needs. Beyond the here and now. If we're looking for joy, let's mine it for all it's worth. Joy expands us beyond self-preoccupation. It frees us up to think about others and broadens our horizons so that we see ourselves as part of a collective. With that power, there is no limit to what we can achieve.

Follow me as we embark on a journey of expansion, discovery and joyful change.

3

No one is Telling Us What Joy Is

It seems to be complex, this joy. We have it innately, yet we lose it.

Joy is one of the deepest and most elusive mysteries of creation.

Do you know what genuine joy is? Can you describe perfect joy?

Every time I was presented with this stumper during my initial joy-discovery process, I searched frantically through my mental files, groping for a satisfying answer. Even after I'd sifted through a good amount of Torah sources on the topic of joy, when people asked me "what is *true* joy?" I found myself mystified.

True. Perfect. Authentic. Genuine. Pure. Is there any sense to those labels? Is there a specific meaning for each term?

I'm looking for products that have Genuine, Pure, Authentic, Organic on the label.
Oh, you're into health?
No, but it's so "in."
Ma'am, it's not what's on the bottle, it's what's in it!

I was on a quest to answer these questions. On my friend's enthusiastic recommendation, I downloaded a lecture by Dennis Prager, a nationally syndicated radio talk show host who has also authored a popular book called *Happiness is a Serious Problem*. I listened to samples of his weekly radio program called the "Happiness Hour." His message was novel and useful, thought-provoking and entertaining.

Mr. Prager reminds us, with his rich and practical humor, that we should not allow miserable people to bring us down. Whereas most people think pursuing happiness is an egotistical activity, he proposes that, on the contrary, it is egotistical to be **unhappy**, and we have no right to inflict our own misery on others. Even when we may be unhappy, out of consideration to others, as well as for our own benefit, we could **act as if** we were happy.

All this is useful, powerful and persuasive, but we're still left with our question: *what is happiness – or joy*?

As I mulled over the content of the talks, I realized that it is not *happiness* he and many other experts expand on, but the nastiness of *unhappiness*! What we usually hear is, *why* we're unhappy and how to get over it. I experienced a *Eureka*! moment as I gained a new understanding of the power and sway unhappiness holds in our contemporary world. We naturally relate to our current reality and experiences, and right now our lives are marked by struggle, pain and *unhappiness*.

One day, joy will be our currency. Right now we're here, deep in the galus culture. Right now, frankly, the futuristic joy of the Redemption, while appealing, is just not relevant. The language here is tzores, troubles. That may be why we talk endlessly about *lacking* joy and *needing* joy, but...

No one is telling us what joy is.

I asked Aviva, an insightful Israeli-born teacher if she can define joy. She considered the question thoughtfully. "Unhappiness is complaining...feeling sorrow. So, happiness is *no* complaining...*no* sorrow..."

"But you're using *unhappy* terms to describe happiness! Can you give me information about *happiness*?"

Aviva was stumped. "You chose a difficult topic to write about!" she conceded.

Pure, perfect joy is a mystery to us because we have never – yet – experienced it. Since Adam and Chava were evicted from Gan Eden, a series of unending troubles has been our lot.

Despite all that is written and said on the topic of joy from Torah sources, as well as a ceaseless stream of articles in all kinds of journals, people have a limited grasp of what joy actually *is*. We know about *yomtov* (holiday) joy, *simcha shel mitzvah* (joy which is attached to doing a mitzvah), chicken-soup-on-Shabbos joy, but perfect, pure joy, all on its own, is a mystery. It's part of the mystique of the unknown future.

And – this may come as a shock – but *even the eras of the Holy Temples, the height of Jewish glory, were not times of perfect joy.*[11] That's right, we've never had perfect joy! Consider this: if the world were perfect and complete during the Holy Temple eras, destruction would not have been necessary. Apparently, there was still work to be done to bring the world to its perfect state – and our joy-in-galus plays a major role in getting us there.

Perfect joy will be experienced only with the advent of the Geulah, the ultimate Redemption, when our mouths will be **filled** with laughter. Filled means **nothing** intrudes. There is no crevice left for anything but joy; the pie of joy is 100% complete. The experience of joy will be perfect, genuine, and inviolable.

Imagine a world of permanently perfect joy.

What a different world we'd live in if we went about our daily tasks and lives with ineffable happiness and undimmed exuberance. Luxuriate in that blissful vision for a moment. Here's a sample scenario: you are marrying off your daughter and there is nothing to mar the joy. All of the kallah's older siblings are happily married. There are no ill people or singles to pray for under the chuppah. And so on. There is just a totality of joy. The joy of the Geulah is this, and then some. This kind of existence was envisioned for us since Creation.

A Perfect Existence.

In addition to joy, there are three areas in which we will achieve ultimate shleimus, perfection, only when the Geulah begins.

1. **The Land of Israel.** We have never completed the process of conquering our Promised Land – three promised territories, the lands of Keini, Knizi and Kadmoni have not yet been acquired.[12] We will finally have full ownership of our Promised Land (and – ahh, secure borders)!

2. **The Torah.** Moshe was instructed to build nine cities of Refuge, but only six of them were established in his time. That means the Torah was never completely implemented – we were only keeping 612 and 2/3 of the 613 mitzvahs! The three final cities will be established when we have full access to our land.[13] And let's not forget this thrilling development: the inner dimension, the magnificent secrets of Torah will be revealed – "A new [dimension of] Torah will issue forth from me"[14] – taking our Torah-learning experience to a whole new level.[15]

3. **The Jewish nation.** The ten tribes that were lost through exile will return, the sin of Adam and Chava will be completely eradicated and Jewish lineage will be properly established. And, after Resurrection, all Jews of all generations will enjoy life together.[16]

Adam and Chava's eviction from Gan Eden opened the way for the *etzev*, sadness and suffering. Sadness is galus. *Get us out of here,* we plead.

G-d has constructed our lives and paths in ways that make joy difficult to secure and maintain, but He didn't mean for us to be trapped in sadness and suffering forever. He has an ideal world awaiting us. We have been working towards it since Adam and Chava's eviction from Gan Eden.

"Working towards it" means we have a hand in it. What can be done to bring the world to its perfect state?

We must flood our lives with more and more joy, until we outpower all vestiges of darkness.

"We must fight the darkness with great Simcha...only by add-

ing in light can we truly overtake the darkness."[17]
"Simcha...breaks through the person's limitations, the limitations of this world and the limitations imposed by this dreadful darkness of exile..."[18]

Practice joy. Increase in Simcha. Simcha is redemptive! We do not need to feel chained, passively watching the ticking clock as it creeps closer to the perfect Future. We can practice a specific kind of joy right now that has power to bring it closer. We will find out what kind of joy this is as we proceed.

4

Transition Time

G-d didn't mean for us to be trapped in a world of limited, imperfect joy forever. An ideal world awaits us.

J oyce and her fellow alumni were getting together for their thirty-year class reunion. It was exciting to meet old class-mates, each with diverse paths in life. Each had had their array of ups and downs, their individual mountains to climb. At the reunion, a speaker led a discussion on happiness, asking each one to share her happiest moment. Whatever each partici-pant offered, the speaker responded, "Well, and the day after?"

At the end the speaker explained, "You are all telling me about the happiest day of your life. No doubt each one of these was a moment of joy and elation. But what happened the next day? Are we just as high-spirited as the days, weeks and years pass?"[19]

For us, the best day is yet to come. There is a new tomorrow on our horizon, a Shabbos such as we've never experienced, a Shabbos of everlasting joy. Each passing day will surpass the preceding one.

Shabbos doesn't just show up. Every restful Shabbos oasis is preceded by a hectic Friday. Friday acts as a transition between the weekday whirl and the sanctified Shabbos world.

I love walking into a house on Friday afternoon and being greeted by the aromas of the erev Shabbos cooking, noting a rich white tablecloth spread on the table and a gleaming Shabbos candelabra ready to be lit, all in preparation for the Shabbos queen. And, we're not satisfied just to delight our olfactory and visual senses. It is a mitzvah to sample the Shabbos foods as well[20] so that the anticipatory pleasure should warm us from the inside out.

No matter what day of the week you're reading this, it's "Friday afternoon" now. And I'm going to offer you a piece of kugel. Well, sort of.

You see, there are two ways to calculate time. One is based on the seven-day cycle in which each day takes twenty-four hours. The other is based on a broader calculation – seven millennia, in which each "day" lasts one thousand years. The seventh millennium will be an everlasting Shabbos. In the year 5750 (1990) we entered the last quarter of the sixth millennium since Creation – it's Friday afternoon! In the Zohar[21] the following prediction is recorded:

> In the...sixth millennium, there will be an opening of the... gates of wisdom, preparing the world for the seventh millennium, like a person who begins to prepare himself for Shabbos on Friday, when the sun heads downwards.[22]

It's transition time now and the best is yet to come.

Just like erev Shabbos, the aura of the upcoming seventh millennium already pervades the air. The joy that will reign at that time is already casting its warm rays on us. This is not mere imagination. Just as the Shabbos foods are already available and can be tasted and enter our bloodstream before Shabbos, the joy of the Geulah is truly accessible today.

Where *is* that kugel? Why it's almost gone! Someone ate almost the entire kugel. Was it you?

Don't feel bad. It happens to me, too, every time I step into the kitchen on erev Shabbos. I start off planning to have just a sliver, but once I bite into it, my appetite kicks in, and before I know it, half the kugel is gone.

It works the same with joy. A taste of joy, the food of Geulah, kindles our craving and gets the joy emotion into motion.

Joy-in-advance is available now – as are all the calories of the kugel I downed.

Kugel is the appetite facilitator, and joy is the Geulah activator.

The piece of kugel that we enjoy erev Shabbos is a palate-pleasing, stomach-appeasing, materialistic pleasure. Somehow, though, it assists in the transition from "mundaneness" to holiness. Oh, what a long week this was...

The Midrash[23] describes the famous sage Shammai's method of preparing for Shabbos. Whenever he would see something nice, he would buy it and set it aside for Shabbos. In this way, Shabbos was a focal point of anticipation throughout the week.[24]

As you savor the fresh, sizzling-hot piece of kugel between your tongue and palate be mindful that you are enjoying your first taste of "joy-fusion" (just so there's no con-fusion – note that this will be further elaborated in Chapter 16).

There is a new joy in the air that is now available for us to tap into, more than ever before. It's got a quickened-pulse erev-Shabbos feel to it, an anticipatory pre-yomtov scent about it, a wedding-celebration-expectancy that is about to unfold. Visualize this scene: The choson and kallah are about to enter the wedding hall. Everyone is waiting with bated breath for them to appear. The moment they enter, simcha will explode with the downbeat of the music baton and the suspense of the wedding guests will erupt into a frenzy of dance.

Change...

It's Transition Time. Change can take place gradually, or it can happen in an instant. Sometimes we need to take some initiative to show how sincerely we want it, and that will bring it on.

I'm unstoppable... once I get started.

Change? Who likes change? Things are bad enough. Let's not rock the boat.

Brother, can you spare (me) the change!

Changing ourselves is hard. Many of us (the middle-class joy'ers) always aspired to achieve transcendence over our circumstances, but maybe what we really wished for were different circumstances.

It's easier to wish that our circumstances would change, rather than to change ourselves.

But there's good news: we're not only perched on the precipice of change, the world is already evolving and reflecting positive change in so many ways. In the last two hundred years, the Divine gates of wisdom have "opened" and we have seen the development of many unimaginable possibilities.

- Medical/scientific breakthroughs: stem cell therapy, laser treatment, unraveling of the human genome, neuroplasticity.
- The astounding wonders of technology: space missions and telescopes; exquisitely compact circuitry that drive our mini-devices such as our smartphones, music players and smart wristbands; satellites for communications, GPS, GoogleEarth, weather, and detection of underground systems and resources; and instant global information transmission via digital scanners and audio and video streaming.
- Scientific thinking: the Theory of Everything with its Grand Unified Theory, the String Theory, quantum physics...
- Positive psychology taps the innate strength and goodness

of man's psyche in contrast to Freud's pessimistic premise of man being ruled by his base drives.

Change awaits us just beyond the bend. But we need to take change seriously.

5

The As If Theory

One easy and powerful way we can facilitate change is with AS IF Power (powered by a piece of delicious kugel)

C hange, an ongoing project, is discussed more extensively later in the book. But we will offer a quick fix in the meantime (evoked by the plea of the overwhelmed Jew – "G-d, can you help me till you help me!").

If-only thoughts undermine our ability to enjoy our many gifts. Why suffer in the "land of lack"? Let's dispose of our unhappy *if-only'ness*. But we need not dump it all. We need only to dispose the *limiting* part and recycle what's left into a more productive partnership. *If-only* becomes ***as-if***, a joy-boosting strategy that helps us to mend the missing gaps in our lives.

> *Berel had just returned from a trip and was giving his wife a report. He told her how, while he was on the train in Europe the conductor passed by and looked at him very strangely.*
> *"Why was that?" asked his wife.*
> *"Well, he looked at me as if I had no ticket."*
> *"So what did you do?"*

"What could I do, I looked right back at him as if I did!"

Acting *as if* can really get you places. Even if something is beyond your reach, when you initiate or mimic your coveted goal, and act *as if you can do it*, you are much more likely to achieve that goal.

Are you shy? Act as if you're socially confident. Overdrawn at the bank? Act as if you're in the green. (Don't spend it, just act it.) You may be unsure of your answer but act as if you're well-prepared for class. You may be sad but act as if you're glad. Act the way you want to end up.

What people do, day after day, eventually becomes who they are.[25] We become what we practice most. An interesting halacha (law) is offered to prove this point: we are cautioned not to break the bones of the Pesach sacrifice, the Paschal lamb. The *Sefer HaChinuch* explains why: people of royalty need to eat in a more dignified manner. Unrefined eating manners will make the person become crude, since the person is drawn in the direction of his actions.

A follower of Reb Shneur Zalman, known as the Baal HaTanya, complained to him that a certain other chassid was falsely presenting himself. When he would visit the Rebbe, he would take on the appearance of a devout chassid, in contrast to how he lived otherwise. Reb Shneur Zalman responded, "In that case, then that which is quoted in the last mishnah of the Tractate Pe'ah should befall him."

This sounded really ominous, and the chassid was smitten with self-reproach at having played a role in this dire pronouncement. He immediately ran to find a Tractate Pe'ah, nervously opened it to the last page, and found that it discusses imposters: someone who does not limp, is neither blind nor mute, but pretends to be one of them, is warned that he will not leave this world until he will become one of them.[26] The relieved talebearer realized that his Rebbe had actually predicted a positive outcome, because there is a fundamental Jewish principle that if something is true in the negative sense, it is more true and applicable in the positive sense.

By pretending to be spiritually strong and steadfast, that person is on the road to becoming so, quite literally. Historic precedence has proven the efficacy of this rule of life time and again.

- Basya, the daughter of Pharaoh, saw a basket in the water, and her heart was aroused to rescue the crying baby (Moshe) who was in it, but it was beyond her reach. Nevertheless, she extended her hand, and, miraculously, her hand s-t-r-e-t-ched and she was able to access the basket. Her maternal tenderness had propelled her to act *as if* she were close enough to reach her objective.

- Rabbi Chanina ben Dosa was a sage who lived in the Galil (northern section of Israel). He wanted to express his love to G-d with a gift, but he did not have the means to buy something of real significance. He noticed a beautiful stone and decided this could be used in the Holy Temple when replacement materials were needed. The stone was large and very heavy, but oh, how he wanted to bring it! He placed his fingers on it *as if* he really had the ability to raise it, and with the help of angels sent by G-d, he soon found himself in Yerushalayim.[27]

- Every teacher who ever walked into a class knows the critical role of the *as if* rule. Teachers could never make it past the first day of school if they didn't hide their flutters under bravado *as if* they felt totally confident and in charge.

Are you convinced?

Suppose low spirits have been pulling you down for several days. One thing you can do is focus on your external movements, forcing yourself, if necessary. To the observer, it seems *as if* your heart is filled with happy thoughts. Even though your heart is dead, and not at all interested in acting that way right now, you *simulate the state of mind that you would like to be in.* Your heart will be steered in accordance with your actions and activities.

How can we convince a person who is in the doldrums to fake it? Rabbi Levi Yitzchak of Berdichev[28] would often remind his disciples of the expression in the Tehillim – "G-d is the shadow of a Jew." A shadow mimics the motions of the person. The way the Jew conducts himself below, so G-d does, Above. When a Jew acts magnanimously towards others, G-d acts magnanimously towards him. When a Jew is joyful, or even acts *as if* he is in a joyous state of mind, he elicits Divine reciprocation, and G-d then shines joy into his life.

Even if we fake it, the reciprocation is real.

A similar idea is presented by the prophet Yechezkiel, "As the appearance of man [so it is] Above."[29] The manner and mood displayed by Man in this world sets the stage for what he is shown from Above. We're literally creating the setting, the stage for our own play.

The Magid of Mezritch points out that acting *as if*, smiling, even *making the decision* to form the smile, are relatively small actions. They do not require large investments in terms of extended study, travel, or financial outlay.

My mother, a Holocaust survivor, decided that the years she spent in a forced labor camp were not considered "living," and she deducted them from her age. She lived her entire life after the war *as if* she were many years younger. Years later, she moved in Israel, and we corresponded by mail. One letter was the bearer of a startling disclosure: she revealed her true birth date. The interesting thing was that after she revealed that information, the *as if* age bubble burst. Her youthfulness quickly ebbed and she began to resemble the mid-eighties woman she had just become.

> *The more we act like we want things to be, the more likely that goal will become a reality in our lives. People may call this hypocrisy. That may be so. But, imagine a world in which everyone acted better, holier, more compassionately – and more joyfully than they actually are. "Perhaps what our world needs is some more hypocrisy."*[30]

The Chassidic Railroad Line

A group of yeshiva students in Israel was helping some immigrants from Russia put on tefillin when an elderly Russian-born Jew approached them: "You don't need to help me. I know how to put on tefillin, and I have a story to tell you!

"When I was a youth back in Russia," he began, "I used to attend the secret farbrengens (gatherings) of the Lubavitchers. I also used to pray with them and join their classes. At one farbrengen that I will always remember, the discussion was dominated by the fervent desire to be reunited with the Rebbe, Rabbi Yosef Yitzchak (Schneersohn – the sixth Lubavitcher Rebbe). We fervently sang 'G-d should give us good health and life, and we will be reunited with our Rebbe.' Our intense yearning to be with the Rebbe was almost palpable and was growing from minute to minute.

"In the middle of the farbrengen, a few chassidim suddenly stood up and decided to 'take action.' Grabbing some chairs, they turned them upside-down and arranged them in a row to make a 'train,' complete with beeps and train sounds. Just picture it – grown men behaving like kindergarten children, sitting on overturned chairs and making believe they were going to the Rebbe!

"Most of the others, myself included, stood around watching. We laughed at them and told them they were crazy. What ridiculous, childish nonsense! But, do you know," concluded the man, "within a short time, all of the chassidim who rode the 'train' received visas to leave Russia, and actually did get to the Rebbe. Whereas the rest of us, the ones who 'acted our age,' were left behind. As you can see, most of us did not have the strength to keep up our observance of Torah and mitzvahs, and are only now beginning to catch up."[31]

As if demonstrates our belief that G-d can help us.

Rabbi Immanuel Schochet a"h, a rav in Toronto, Canada often recounted how the Lubavitcher Rebbe instructed him to make a celebratory Kiddush for his daughter who was very ill at the time, which meant, in essence, that he should act *as if* she had already recovered. The tenuous reality of the situation surely made the joy of a Kiddush seem incongruous. Nevertheless, acting *as if* she were already well "did the trick" and the child subsequently recovered.

Act *as if* G-d is about to answer that which we have been beseeching Him daily.

Act *as if* G-d is about to answer that for which we have been praying, for close to two thousand years.

Don't appease your unease with passive sighs, "*If only* Moshiach would come already." Act *as if* Moshiach *is* coming in the next moment. If we all do that, he will. (G-d reciprocates, remember?) When we are joyful now, acting *as if* the Geulah is just about to unfold, we *invite* the future joy into the present.

> *"We must rejoice even in the darkest days of Galus – we don't want to greet Moshiach looking downcast. We must calibrate our lives to live **as if** Moshiach is already here, and when he comes we are ready to greet him in a mode of joyfulness."* *Lubavitcher Rebbe.*[32]

Live the future in the present – fill your mouths with joy and laughter, *as if* it is practically here.

6

Joy: What is it Really?

(and it's not happiness)

It's time to dissect joy.

Let's start by dissecting this innocuous statement: "I just want to be happy!"

What makes us happy?

I took an informal poll among friends and family members, and these were some of the responses: Love. Security. Family. Health. Money. Helping people. Doing what's right. Personal accomplishments. Community. Fame. Making a difference. All these responses express our personal pathways to happiness.

Try posing the question "What do you want out of life?" to people you know. You can expect to hear, "I just want to be happy." Aristotle aptly called happiness the "goal of all goals."

How do we go about attaining the "goal of all goals"? It is a paradox of life that we often seek this greatest of values in shopping malls, restaurants, vacations and home decorating. These are temporal triggers, short-lived sources, and like a drug addict whose high is wearing off, people engaged heavily in these types of pursuits are soon panting for new sources of happiness.

Happiness is not something that can be captured and caged. We live our lives looking forward to the time when we can finally be happy, but our happiness continually recedes. We pursue happiness in life goals, hoping that the next achievement will finally press the magic happy-forever button. *The magic "happiness that lasts" is never found because it is actually impossible to reach a happy plateau and stay happy.*

The American Bill of Rights was wisely drafted. It allows its citizens the right to the *"pursuit* of happiness." No one can claim possession of "happiness," and capture it forever. Don't expect to bottle happiness like a bottle of perfume that emits its fragrance for years to come.

A life based on obtaining happiness will always fall short.

Worse, it can lead to depression unless the person discovers life's deeper truths and purpose. Often, people who managed to climb the ladder of "success" have confessed, "I had everything a person could want. I had every reason to be happy and yet I wasn't. I still felt empty." They realized that in their pursuit of happiness which is the "inalienable right" of every American citizen, the "pursuit" was disconnected from the "happiness."

If simcha is playing hard-to-get, we are chasing the wrong type.

With this in mind, we can appreciate the sage accuracy in the expression "pursuit of happiness." When something is external it has to be pursued. Joy is the natural state of a person's being. It merely has to be *activated*.

The inner truth is a quality we own from birth. We don't need to chase what is already there.

> *Ronen was a fortunate man – he discovered his inner truth, and with it, authentic joy. After graduating with a degree in biotechnology, he landed a high-salaried job with one of the largest hi-tech companies. He vacationed frequently and lived the good life.*

"Yet I began to experience a tremendous feeling of emptiness. I assured myself that with sufficient material wellbeing the feelings would eventually dissipate. But they didn't. In order to quench my thirst, I started exploring my spirituality. I studied alternative medicine, meditation, Bach flower remedy...but the feelings persisted. As a final resort, I bought a ticket to India, hoping to 'find myself' there, but my spiritual hunger grew and intensified, and I decided to return home." There, by Divine Providence, Ronen met a group of young baalei teshuva (returnees to Judaism) who convinced him to join a Rabbi's Shabbos table. He was enthralled. "I saw things that I had never seen before. My search for joyous fulfillment finally bore fruit as I gradually made these practices part of my life."

As Viktor Frankl said, "Happiness cannot be pursued; it must ensue." Happiness will occur as a natural by-product of a meaningful and purposeful journey through life.

Enter Joy

Many use the words happiness and joy interchangeably. What is the difference between happiness and joy?

Simcha is a broad, encompassing term describing a positive emotional energy. Simcha may legitimately be translated as "happiness," but more precisely it refers to a healthy, non-egotistical joyous state. Simcha is a soul state.

In this book, the word "happiness" is used to describe external, superficial joy and "joy" is used for the inner, deeper brand of joy. Happiness and joy are two distinct elements.

There are ten terms for joy relating to the Jewish nation,[33] many of which (*sasson, simcha, gila, rina, ditza, chedva*) feature in the seven wedding blessings for a bride and groom.

- *Sasson:* The physical expression of joy; exertion associated with simcha. It is the full bloom, the satiation, like the satiated feeling at the end of the repast celebrating that joyous event after the salvation is complete.

- *Simcha:* A joy that is constant. The joy of being attached to G-d.
- *Gila:* The joy of being connected to others; joy expressed via dancing; dancing in a circle of connectedness.
- *Rina:* Vocal expression of joy: happy shouts with co-celebrants, joy expressed through singing and prayer (Tehillim!).
- *Ditza:* Jubilation; expressing joy in a way that spreads to others.
- *Chedva:* Inner delight.
- *Tza'hala:* Exulting and sharing the triumph with others, a reveling (as in the verse from Megilas Esther: "...[the city of] Shushan tzahala v'sameicha)."
- *Alizus* and *alitzus:* High spirits and cheer in friendship, harmony and fellowship.

Good fortune comes in many guises. For example, we feel fortunate when we receive gifts. But what kinds of gifts make us happy? That is the often-torturous dilemma of many a husband before his wife's anniversary.

> *Hubby picked a perfume for his wife and as the friendly saleswoman wrapped it, she smiled at him, "A little surprise for your wife?"*
> *"Yup, it's going to be a little surprise. She's expecting a cruise."*

When we are young, we are satisfied with trivial trinkets. As we mature, the gifts and acquisitions that make us happy become more sophisticated. A child thrills over a toy car. When we get older, we want a real car, and maybe we'll only be happy with a more expensive car. Have we really matured? It's a fancier toy but still a currency-based acquisition.

There is another kind of "gift," a result of blessings from Above. These are intangible gifts, like health, income, children and *nachas* (gratification from children). Our concept of gift-quality has clearly matured when we would give up the currency-based category to get the G-d-bestowed gifts. And yet, even these gifts are things we *get*, and our happiness is tied to and contingent on them.

Many of us allow our ventures into and out of happiness to revolve around a few choice words: **house, spouse, child**. You might want to add **job** and **car**.

To illustrate: I need a house. How long must I search to find the right one? I have a house but it needs a lot of work. The mess in my house is driving me up a wall (a dirty one at that). The cleaning lady didn't come; she came but I'm not happy with her work.

Now substitute the word *spouse* for *house*. I want a spouse. How long must I search to find the right one? I have a spouse but he/she needs a lot of work. The mess my spouse makes is driving me out of my mind. My spouse didn't come home (yet). My spouse came home and I'm still not happy.

Now try it with the word *child*: I want a child. How long must I suffer until G-d answers my prayers? I have a child (or more) but he/she generates a lot of work. The mess my children make is driving me crazy. My son didn't come home and I'm worried. My children came home and now they're bickering. How can I be happy?

Try it with job, employees, roommate, tenant, and anything else that's important to you. Yes, you need a job. Why is it taking so long to find one? On the other hand, if you do have one, it can mean a lot of work. Either way, you may have a challenge to being happy.

HAPPINESS	JOY
Externally-based	Internally generated, an inner emotional climate
Success-related	Self-generated, indigenous

HAPPINESS	JOY
Dependent on circumstances and interpersonal relationships	Unaffected by the things that happen to us; an independent existence
When things go well	A state of mind. It sometimes has to be worked at
A response	Proactive
Receives	Gives
A self-centered goal	Transcends our own needs

No amount of tax dollars will make joy available to us (so let's lower taxes – are we joyful now?). Lack of joy cannot be blamed on environmental issues, state of government or life circumstances. Our state of joy is our own enterprise and we are the executive CEOs.

A neat, handy way to sum it up and remember it is with this word association:

*Ha*ppiness and *ha*ve begin with the same two letters. (Indeed, **happiness** is based on things we **have**.)

G-d and **Joy** have a parallel construct –both are three-letter words with an "o" in their centers. **G-d** and **Joy** go together.

Happiness is a relationship with ourselves. Joy is a relationship with G-d.

How did "happiness" come to be?

Before Adam and Chava ate from the Tree of Knowledge there was only joy. The world was drenched in G-dlight. There was no personal wish list, so "happiness" did not exist – knowledge and pleasure were not subject to personal interest and consideration. Chava wanted to make Supernal joy available for mankind as a powerful tool to serve G-d, so she set out to harness pleasure. It would be personal but selfless, a human brand of Divine joy. Despite her good intentions her subjective delight got in the way when she acknowledged the fruit's pleasure. She was personally aware, rather than totally committed to the Divine truth and purpose.

And that's how "happiness" was born (and, unfortunately, unhappiness as well). The "I" debuted – the "I" that says "I like... therefore I am happy..." (and, too often – "I am *unhappy* right now"). It is the voice of the ego! Now that the ego was unharnessed, there was no turning back – anymore than you can get a newborn baby back into the womb from which it emerged!

Transplanting sublime joy into humans is a delicate maneuver. No unholy matter may infiltrate. The serpent didn't take full possession of Chava, thank G-d, but she now had to deal with two inner voices vying for attention – G-d's voice and the serpent's prodding. According to mystical teachings, Chava meant well and wanted to turn this amazing joy that drenched our Gan Eden existence into a sanctified marketable product. But the serpent was too cunning at promoting *his* product – the ego. He succeeded and she failed. But, Jews are optimists; we see how this was good. Because of the Tree of Knowledge fiasco, we all became partners in bringing G-d back into the world through our moments of spiritual ardor and transcendent joy, those rare moments when our soul bursts out in Jewish ecstasy.

The natural state of the neshama (the soul), is joy, but joy is not the natural state of the body. The body is self-absorbed, so the body wants more material gratification and the elation can't last.

We are hard-wired to never be satisfied.

What makes the body crave materialism? It actually filters in from our G-dly soul's insatiable hunger for G-dliness. G-d is infinite and therefore a person's G-dly soul cannot feel contented. Even a person who has no religious affiliation and does not see himself as "G-dly," has a soul, and that soul is sending a subliminal message to want more. The animal soul translates that craving into the desire for more and more material pleasure.[34]

Being human means never being whole. We can never fully satisfy our desires and we will always remain sensitive to that which we are missing.[35]

This book is not about happiness. It is about joy, and our quest for perfect joy.

Had any cravings lately? There are two things in life that people insatiably crave: sugar and joy. I don't know which people crave more, but I know which is healthier...

7

Forward Thinking

Are we ready to invest?

The next chapters will move us forward. We will reveal the extent of genuine joy so we can appreciate its value up close, immerse in it, and learn things we never knew. We will harness joy to help us change our circumstances. But before we do, let's stop and ask ourselves some questions.

Are we ready to invest? Are we emotionally available?

Are we ready, willing and able to clear a space in the clutter of our daily lives to revel in a world-state that seems far off?

These are good questions and they deserve honest answers.

Emotional readiness

Who can talk about joy with all our pressing life issues? Right now, we want and *need* to talk about our problems – even the Torah counsels that when we have a problem we ought to discuss it with a friend.[36]

The truth must be told. We *love* to talk about problems. The media loves to report about problems, and we diligently read and agonize over the reports. Anti-Semitism in Europe, anti-Semitism on campus, anti-Semitism around the corner. Terrorism in Europe and terrorism lurking at every bend. And if that's not enough, we've got our own problems. A sample in-house news report: overdrawn bank account, my child hates school, I can't sleep! It's simple arithmetic. The negatives outweigh the positives, so the negatives win the day!

> Sure I want to talk about joy – as soon as I get a chance, but right now I'm busy. I have to do my daily exercise, say Tehillim to pray for my sick neighbor, deal with my bug infestation. And this pain in my knee is killing me... By the way, did you hear what happened to my uncle's brother-in-law's cousin? Isn't that terrible? Okay, gotta go or I'll miss the news. I must find out what the Ambassador had to say about...

Do we want to stay in this negative mode forever?

Facing forward

"How can we declare this to be the time just before the coming of Moshiach, when we see the sorry state of the world?" This is a very good question, and it was posed to the Lubavitcher Rebbe. He responded:

"It depends in which direction we look."

> Two old friends ran into each other on the outskirts of town and were catching up on the latest. One commented, "How decrepit this city is. Look at all the garbage, the sordid commercial buildings, these abandoned lots. The other said, "What are you talking about? Don't you appreciate the lush gardens, the grand promenade and the spectacular palace?"
> The perspectives of these two people were not colored by their being pessimists or optimists. Their views were influenced simply by which direction they were facing.
> The first person was facing the city, and therefore saw the di-

lapidated outskirts of the city. The second person was looking ahead, to where he was going; he was on the way to the palace to meet the king.

We are at a crossroads now between our past and our future. We could focus on the brokenness of our galus lives. Or, we could invigorate ourselves by keeping our gaze fixed forward, as we draw nearer, toward our future Geulah.

We could ante up the joy of anticipation and experience the joy in advance.

Science is helping us move forward

Many people grew up with the belief that we are passive players in a predetermined whirl of fate. At the same time, if everything is predestined, there is no possibility of free will. This free will conundrum has been debated over the centuries, with many proposed resolutions.

Recent scientific findings have enriched our perception of true free will, the power to choose. Moreover, they reveal the power we have to *change* our circumstances.[37]

> *Quantum physic experiments demonstrate that when a person observes particles of matter, they literally change course simply by a person looking at them. The person's observation has affected the conditions and determined their state.[38]*

We humans have more power than we thought. We are active participants in this universe. What an empowering perspective!

> *"The Jew becomes a 'partner with G-d'...in bringing the true and complete Geulah."[39]*

New perspectives can take us down exciting new roads. Valuable nuggets may be mined. We may even completely overhaul our lives for the better. And yet, we sometimes lack the flexibility to open our minds to our power. Our personalities, prejudices and pre-conceived notions color the new information to fit in with our old, familiar perceptions. We spurn new ways of thinking. We reject logic and dispute proofs. We like to call ourselves open-minded, but are we?

It all depends on our perspective:

One of the main principles of quantum theory is that the human observer determines reality.

For many years, there was a major debate among scientists as to the nature of light. One theory posited that light is a series of particles; the opposing view was that it is a wave. The development of quantum theory effectively ended the debate and rocked the world of physics. It concluded that both theories are correct. Sometimes light manifests as a wave and sometimes as particles. The observer's perspective is the determining factor. His assessment (measuring) of its components effects a change in the state (outcome) of that which is viewed.[40]

It was initially believed that all is inevitable and predetermined. Quantum mechanics experiments have demonstrated that each event is able to occur in a number of ways. The precise way will not be determined until it is measured by a conscious observer.

Eugene Wigner, a Jewish physicist, made a very Kabbalistic and metaphysical statement. He said that the human conscious observer puts the particle into one state or another. He effects reality. This is a very strong manifestation of free will. The inexplicable results of the experiments led him to conclude that conscious beings play a different role than does an inanimate measuring device.

Another very prominent physicist, John Wheeler, said the following: "It is often stated that the development of life is accidental and unimportant in the scheme of things. Quantum mechanics has led us to take seriously and explore the directly opposite view – the observer is as essential to the creation of the universe as the universe is to the creation of the observer."[41]

It wasn't easy for scientists to accept this groundbreaking model of reality. There was a lot of resistance. Even Einstein strongly resisted some of its conclusions. Noted physicist Richard Feynman warned about the limits we should place on 'our old-fashioned' ideas (inadequate models). It takes time for people to accommodate to new, progressive thinking patterns. Eventually, after repeatedly hearing about them, we reprogram our brains.

New-way positive thinking and optimized personal empowerment *can* become second nature.

Our perspective can shape reality

Reality isn't static; it's dynamic.[42] We can be dynamic by the way we regard the unwelcome events in our lives, not only of the moment, but also our past and future.

The present: When we learn a brighter way to view the problems sitting in our laps *right now* we change their course and provide positive momentum.

> *Someone came to Rabbi Avraham of Parisov[43] and spilled out his bitter heart. "I have not a drop of joy or nachas. Suffering and more suffering are my bitter daily lot."*
>
> *"Who says that your problems are the cause of your sadness?" responded the Rabbi. "Maybe your sadness is the reason the problems are attracted to you. Pull yourself together and fill your heart with some simcha, and you will see that the problems will disappear."[44]*

The past: *It's over...It's behind us.* But is it really over? Misfortunes in our midst often leave behind emotional aftershocks. We can liberate ourselves from our problems mode. Each of us already knows and practices some strategies that helps free us from unpleasant events that we endured. Here's an example of a strategy I often use to deal with a "terrible" experience:

The information doesn't make the story – our interpretation does. Here's a great story to prove the point.

Steve did not know he was adopted until a neighborhood boy told him so. He was devastated to discover he was 'discarded' goods and cried for hours. Finally, his adoptive mother had a talk with him. She told him, "You were not abandoned or discarded. That is not the way the story goes. On the contrary, you were chosen, selected." That became his story. He was ready to move forward once again. And he did. He moved on to become co-founder of Apple, Inc., Steven Jobs.[45]

After particularly trying tragedies, community leaders and friends will often call for gatherings to offer support, to find healing and meaning. When we invest an event with meaning and purpose, it restores some measure of equanimity. And yet, tragic events take us backward into the unanswered *whys* of the galus world. We've had enough tragedies. Enough!! We are not looking to invest tragedy with meaning. **We are looking to move forward and leave tragedy behind.** Forward on the path to a pain-free world: Geulah.

Backward is pain and sorrow. Joy is forward thinking.

The future: Experiments demonstrated that shining a light on particles of matter provides momentum.[46] When we rise above the fray of our daily problems to visualize a brighter future, we provide forward momentum. We can be dynamic about our global circumstances as well.

Meditate on the perfect future world.... An experience of joy that is more sublime, with more soul-stirring ecstasy than anything we've ever entertained. It seems off in the nebulous future, but it's just around the bend. Visualize it with joyous anticipation. It is so close, we might as well begin laughing right now!

On the belief in Moshiach, Maimonides writes: "He who does not believe in him or does not **look forward** to his coming denies... the Torah and Moses our teacher."[47]

It is not enough to have faith in Moshiach's eventual arrival. Just

In order to move forward and get into that anticipatory mode, we need more information. What we know so far about joy and its whereabouts is just the tip of the iceberg.

Tests

Iceberg is an apt metaphor. It often feels like our lightness, carefree joyousness and optimism are trapped under a giant iceberg. We may want to move forward, but we may be so snowed under by our problems that we are frozen into immobility. We may lack the energy and motivation to chip off the icicles that conceal joy.

We don't see the whole picture, the design behind it all. So, let's examine the tests that conceal joy.

G-d designed the world in a way that conceals His true motives. Since He is the source of Goodness, everything He does is Good, but it may leave us scratching our heads. His ways are inscrutable and He is not providing us with explanations – intentionally.

Tests are difficult. A test looms over us like a giant iceberg. It can freeze our smiles and cool the passion that pulses in a warm Jewish heart. We may think "Life is unfair," "G-d is far away," "He doesn't care."

The same G-d Who sent us these joy-blockers has the solutions.

The test can bring us closer to G-d – it's intended to. As the wise men say, it's not a challenge, it's an opportunity. As soon as we remember that He is the designer of every iceberg and waiting for us to turn to Him, we can sail right around that joy-blocker and rediscover G-d.

The difference between a mitzvah and a *nisayon* (test). The purpose of a mitzvah is to bring G-dliness down into the world by

> elevating material matter of Creation. The purpose of a *nisayon* is
> to elevate ourselves.

To get a better understanding of tests, we will need to burrow all the way under them, to uncover the roots and reasons of these tests.

The tests they give in schools are designed to check our knowledge. Spiritual tests are loyalty assessments. They gauge our loyalty to G-d by noting our joy-levels in a variety of situations. Are we retaining our joy, or losing it?

Suppose we are on a sailing expedition with our newly refurbished yacht, and suddenly we ram into an iceberg. Our grand vacation plans are in danger of being thrown off course, and the expense of repairs is an added stress. Is this a good or bad thing? It looks bad. If it is bad, we have a right to be upset. But if keep our wits about us and recall what we learned in Judaism 101, that

1. Everything G-d does is Good
2. Everything is designed by G-d – so it must be Good, because He runs the world down to the most trivial details[48]
3. G-d is present in every tight spot – not only is He on the boat, He is even in this iceberg
4. The G-dly presence is joyful, therefore we can be joyful

...then we can turn that predicament into a positive event.

How to Take a Test

There's a way to manipulate the results of a Divine Test, and it's totally honest. Up in those hidden realms that are beyond our comprehension, "bad" things are really good. Although they *feel* bad to us, they are blessings in disguise.

We are able to transform them to user-friendly blessings. Here's how:

Show, by your abiding joy that you know G-d is Good. When we reveal the Test's G-d-connection, which is also its Good-connection, we draw its Goodness down into our revealed world, into the plane of existence that we experience. We cause its inherent Goodness to be manifest and enjoyed on a human level.[49]

This is exactly what quantum theory proposes. *When a person observes particles of matter, his observation causes them to manifest as a definite state.*

The way we observe the Test impacts its outcome. When we observe the particles of the Test as "a good thing," with joyfulness and trust, that observation takes on a positive state, inviting palpable blessings into our lives.

This concept is strikingly similar to words in the Zohar (184b): "When a person puts on a radiant countenance in this world, there will be a flow of abundance from Above. The joy of man draws down on himself more joy from the worlds Above."

"Adding bitachon, trust, and simcha from below evokes these qualities from Above."[50]

> I believe that G-d knows about my predicament and that He sees from one end of the world to the other and from the beginning of time until the end. Furthermore...
> "G-d is always Good. G-d's wisdom is the source of life, goodness and delight. 'In the light of the King's countenance there is life.'[51] And therefore...before everything, man ought to be happy and joyous at every time and every moment... It is for the sake of this faith that man was created; the main purpose of his creation is to test him to ascertain what is in his heart." (*from the Tanya*)[52]

There are many kinds of tests. There are, for example, Iceberg tests, which cause us to recalculate our routes. And, certainly, there is intrinsic value in the new direction our life takes. Then there are Cloud tests. Cloud tests also test the tenacity of our trust, but their fabrication is different. There is no need to reroute. We stay our course and proceed as if **Forget about some sunny island. Let's pick a cloud and hang out on it.**

there were no obstacle whatsoever. Our air travel experiences provide a visual paradigm – if you've flown in cloudy weather you've seen how the aircraft lifts off the runway, right into a mass of obscuring clouds. If we didn't know better we'd think that it's impossible to cut through them. But we do, and suddenly the world is bathed in sunshine. The world above the clouds – that's the true reality.

The "badness" is imagined. When we move faithfully forward *as if it didn't exist*, we discover that it poses no obstacle.

The Roots of Joy

Mystical and Chassidic teachings shed light on the inner dimension of tests. They help us transcend the gloom of galus and connect us to the Divine joy that is always available. As we have been getting closer to the end of our galus journey, the mystical roots of joy have become increasingly revealed.

Rabbi Shimon bar Yochai[53] revealed the deepest secrets and truths of Torah, collected in the Zohar, the fundamental work of Kabbalah. Aptly, he turned the anniversary of his death on Lag B'omer[54] into a day of joyous celebration. When the inner dimension of "bad" is revealed, a tragedy can become a landmark of intense joy. The Kabbalistic teachings of the Arizal[55] were the next major step in the revelation of joy. The Arizal credited his tremendous spiritual accomplishments and insights to his exceptional *simchah shel mitzvah* and asserted that we should serve G-d with palpable joy.[56] Even more joy was revealed through the Baal Shem Tov, who thrust joy into the forefront of Jewish life. "The ability to be joyous, by discerning the good and joyous within every experience, is considered by chassidim as a biblical command!"[57] "A person must *always* be joyous,"[58] not only when he is doing a mitzvah.

Rabbi Schneur Zalman, author of the Tanya[59] presented a holistic plan wherein the intellect holds the key to the emotions and through it, to the soul. Studying the inner dimension of Torah brings vitality, joy and G-dliness into our every aspect of our lives. The Tanya expounds on the joys of faith and relationship, joy of teshuva, joy of prayer, joy of daily redemption, and more.

Rabbi Nachman of Breslov maintained that only through a state of joy can one be close to G-d and that, no matter what, we must strive strenuously to remain joyful. Obstacles are given to increase our yearning to come close to G-d.

The revelations regarding the power and deep roots of joy have continued to accelerate. They are helping us make a transition from the galus mindset to the Geulah state.

A fascinating "Supernal inside scoop" on the mystical interplay between pleasure and joy is discussed in depth in a series of discourses[60] called *samech t'samach* (you shall make joyous). It highlights the dominant and powerful role of joy in the trajectory of Jewish history. Some points have made their way into this book (see Tiers of Joy, Chapter 14). An apt subtitle for this discourse might be *"Pure Joy."* The call of the Lubavitcher Rebbe for *pure* joy to hasten the coming of Moshiach is constructed on concepts in this discourse series.

And about those icebergs…No icy entity can hold its own against the warmth and fire of Torah, particularly the inner, mystical dimension, which ignites a fire and passion inside us.

8

"Can You Give Me Joy in a Nutshell?"

A friend appealed to me, "I hope you wrap up your joy theory in the first few pages of your book. A person needs to be able to find it quickly." She is one of many who are gasping for joy-air and needs the information succinctly presented so she can quickly inhale its life-giving oxygen. It would be nice to provide a thesis statement for joy, make it accessible in a few easy how-to steps. (Get rich quick! We sell "joy in a nutshell"!) People want quick solutions. We seek easy shortcuts.

> *Magazines love to feature "how to" articles. One magazine editor received an article entitled "How to make your own mink coat." He was really excited, thinking how many people would buy the issue with an article like that. Then he read the opening sentence, "First catch 96 minks...."*
> *Beware of easy solutions and freebies.*

A large coffee mug was on display in a shop window. On its side was emblazoned: INSTANT HUMAN.

We need "Instant Joy!" This appeal should not be dismissed lightly. The plea is an urgent one. People are desperate.

How can we pack all the dazzle and dynamics into a few lines? There are so many aspects to joy, and to do justice to it, we must unfold its splendor and display its beauty facet by facet. I am reminded of an unforgettable sight when I toured Yosemite National Park with my family. We drove to one picturesque scenic point after another. The viewing point we saved for last was touted to be the highlight, especially during sunset on a clear day. From there, the valleys and mountain peaks we had seen from the various vantage points during the day could be taken in all at once. The view from that lookout offered a panoramic expanse of stunning beauty, a visual feast swathed in brilliant colors. The grandeur of this magnificent sight caused me to catch my breath with a gasp.

Our imminent discovery of the breadth, depth and heights of **joy** will evoke that mountain range as magnificent new peaks are discovered one by one. When we are done, we will have the entire exquisite range of joy arranged before us.

But we will not be satisfied to merely view the peaks. We want to soar. To do so, we need something that is higher and greater than those peaks, a strong hand from Above, the Divine strength-of-joy that provides a sturdy line to grasp and makes forward momentum possible.

There *is* a way to encapsulate joy-in-a-nutshell. But, in order to benefit from the brevity, we need more groundwork. It's like the last speaker at a conference whose turn comes after exhausting hours of lengthy speakers. He approaches the podium and makes a powerful three-minute speech. Admirers ask him how he did it. "Simple," he shrugs. The longer he prepared, the more he was able to strip away.

> S & L was trying to get their client to pay a bill. However, their client insisted that he had already paid the bill. After a year the account payable department sent their client a message:
> DEBT NOW ONE YEAR OVERDUE. PLEASE REMIT AT ONCE. WILL WAIT NO LONGER.
> The boss checked the text before it was sent. "Who needs so

many words? You couldn't make it shorter?"
"I don't see how," said the secretary.
The boss grabbed a pen and scribbled one word: NU?
The very same day, they received a reply: SUE!

Hmm, can we capsulate joy into a mere two words? I like the challenge, let's wait and see....

That's the kind of challenge I like – the one I choose myself.

Section II:

Prisms of Joy

The story of joy in its full glory

The beauty of a precious gem is enhanced by facets that bring out its brilliance. Joy is like a gem. Its many facets contribute to its sparkle and depth. But joy has an advantage – while a gem is beautiful, it needs to be guarded. We do not need insurance to protect this priceless asset. Like a mezuzah that shields a home, simcha will spread its protective wings over us. It will return to us more than we invested in it.

Joy is more enriching and valuable than jewels and we don't need a bundle of money to acquire it. Like a precious gem, we need expertise to appraise the beauty of joy and appreciate its value and many inherent features.

Some readers may be wondering, why do we care what joy is made of, as long as we're happy! Why bother to dissect and analyze it? An experience I had showed me the effort is well worth it.

I was preparing a Torah class about an upcoming holiday. I had just the right concept ready, complete with fascinating insights and historical background. There was an Aramaic passage in one commentary, but not being versed in the language, I figured I would navigate around it and still present a cohesive delivery.

I reviewed my points a day before the class and realized I lacked emotional involvement in the material due to the missing commentary. This would not do; a dispassionate delivery would not hold my audience.

My husband, my scholar-in-residence, came to my rescue. With the murky passage demystified, the entire Torah concept took on a new life. I was able to plan a much more interesting approach. I could manipulate and unfold the ideas in a variety of stimulating ways. Now that I had mastered the information to its very foundation I felt in control.

That's the way I feel about understanding joy with all its components. When we uncover the deepest elements of joy, we can manipulate our findings to fit a variety of life situations. We can become masters.

In the next chapters we will unveil the powers of joy, reveal its lights, refine our mission, and scale its heights.

9

Joy Plus

Spotlight on joy's many features

Just see what comes along with this gem, as we carefully unwrap and extract this precious element from within the crevices of our richly endowed spiritual selves. So many useful and important features and valuable bonuses were thrown in at no extra charge. Here is a sample of the features accessible to each of us within ourselves.

Love: Love and joy go hand-in-hand. Joyful people are more loving people – *like* turns to *love, dislike* to *like*. A six-year-old demonstrated this phenomenon: She was feeling like a million dollars helping the grownups in the kitchen before Passover. At one point she started to send up euphoric "joy balloons": "I don't *like* to peel carrots; I *love* to peel carrots." Then she told her Mommy "I don't *like* you; I *love* you. And, of course, in turn, love promotes joy. It's a positive feedback loop.

Superior intellect: Research has revealed that pleasure chemicals (notably Dopamine)[61] released by good feelings activate brainpower and promote motivation, memory and cognition – in short, better learning.

Unity: The completeness of simcha is experienced specifically when together with others. A happy person feels more generous and willing to cooperate and include others.

Peace: A joyous frame of mind can help people make peace with their enemies. The Talmud tells of two jesters who would entertain people and get them to laugh.[62] In this mellow atmosphere they succeeded in making peace between people with disputes.

Humility (bitul): A state in which we experience G-d's bigness and our smallness. When we "feel" G-d more, we become less involved with our "self." The instinctual impulses to compete just melt away, as do perceived ego threats (such as from the fellow who is getting all the attention at the table).

Enduring education: When children see that the Jewish way of life is joyous they will be motivated to maintain it. (Don't preach it – *do* it and *be* it!). That's why schools make a big deal when their young students get their first Siddur or begin learning Chumash. All those *siyum* parties (celebrations for completing a section of learning) may seem like a waste of learning time, but they have enduring value.

Every accomplishment and milestone that is fussed over with lots of positive, enthusiastic feedback tells the child this matter is important to us. It is registered in the mind as a good kind of "big deal." There are so many of the negative kind of "big deals" in a child's life! The event gets etched with permanent ink into their memory logs. *Commotion + positive emotion equals commitment.*

Resilience: Joyous people have good recovery skills. They don't overreact because they know that snags usually work out. Jews are historically the most resilient of all people. No other nation has shown this ability to self-generate after being subject to unrelenting attempts at annihilation.

> **Resiliency checklist:**
> There are four types of people: People who are happy when things are going well, people who are sad because things aren't going well, people who are sad – maybe a bit grouchy – despite the fact that things are relatively fine, and people who are happy despite difficult circumstances.

Health: Positive thinking releases chemicals that boost the body's immune system. Chronic negative-thinking stress is the #1 source of illness.[63] Some sources of stress are anger, anxiety and fear. Guilt and worry

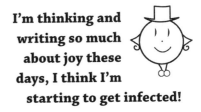

I'm thinking and writing so much about joy these days, I think I'm starting to get infected!

are notorious as well. But *humility* tames anger, and *bitachon* banishes anxiety, fear and worries. (Now all we're left with is Jewish guilt.)

Strength: A joyous person can remain strong and steadfast in the face of opposition and uncover inner resources and hidden potential. As expressed in Psalm 19:6, joy empowers a person to run the course – a marathon runner!

Of the many rewards associated with joy, *strength* enjoys an elite status. It teams up with joy in an oft-repeated verse. *"Strength and gladness are in His place – oz v'chedva b'mkomo."*[64] These words are part of a song that the Leviim sang during the holy service in the Holy Temple and feature in our daily Shacharis (morning) prayers.

> Not only is there a bonding of Strength with Joy; it all takes place **"in His place."** Where is "His place"? Everywhere. He is with us wherever we may be. Even in our challenges. The fact that G-d is everywhere should encourage a person by strengthening his trust and thereby fill him with joy. Whatever predicament a person finds himself in, G-d is there too, as is His "strength and gladness."[65] It's a positive feedback loop between trust, strength and joy

Bitachon: Optimism + Confidence.

Optimism: Joy enables us to see positive possibilities and successful outcomes.

Confidence: We proceed with the certainty that our Father in Heaven will provide what we need. There is no worry where there is confidence.

Expansiveness: This is the entrepreneurial expression of joy. Where there is optimism and confidence there is serenity and courage. This shifts us into an expansive mode. We feel more competent and communicate more confidently. We may be small, with limited abilities, but G-d is big. We may be constricted, but joy aligns us with G-d. We feel larger than life and its challenges.

Prayer augmenter: We achieve more with our joy and delight than with weeping. True, the Tehillim-with-tears method brought us salvation countless times through the centuries. Yet, while those tears unlock the gates of Heaven, joy absolutely demolishes the very walls and barriers Above!

Our prayerful tears are effective only because we mix them with a special ingredient – the joy that is at the base of every yiddishe neshama. When Pharaoh's daughter went to bathe in the Nile River, she heard a baby crying and declared, "This is one of the Hebrew children." How did she know the baby was Jewish? Because a Jewish cry is unique; even when he weeps, a Jew is filled with hope. And optimism. And Jewish joy.

> *Doctor, this joy stuff is giving me so many side effects.*
> *Positive?*
> *Yes, positive.*
> *Okay then, keep it up. And double the dose when you're down.*

Don't you appreciate the convenience of one-stop shopping? Look at the array you could throw into your cart in just one outing at the joy-mall.

Close-up on Joy's Power
Spotlight on Strength: Mighty as a Monarch

> *The President of the United States was scheduled to speak in a school in my neighborhood. Signs were posted days in advance notifying us that all the main thoroughfares beginning from the helicopter landing site, all the way to the school – a four-mile swatch – would be closed to traffic hours before his arrival. The road had to be completely free and clear. Incon-*

veniently, the route ran through the major shopping artery of the neighborhood, and worse, it took place on a Friday when the streets are their busiest with the hustle and bustle of pre-Shabbos shopping.

Eventually, some motorcycles roared by. No, it was not the real thing yet. And then, the President's motorcade whizzed by. At the rate they were going, I would estimate that they traversed the entire stretch in less than three minutes.

The President of the United States is a powerful position, but nowhere as powerful as a mighty monarch. There are no limitations for the monarch.[68] As the Talmud tells us, to facilitate his access to his destination, mountains may be razed and private properties commandeered. A monarch is accustomed to having his needs met, unequivocally.

Joy is as mighty as the monarch. The expression *"simcha poretz geder,"* joy breaks through boundaries, was coined by the fifth Lubavitcher Rebbe, Rabbi Sholom Dovber. It parallels the phrase *melech poretz geder*, a king breaks through boundaries. A breakthrough experience shatters physical and spiritual barriers and blockages.

Joy can break through barriers. A joyous person can "move" worlds.

Speaking about breaking... Children break things too. The difference is – children break things you want and joy breaks (through) the things you don't want.

When we are in a state of joy, we take on the imperial strength of a sovereign. Our joyful trust in G-d is based on the premise that we'll succeed, just like the monarch who is accustomed to getting his way. He proceeds right along with the confident expectation that he'll get what he wants.

I'm discovering many uses for my sovereign strength...

Spotlight on Bitachon

*Searching for a parking spot daily in the congested neighborhood where I work is no fun. One day it occurred to me that I should replace the timbre of my inner thoughts from the uncertain, "(How) will I **ever** get a parking spot around here?" to the confident "I am **sure** G-d has a parking spot for me – as He provides for all my needs."*

It worked! And has been working since, as long as I keep my part of the deal – taking a moment to sing thanks to Him. My parking spot search became my daily run at confidence and trust, and a fountainhead for my daily gratitude. Now and then I need a wakeup call, which G-d considerately arranges for me: When I encounter difficulty finding a parking spot several times, I am reminded that my enthusiastic thank-you's had slacked off! I had lapsed into the take-it-for-granted syndrome.

> As I continue to perfect my style, I am learning to make gratitude become a live emotion in my heart. Hearts don't talk, but they can s-i-n-g their heartfelt thanks. I am grateful to have my daily bitachon runs to develop a heart brimming with gratitude and love for a G-d Who takes care of us.

What was the daily challenge of our ancestors in the desert? They certainly did not need parking spaces, and all their basic needs were supplied in a miraculous manner. The Torah describes how their food was delivered daily from Heaven. For them the daily bitachon test was *the way* their food was supplied. The manna fell daily, but they were not allowed to leave any overnight. No extras tucked away "just in case." G-d could easily have set it up to fall in larger batches and provide them with a week's or month's supply, but...*everyone needs a daily bitachon run. Find one that works for you.*

Yes, like finding a cleaning lady that works (for me).

Spotlight on Optimism

> *A patient's medical condition had eroded his emotional well-being. "Rabbi, how can I prepare myself for the worst?" the patient asked.*
>
> *"As Jews we prepare ourselves for the best, not for the worst," was the Rabbi's rejoinder. The Rabbi helped him find three good deeds he could commit to in prayer, charity and repentance. Twenty minutes later, the first in a series of good news started to come in: the doctor came to tell him that, completely unexpectedly, his liver had started working again. Three days later, more miraculous results from his lab work. He was discharged in perfect health.[69]*

There's a distinction between the faith of emunah and bitachon. Emunah is believing everything G-d does is good. Bitachon is the belief that circumstances can actually change for the better, to the extent that we can cast aside the worries from our mind. It's hard work, though! It's much easier to respond to a crisis with tears rather than with trust and cheer.

Why would we expect G-d to give us what we want? Are we deserving of it? How would we know we are worthy?

It *is* quite possible we do not deserve His help (according to the "bookkeeping"), but the very fact that we are relying on G-d's omnipotence gives us the credits to tip the scale. When He sees that rather than wring our hands we exhibit cheer and confidence in His ability to take care of us, He is so impressed that he reshuffles conditions to bring salvation. [70]

Joy, confidence and trust contribute to an expansive broadness within us.

Spotlight on Expansiveness

When our own can-do mode is turned on, it makes people happy to join our venture. When we access our inner strength-of-joy, we are like the powerful sun, beaming light on those around us. Here is a result of an experiment from my joy-lab.

I had taken overly long to return a sweater to a store that was known to have a strict return policy. Admittedly, the plastic wrap was rather crumpled as well. Instead of approaching the counter defensively and worrying "How is this gonna go?" I went into an expansive mode. I waited in line exuding sanguine positivity. Life is always wonderful -- I just made it my business to keep its wonderfulness in the forefront of my mind and not allow annoyance-in-advance of the expected refusal to refund or exchange to intrude. The saleswoman approved the exchange – cheerfully. Expansiveness is contagious!

We're bound to have greater success on a day when we're in the joy mode. I invite you to create your own success stories.

Come join our circle.

A serenade of strength, optimism, bitachon and joy:
The Eishes Chayil is a beloved prayer that is sung every Friday night before Kiddush. It lauds the Jewish woman, and allegorically, all of *knesses yisroel*, the Jewish people. It weaves the strength, optimism, bitachon into a beautiful tribute. There may be plenty of trials and tribulations, but all become golden opportunities for praise. "Strength and honor are her garments, she smiles – laughs confidently – at the future."[71]
The immediate future ~ she maintains an optimistic demeanor in the immediate crisis.
The ultimate future ~ she lives with joyous anticipation for Geulah.

A happy **wife** gets through her daily chores and tasks more quickly. She is stronger and more loving. A happy **mother** deals more effectively with the challenges of parenting. The present may appear cloudy, but the Jewish **woman** looks beyond the present, gains strength from her optimism in what is to come and infuses today's life with it.

Spotlight on Prayer

A poor man was admitted to the king's chamber and tearfully petitioned the king to grant his request. The king granted him a pittance. Then another man entered, and, in stark contrast to the pitiful complainer, lauded the king with an expansive and exuberant demeanor. The king awarded him a lavish gift as befits nobility.[72]

This tale, offered by the Baal Shem Tov, highlights the advantage of prayer with joy. But that was just the first step. The Baal Shem Tov demonstrated that joy plays an even more prominent role:

One year the Baal Shem Tov went outdoors with his chassidim to recite the Kiddush Levana blessing (heralding the moon's rebirth) immediately after Yom Kippur,[73] *but the moon was concealed by clouds. Returning to his room, the Baal Shem Tov prayed fervently and tearfully that the moon be revealed. Still, the clouds did not part. Meanwhile, the chassidim broke out in joyful dancing in gratitude to G-d for the Yom Kippur they had properly spent. The Baal Shem Tov, drawn by their joyous spirited dancing, joined them. Suddenly, the clouds moved aside to reveal the moon. The Kiddush Levana was recited with great ecstasy.*[74]

After this episode, the Baal Shem Tov would say, "What I could not bring about with my prayers and holy unifications of G-d's name, the chassidim were able to accomplish with the power of simcha."

Like *tefila* (prayer), simcha is a "service," a very lofty mode of Divine service, above and beyond anything attainable through the avoda of sadness and bitterness.

The Baal Shem Tov opened the path for a new way of dealing with crises; transforming bad news through simcha, quite literally. Over the generations, Chassidic lore accumulated stories that show joy's power to bail us out of difficult situations, even replacing tefila. Our Chassidic leaders taught by example. This story took place several generations after the Baal Shem Tov.

> The Mitteler Rebbe, Rebbe Dovber,[75] had a kapelya (singing troupe) of musically gifted chassidim as well as a group of agile horse riders who would be asked to perform on special, joyous occasions.
>
> Once, on an ordinary weekday, the Rebbe suddenly called for a performance by both groups. In the course of the performance, the Rebbe's son, Reb Nochum, who was one of the performers, was thrown from his horse and appeared to be seriously injured. The intuitive response would have been to stop the performance immediately, pick up Tehillims and pray ardently for his recovery. Instead, the Rebbe waved them on to proceed as if nothing had happened. An update soon arrived that Reb Nochum's condition was less serious than the original prognosis.
>
> Later the Rebbe explained his unusual actions: "I became aware of a harsh decree being passed in Heaven on my son. However, joy sweetens the attribute of severity, and so I called upon my choir to sing and the horse riders to gladden everyone with their antics.
>
> "The simcha helped; his condition was no longer considered critical, but a small portion of the decree remained. The continuation of the performance lessened this residual decree as well, and, G-d willing, my son will recover in the very near future."[76]

Joy is loftier than tears. The Heavenly gates of tears are never locked[77] – they must remain open because sadness lacks the power to pry them open. Joy has the power. It not only gets through the gates, it can break right through the walls.[78] We can aim our joy like a cannon; a few booms and the barrier is gone.

"Battles are won with joy, not tears. A soldier enters the fray of battle to the tune of a joyous march. It is by the power of his joy that he is victorious even in the most dangerous and challenging endeavors."[79]

Joy in Our Time

Gradually, the joyous approach to crisis has become more familiar and accepted. Many of us may need a push or reminder, but some people are strongly anchored and have the presence of mind to take the high route independently, as the dancing father-to-be in the story below. I have seen the transformative power of joy many times, but this story is one of my favorites.

I arrived at the hospital to support a friend who was having a difficult labor. The doctor was on the verge of performing a C-section but wanted to avert surgery due to high risk factors. Adding to her woes, the laboring mother was exhausted from the extended labor. She needed some new strength and vitality. How? From where? What is more invigorating than joy, I thought. Reb Bunim of Pshische had saved a drowning man by using humor to infuse him with a surge of new strength.[80] (Of course, the humor had to be tactfully aligned with the women's temperament.) Well, it worked – the mother got the baby out just in time to avert surgery and the doctor thanked me for saving the day – with a gem of a story.

A laboring mother, member of a Chassidic sect, was in a precarious situation. The father-to-be began to dance, right in the labor room. He invited the doctor to join – who promised he would, in his private office after the delivery. The danc-

ing was effective. The crises abated right after the dance and the birth was swift and smooth. And yes, the doctor kept his word and danced with the new father.

Joy is a powerful way to pray. More than that... **joy *is* a prayer.**

"The service of a broken heart is not suitable for our times," declared the Lubavitcher Rebbe in a talk in 5746.[81] One reason, he explained, is that people in our times do not have sufficient emotional stamina. A broken heart may degenerate into a melancholy one. Therefore, even a baal teshuva should take the joyous road of remorse and contrition over his past deeds.

Broken-heartedness is not suitable for our generation (except for pre-specified times) for another reason: It is not in synch with the erev Shabbos atmosphere. On Friday, fasting and sorrow-inducing activities such as Tikun Chatzos (a spiritual accounting characterized by contrite prayers) are prohibited. Since we are now in the second half of the sixth millennium, corresponding to Friday afternoon, sadness is banned. A Jew must be in a state of joy as he prepares to greet the holy Shabbos.

In earlier generations, our all-around service style was in accordance with the Thursday night Tikun Chatzos spirit. However, in our generation, as we are standing on the threshold of the eternal Shabbos, the day that is all light and joy, our avoda must be specifically through joy.

10

I Want Perfect Joy

It's time to reveal one of the best-kept secrets about joy

What is the shortest sentence you can come up with that has *perfect* and *joy* in it? Here's mine: "I want perfect joy!" (We deserve it. It's high time, don't you think?)

I want perfect joy. Let's savor it and roll it around in our mouths. And then, let's examine each word with a microscopic lens and make exciting discoveries about ourselves and what we're doing in this world. This redolent four-word sentence seems short and to the point but there are actually words in it that are taking *away* from the joy! Can you guess which?

A little editing will help us edge closer to our coveted goal. "Perfect joy" is a most admirable goal. We don't want to tamper with it. But is this statement focusing on the *perfect joy* or on the *I want*? The beauty of joy is that it has no ego. And because it has no ego, joy is sincere and wholesome. No wonder we like to hang around joyous people!

The word "I" is usurping the perfection of joy. To achieve joy, I need **less of myself and more of G-d.** My friend Brachie objects to this statement. She says, "A woman is not a little pregnant. She is either completely pregnant or not-at-all-pregnant. Joy can work only if it's 'all of G-d and none of me.'" In plain, street-talk, if you want joy, get "yourself" outta here.

**For a happy Jew, true being is non-being.
Remembering G-d, we forget ourselves.**

It's like an eclipse. When two orbs get closer to each other, there is a partial eclipse. When one orb is totally superimposed upon another, we see only one orb. When we become completely congruent with G-d and the joy that He provides, rancor fades, complaints dissolve. Real or imagined slights melt away. We forget about ourselves and our have or have-not state of mind.

When we surrender to an opponent in a chess or tennis tournament, the concession insinuates a weakness in a player's skills. When we surrender to G-d, however, we gain. We gain access to G-d's own brand of sublime and unlimited joy. Strength and surrender seem strange partners, but joy makes it work.

Strange partners! We surrender – to gain.

Give it up... Give it to G-d

The aftermath of Hurricane Katrina was notorious for the belated processing of insurance claims. My friend lives in New Orleans, the hub of the impacted disaster area. She had to wait many frustrating years for financial redress for her water damage and could not rebuild her home until her application was approved. Naturally, it was very frustrating to be stalled year after year, during which a normal quality of life remained in limbo, tied up in the red tape of bureaucracy.

She decided to make two lists of things that needed to get done. On one list she wrote all the things she could do, and on the other, she wrote things she could not do, such as inviting guests or replacing her ruined washing machine. The first list was for herself, and the second list, the things that were beyond her control, she "gave" to G-d.

The "two-list strategy" cleared the way for joy.

Joy lets G-d in. It's not about you, or me. It's about G-d. Are we connected?

So many things are buzzing around our heads and interfering with our happiness: I must get a new kitchen floor; I must have x, y and z living conditions. Whether they are necessities, luxuries or fantasies, we can write the item(s) on a piece of paper like a grocery list, and then **cross the items off the list**. We surrender them. They're gone. Ah, now joy can enter.

Clear the way for joy

Chana, an empathetic neighbor, related that once, as she was shopping in the fruit store, she noticed a woman whose face and posture bespoke utter dejection. In her forthright manner, Chana invited the woman to tell her what was bothering her. The woman began to describe her insufferable situation. Her daughter was getting married, and her ex-husband and his wife were making her feel superfluous and unwelcome at her own daughter's wedding.

Chana asked her, "Are you happy your daughter is getting married?" "Yes!" "Do you have something nice to wear to the wedding?" she questioned further. "Yes." "Then go to the wedding and have a good time!" "You should have seen the woman's face light up," Chana reported, "as she mentally removed those things she could not have off her list and focused on what she could have." Once the woman had surrendered the ideal scenario that she was carrying around in her mind, she was able to enjoy the blessings of the moment.

When we empty ourselves, we are making room to receive G-d's munificence.

We used to return from our *chol hamoed* (intermediate days of the major holidays) amusement park trips with a car of disgruntled children. Invariably, when it was time to go home, they each had one more ride they wanted to go on. Never mind the seventeen wonderful fun rides they had enjoyed. To them the trip was a failure because of that one last ride they didn't get to take.

As adults we don't do this anymore. Or do we?

> We learned to preempt this by having a "happiness discussion" and visualizing the end in advance. Do you enjoy amusement parks? What happens if we only go on six rides and not on seven? Would you still want to go? Will you still enjoy the trip?

*A joy-genius strategy is to "enjoy the things we already **have**" instead of focusing on "all the things we **want**" (and all the things we "deserve").*

Joy of Purpose

When we help someone feel better, as Chana did, we feel good about it. Every person needs to feel useful, a sense of gratification that he or she has added something to this hodgepodge world, a payback for all the trouble of hanging around for a lifetime.

When we have a sense of purpose, we're not centered on what "we need," but rather on "what we're needed for."

Well, isn't "perfect joy" a noble purpose? I'm not soliciting for ice cream or other petty gratifications. Joy is an honorable objective, isn't it?

But notice how the "I" is infiltrating – "*I'm* getting the simcha, *I'm* filling up with joy." And the next thing, we're wondering, "Am *I* happy yet?" which leads to kvetching, "I'm not happy yet!" That is not the voice of a happy soul.

A strange idiosyncrasy of our language is its large I and small "you." Here's a solution: Let's change the capital "I" of "I want…" into a small i. Now that we are no longer the center of our universe we are free to see how we can make the world a better place for others.

The next level is to bring in the big You – G-d. I shift the focus from myself and **"rejoice with Your joy…"** Let's not think about our own pleasure, for a change, but *what gives G-d pleasure*! G-d rejoices as He sees that we are making this world a dwelling place for Him (Tehillim 149:2, also in daily morning prayers).[82] How magnificent it is to "levitate" and see it from that lofty perspective. We're truly on top of the world when we reach the true ideal – putting G-dliness above our "self."

Are you capable of thinking beyond your own needs and happiness? Are you capable of truly rejoicing for others? To become your greatest "self" you must think beyond yourself.

Suppose a friend gushed excitedly that she won a cruise. What would your response be? "I'm not happy for you. Don't send me any pictures," or, "That's so nice! I am so happy for you!"

Granted, it's human nature to be jealous. But the winner's personality may influence our response – it's hard to rejoice in the good fortune of a selfish person. It's certainly easier to be happy for someone who cares about us as well. Who cares for us more than G-d, the Epitome of Giving and Selflessness? He has no needs for Himself whatsoever. It shouldn't be that hard to say, "G-d, I'm happy for you."

What a wonderfully happy world this would be if we all woke up and said, "Let's be done with petty politics, for G-d's sake! Let's set aside personal interests and do it for G-d's sake!"

If we set out to live life with the goal of "I want perfect joy" we will not find it. When we drop the big "I" and refine the "want," perfect joy can emerge.

A participant in a workshop on joy was a giant step ahead of me. She assumed, when I presented the words "I want perfect joy" to the group, that the word "I" was not the egotistical voice of the body but the selfless voice of the soul. Frankly, it had not even occurred to me to think so nobly. But yes, when the voice of the body becomes congruent to the voice of the soul, we are well on the way to perfect joy.

Simcha is derived from the realization that the most important point is not "me," what I want and need. Ultimately, it's what You,

G-d, want. And what does G-d want? He is happy when we make His children happy, when we focus on each other's needs – this is the ambition of every parent. This is a real unity of purpose!

A chassid learns a lesson

> A man whose business was in a precarious state was admitted to the study of the Alter Rebbe (the Baal HaTanya). The distraught disciple listed the problems from which he needed immediate deliverance. The Rebbe waited until he finished, and then said, "So far you have been telling me everything you need, **but not what you are needed for.**" It happened that this man was a refined, eminent individual, dedicated to the service of G-d and the community, but, in the anxiety of impending loans he could not cover, he had forgotten all but his own needs. The Rebbe's reminder that he had forgotten to put G-d on top of his list of needs hit the chassid with such force that he fainted on the spot. After he was revived he spent the next few days in prayer and study, putting all his worldly concerns out of his mind. Several days later, he was re-admitted to see the Rebbe who blessed him with success, and indeed his business fully recovered and he was able to continue helping people, even more than before.

It's not about "me" and my needs. It's about doing whatever it is we were sent down to this world to achieve.

The good news is **we have everything we need, to do what we are needed for** – no matter what we think we're lacking. Young and old, rich and poor, healthy people and hospitalized ones all have the ability to make this world a welcoming one for G-d Above and Man below.

About "having" and our happiness index.
A comparison study was done between people who became paralyzed in traumatic accidents and those who had an unexpected

turn of good fortune, such as winning the lottery.[83] The former were found to be just as happy, over time, and even happier than those from the latter group.[84]

G-d alone knows why he picks specific people for specific challenges. We wish everyone a happy, eminently enjoyable life. But, just in case we do encounter a challenge, it helps to remember that...

There is a joy in purpose and a purpose in challenge.

Let's take a moment to rejoice in our purpose. People may take years to find their calling – something that makes life meaningful and purposeful. Jews have a built-in calling, an elevated life defined by commitment to the Torah and mitzvahs. What a joy to have a mission like that.

"With purpose comes inner joy. With purpose, your life belongs to you. And it is eternal life, as your purpose is eternal."[85]

Being purposely focused on a mission of value gives our egos less time to stir up trouble. When we discover a nobility of purpose, our lives are uplifted.

Haman, the infamous villain of the Purim story, is described in the *megila*, the Book of Esther, as coming home from the palace in a great mood, but, as he confessed to his wife, there was one thorn in his side – Mordechai the Jew. He had everything he wished for, was at the top of the world politically, but one Jew who would not bow to him interfered with his happiness.

G-d keep all Hamans far away from us! But this behavior does sound familiar. Our joy can be marred by another person's success...someone's better than me...someone's getting more recognition than me.

To tune into others we have to tune out of ourselves. This means working against our default. Try this shortcut: **tune into others and you'll forget about yourself!**

Purposefulness is an effective remedy for pettiness.

We're still working on refining perfect joy, but, hopefully, we have succeeded in removing some of the *imperfect* joy. I guess you might say we're sweeping up before bringing in the new furniture. So there is a purpose in it – and there's joy in every worthy purpose!

11

De Light of Joy

There is so much beauty around us but without joy we can't see it

J oy is a de-light! Truly, the two – joy and light – are closely aligned. Joy is usually represented by the color yellow, due to its luminous quality, and light is defined in physics as a luminous or radiant energy. Joy is the ultimate metaphor for the Divine (light) as it is the most ethereal of creations and imitates many spiritual properties.

As sure as there is light in the world we all have the delight of joy within us. Even if we are depressed, we still have joy within our souls. Remember? Wherever G-d is present (He is certainly in our souls), there is "strength and gladness."[86]

Shadows of light

Do you wish you had more "internal light" in your system? Some people have lots of light – joy, positivity, kindness. Others seem drawn to darkness. Perhaps, after many years of living in its shadows, they've become accustomed to it and don't have tools to deal with the light. The optimists, those perennially positive people that are naturally equipped with "light" seem to be the fortunate ones. It's not pleasant to be living in the shadow of pessimism.

- A pessimist is preoccupied with how dark the clouds are, but the optimist doesn't see the clouds. He's walking on them – and getting all the bright sunshine.
- A pessimist turns his opportunities into difficulties. An optimist turns his difficulties into opportunities.
- A pessimist, when talking to G-d, tells Him how big his problems are. An optimist tells his problems how big G-d is. One moans; the other sings.
- Always "read" the bright side of life. It's not possible to see in the dark.
- A pessimist's blood type is always B-negative.
- The pessimist fears that things are so bad they cannot get any worse. The optimist saves the day by assuring the pessimist that things have the potential of getting far worse than they already are. (This one was clearly composed by a pessimist.)

But give the pessimist some credit: The optimist may have invented the airplane, but the pessimist gave us the parachute.

Actually, each personality type has its challenges. An optimistic person may have so much light in her system that she doesn't know how to handle the darkness. One such person was bemoaning her inability to set limits. She couldn't say no to people who had no concept of boundaries and were abusing her smiling, unending goodness. So enjoy what you have. The grass is green on your side as well.

I was reading a paragraph about light and was struck by how the words *light* and *joy* are interchangeable. "Light [joy] does not create anything new. It only lights up [reveals] that which is already present. It removes all doubts engendered by shadow, darkness, by mistaken notions and blindness."

Let there be light...

"We must increase in light and not just any light, but spe-cifically the light of simcha. Simcha breaks...the limitations imposed by this dreadful darkness of exile..."[87]

"The greatest light comes from within the darkness itself...we must fight the darkness with great simcha... only by adding in light can we truly overtake the darkness[88]

"When we see the darkness, it is evident the forces that op-pose holiness are still active. Apparently, the joy that was achieved up until now was not great enough to nullify it. Simply put, there must be an increase in joy of holiness. The obstacles should not affect us. On the contrary, we must add, with greater strength and force, in all expressions of joy."[89]

Conclusion: It's not enough to shine a little bit of light, the bare minimum that keeps us from "bumping into the walls." We must flood our lives with more and more joy, until we outpower all vestiges of darkness.

What is the best word choice? Are we *combating* the darkness, *chasing* away the darkness, *nullifying* it, *overpowering* it or *lighting* it up? It may be that each has merit. We know one thing: When the light we generate with our joy will be greater than the darkness, the darkness will cease to be.

A blind man was sitting on the sidewalk of a commercial thoroughfare. Next to him was a sign. "I'M BLIND. PLEASE HELP." Occasionally a pedestrian would stop and throw something into his collection can. After a few hours, he had barely accumulated a few cents. A passerby who surveyed the scene, stopped, picked up the brown corrugated cardboard sign, and wrote a new message on the back. Suddenly, the change was pouring into his plate. What was the magic mes-

sage that generated this remarkable turnaround? The new message read, "IT'S A BEAUTIFUL DAY AND I CAN'T SEE IT."

Why was the new message more effective? Our systems have a built-in pain protection mechanism to shut out negative input. So, when the environment sends a message with a pitiful tone, we may try to avoid it by turning a "blind" eye to the unfortunate person's plight. But when the message we receive is one of joy and celebration of life, of the beauty of the day or the moment, it evokes a corresponding sense of joy in the listener. Our feel-good side has been aroused. Happy people are also more prone to sharing – and the blind man's collection can was the happy recipient.

We need each other to add light to every corner of the world. Don't wait for people to come and add light to your life. Be proactive about your joy. Shine your own light out to the world; the world is bound to reciprocate. No one's world is so dark that they don't have some light to offer and share.

Joy, like a candle, can share its light with many others and not be diminished.

It's always a perfect day, even if we don't see it.
You know those stories where you're in the right place at the right time and everything works out "perfectly"? My summer job finished earlier than expected, as some students had gone on last-minute vacations. I had some free time and went to check on an adorable but challenging child I'd worked with that year. As I approached the building, my replacement teacher for the summer session was walking towards me. "I booked tickets to Israel last night. Do you know anyone to replace me?" she asked. Yes! I was available, and it was exactly what I wanted: more time to work on the child's skills, a supplemental income opportunity, and I would still have time left for a vacation.
I commented on the neat chain of events when I introduced myself to the camp director. "Perfect!" was her comment. I remember

thinking wryly, "Wouldn't it be wonderful if that were always the case?"

Well, as real life goes, my first Monday on the new job, neither my new nor old students showed up. "It's still a perfect day," I told myself, even though I didn't see it. (Writing about joy has made me more willing to agree that G-d is running our world perfectly well.) It seemed to be a wasted morning and purposeless commute, but we know there's a reason for everything. If one plan doesn't work out, G-d must be opening the door for a better plan. I used the unexpected slot of free time to make another attempt to book a mileage ticket to Israel, though I had sort of given up; there were just no mileage slots available. Fifteen minutes later I had the reservations I wanted – right at the height of the travel season. I began organizing the travel details at once, gratified that I would be leaving for Israel right after my "perfect" job ended.

It was a perfectly beautiful day after all.

It's a beautiful day and a beautiful world. Without joy – we cannot see it.

12

I See You, Joy

Good things should be shared

Does your joy spilleth over? Try to "read" the people around you. People can be inscrutable. *Are* they happy on the inside? Who's to know? I wonder if they even know.

"Joy is my own business," many of us think. "It can be a quiet presence. It doesn't necessarily have to show to the outside world." We can experience inner joy.

Happy Walls

Some people wish their houses were noisier. It's sometimes just them and the four walls. Other people wish their houses were quieter. They have a hard time with the noise level in a house with a bunch of energetic children.

The sounds of a wholesome lifestyle should fill the air with joy and positivity. Joy, when it's utterly real and full, makes its presence heard. Even if you're living all by yourself, your walls need to hear about your inner joy.

Rina was getting annoyed at the way her brother was eating.

"Do you have to make so much noise when you eat?"
"Our teacher told us to start the day with a sound breakfast."

When Moshiach will come, the stones on the walls will cry out to protest impropriety.[90] What *are* those walls hearing now? When we fill our minds with happy thoughts, our mindstream flows naturally into "happy speech," producing a lovely surround-sound environment.

Women specialize in creating a warm and welcoming home environment. We decorate the walls with hangings and pictures. We fuss about just the right shade of paint. We can "paint" our walls with happy sounds.

Inner joy is a good starting point, but a full-bloom gladness will manifest itself visually and verbally when the fullness of the joy forces it out, like a succulent fruit whose juice drips out when it is cut. The ultimate manifestation will be in the future: *az yimalei schok pinu* – when Moshiach comes our joy will be so great that it will spill over into laughter that can be *heard*!

One word, three meanings: Simcha – revelation – redemption...

The words *gila* (rejoicing), *gilui* (revealed) and *geulah* (redemption) share a common word root. The three are interconnected. Joy is a *revealer*. When everything is saturated with *joy* we see goodness around us. Our eyes open to see a different, better world. Thus, we can feel the *Redemption* even during the exile.

Joy is a Geulah state. The more joy we put out, the more Geulah we bring in to the world.

Here's another exciting word association highlighting the connection between simcha and Moshiach: *Moshiach* ("anointed one") shares the same four Hebrew letters as the word *yismach* ("let him rejoice").

We have to see it to believe it

Would you hire someone for a sports team just by talking to him? No, you have to see him in action.

When something is seen its existence is vouchworthy. When G-d gave the Jewish people the Torah, millions of people were there to testify to it.

Did man really set foot on the moon? Honestly, those simulated telecasts in advance looked exactly like the real thing.

Did anyone see your joy in action? We're looking for authentic, verifiable joy. You may be experiencing some measure of joy but unless it is seen it can't be vouched for.

"Seeing" is a special gift.
"Whoever did not *see* the joy of Simchas Beis Hashoeva (Ritual of the Water Drawing in the Holy Temple) has not seen true simcha."[91] Whoever has not *seen* authentic joy cannot fathom the depths it offers.

A toddler hears many warnings, "Hot! Dangerous!" but after she burns her fingers she has a new level of perception. "Ah, now I see what hot means."

Simchas Beis Hashoeva[92] was a joy fiesta during the holiday of Sukkos with all stops pulled out. The joy was so passionate that it could not be contained internally. Simchas Beis Hashoeva is a code word for a see-able joy. We have not – yet – had the privilege to be part of that extraordinary joy, but we can see it by making it vivid in our hearts.

Once you are aware that joy can go deep, try to reach for it.

Authentic joy is a – physically – "moving" experience

How does joy display its face? After all, it has no hands, feet or assigned limb to express itself. Joy has no hands but can animate hands.

It has no feet but can make feet dance. It has no mouth but loosens tongues and curves lips into smiles. When joy fills every crevice, it spills over. Joy is one of the most moving experiences. It makes body parts move, hands gesture, feet jump and pirouette, and bodies spin.

Fortunate is the person blessed with the equanimity that keeps him on an even keel through life's occasional shakeups. But sometimes we need to be shaken up in a positive way.

> *The little boy was jumping up and down after taking his medicine. His mother asked him "Why are you jumping?" The little boy pointed to the label of the medicine bottle. "It says here to shake well!"*

The emotions of joy and laughter are medicines that shake us up in a curative, restorative way.

There was a couple who had hoped, prayed and tried for many years to merit the blessings of children. Finally, they received the news that their efforts culminated with success – the wife was confirmed expectant with their first child! The would-be father describes his reaction: "Words simply cannot describe the feeling of sheer joy that enveloped me and my wife at that moment. My legs literally lifted me off the ground, and I could jump three steps in a single bound. I felt like I was flying."

This is the very reaction that Yaakov our Forefather had when he heard the good news G-d had in store for him. The Torah records that after G-d appeared to him in the famous ladder dream he "lifted his feet." Once the good tidings – the assurance that G-d would be guarding over him -- were imparted, his heart lifted his feet and it became easy to walk.[93]

> **Emotion creates motion.**
> There is a concept called emotional running. When our sages urge us to "run" to do a mitzvah they are not necessarily advocating a physical sprint but rather the state of mind that precipitates action. (Like the daily bitachon run we spoke about.)

Full-blown joy

Kids love Chinese balloons – those long, skinny bands that swell into a long, inflated tube. As you keep blowing, the air you blow in will reach deeper and deeper until you've inflated the furthest end. Of course, if the balloon is stretched beyond its maximum, it will pop.

Blowing Chinese balloons is not a joy-filling task, but the expansive quality of joy within us is well served by the balloon metaphor.

Typically, joy only partially permeates a person. It does not strip away our outer shell of reserve. The innermost, deeply entrenched areas of our psyches remain constricted and unaffected. Keep pumping – the deeper the simcha reaches, the more oomph we have to soar and light up our surroundings. If you pop the constraints, the emotions are free to expand as they please.

> *What's the difference between balloons and joy? A popped balloon has reached the end of its career, but a Jew connected to spiritual joy will forever grow and flourish.*

How do we know when the joy has fully inflated? When the tingle of joy reaches from our heads to our toes, when we suddenly, irresistibly feel like dancing, then we know our system has reached full-blown joy-saturation.

Famous for their joy-dancing are...
- Miriam leading the women in song and praises as they danced with tambourines after the miraculous crossing of the Red Sea.
- King David whirling and skipping before the Ark of the Covenant.

One who has acquired Torah, say the Sages, should not keep it for himself.[94] I ask you, if you have joy, why would you keep it all for yourself?

Happiness may be an inside job, but *ahavas Yisroel* (love for your fellow man), asks that you share it with others.

13

Optimize! Controlling Climate Conditions

Tips on helping Authentic, True and Genuine joy flourish

Good produce needs fertile soil – the richer the soil, the better the produce. The produce also needs the right climate and weather conditions – water and sun.

Genuine "organic" joy as well needs the right climate and growing medium to flourish and develop sturdy, life-sustaining roots. There are three facets that enhance and fertilize joy – seriousness, awe and humility – but teaming them with joy makes for seemingly paradoxical combinations.

- **"Serious" joy.** Does that mean we should banter seriously?
- **Fear (awe) and joy.** "Serve G-d with fear," exhorts the psalmist[95] "and *rejoice* with *trepidation*." How can joy and trepidation co-exist?
- **Humility and joy.** These are two apparently contrary concepts: the former is constrictive, the latter expansive.

Paradoxes can be fun. Here are some: Waterproof sponges. Glow-in-the-dark sunglasses. Fast food cholent.

Paradoxes can be fun, and joy can be uplifting. But it isn't anything-goes-to-get-joy-going. We need to know what we're doing. In order for joy to flourish, it needs to germinate in a nurturing climate of seriousness, awe and humility. Without these underlying elements, the joy we are experiencing will be deficient and truncated.

Joy is exhilarating. It can elevate a person to lofty heights. Joy is powerful. It can dismantle blockages. That's why it's so important to know what authentic joy is. Let the wise men come and teach us.

Reb Mendel Futerfas,[96] a legendary chassid and educator, would caution his students to watch out for two concepts that seem similar but are actually vastly different – **simcha and holelus** (frivolity and unruly wildness).

I. Joy – Seriously!

Connect to Authentic Joy

I think back to my parents' Shabbos table. There was joy, but also an underlying gravity and earnestness. From an early age, we were reminded to listen attentively and stand straight for Kiddush. On Purim as well, when high spirits were supposed to sweep us off our feet, my father attended to the mitzvahs of the day with deep reverence. You can be serious and still have fun. Conversely, having fun does not mean you cannot be serious!

My father was a real-life demonstration of the ability to unify seriousness and joy. Love and Awe of Heaven weren't potential ideas for him – they were active emotions. He radiated a full-bodied joyfulness and inner pleasure in serving G-d, but when he sensed a breach in a mitzvah or halacha, he was fierce as a lion (although he would not kill a fly and was incapable of spanking a child). Just by looking at my father, I could feel G-d's awesome and loving presence because I could see my father sensing His closeness.

My father's vitality enhanced his every activity. Despite the many years since his passing, I vividly recall how he would offer his visiting grandchildren three pennies to drop into the pushkeh and then have them shake the box to hear the coins jumping around. The children were so enchanted with the blissfulness of the mitzvah, highlighted by their Zeidy's radiant pleasure, that it outshone the lollipops their Bubby would offer afterwards.

How do we know if jolliness is tethered to *holiness* or has disintegrated into *holelus,* empty levity? The joy of Purim offers an ideal setting to examine the subtle differences. Let us zoom in to that zenith of joy.

On Purim we're eager to be "up-there," to fly away on the wings of our joy. To help us turn on the magic joy button, we take a little l'chaim, which is actually desirable on Purim. But the same cup of wine that could elevate us to the lofty level of *ad d'lo yada* (a holy oblivion in which our soul empowers us to transcend the limitations of rational nature[97]) can also fling us into the gutters. (If we are dependent on l'chaims all year round to generate bliss, we should seek counsel.)

Authentic joy connects us to G-d. Loose behavior takes us away from Him. Authentic joy has gravity and substance, roots and depth, and is regulated and meaningful. Holelus is hollow, derived from the elements of air and wind, a superficial pseudo-joy. This shallow joy looks for sources to feed the emptiness, which it may fill with antics. When a partying group becomes raucous, feeding on cheap jokes to draw laughs, or degenerates into drinking and other vices, it exposes the painful, unfulfilling void of holelus.

You can't be in control of your life but you can be in control of your joy.

A profound point, and those who master it have mastered life itself. Notice also the double meaning in the second part. Our joy has to be controlled. Demonstrative joy is precariously close to crossing the line into *holelus.* Joy is powerful, and our external displays of simcha must be carefully monitored so they don't run loose.

> **Authentic joy doesn't crumple in difficult situations.**
> When you are distressed, the superficial joy won't hold up. It lacks
> depth; it is not connected to a solid source. It's like a match – one
> blow and the flame is gone. But you can fan the flames of a smol-
> dering coal – the simcha within us is that inner flame which may
> only be smoldering but comes out when a person is faced with the
> challenges of life.

A distinguishing marker of authentic joy is the way it pushes us
to include others. Simcha is associated with unity.[98] Authentic joy is
a "connected" joy. We rejoice *with* G-d and *with* people. Holelus sepa-
rates people with its derisive, demeaning style. It pokes fun at others' expense. Contrast Halloween's hands-out-for-treats mode and
its demonic costumes, with Purim's giving and sharing and its wholesome costume themes. Two of the day's mitzvahs involve giving and
sharing. "There is no greater or beautiful joy than rejoicing the hearts
of the poor and orphans, widows and converts," says the Rambam.[99]
When a "l'chaim" is shared, it is an opportunity to mutually exchange
blessings. There is tremendous power in it.

> *A story is told of a cheerful group of chassidim enroute to their
> Rebbe who encountered a dejected Jew staying in their inn.
> "Why are you so downhearted?" they asked him.
> "Why? My situation is hopeless. The Rebbe that you are trav-
> elling to see has not only rejected my plea for a blessing, he
> ordered me to leave." The chassidim had never heard anything
> like it. To be rejected by the Rebbe? The only thing they could
> think of doing was urge him to join them in a l'chaim. In a joy-
> ous atmosphere, they lifted their cups and blessed him to find
> salvation from his troubles. The next morning, they insisted
> he accompany them to the Rebbe. This time the Rebbe greeted
> him warmly! The Rebbe explained that when the Jew came in
> to see him he had seen a decree hanging over him that he was
> unable to rescind. The joyous l'chaims of the chassidim had
> succeeded in breaking the decree.*

A Seriously Joyful Rabbi

A Rabbi from California was visiting Israel when a religious man approached him with great excitement. "Rabbi, you're the one to whom I owe all my Yiddishkeit!" He told Rabbi Levitansky that he became a baal teshuva all because of a short visit one night at the Rabbi's house.

He had met Rabbi Levitansky through his participation in his public school's released time program (a weekly one-hour religious instruction class). The Rabbi had invited him to the seder but unfortunately, his parents did not allow him to join. Rabbi Levitansky thought of a second-best plan. He invited the young student to attend a pre-Passover ceremony called "bedikas chometz" (the search for chometz).

The guest showed up at the designated time and saw how the Rabbi wrapped ten pieces of chometz, and then the family hid them. Then the Rabbi recited a blessing and went from room to room with a lit candle, searching the house for chometz and collecting the wrapped pieces which were placed around the house.

To the guest's amazement, the Rabbi went "nuts" when he couldn't find one of the ten pieces, and the entire family was enlisted in the search. "The Rabbi was completely focused on this one little piece of bread. He was oblivious of the guest and all the preparations for Pesach. He checked sources in seforim (holy books) and consulted with rabbis. All because a small, wrapped piece of chometz had disappeared. What struck him was the stark contrast of Rabbi Levitansky's notably jovial style with the sobering and genuine depth of "the word of G-d."

"When I saw this, I realized that Judaism is serious, much more than I had thought until then, and I wanted to devote myself to learn more about it." He enrolled in a yeshiva, became religious, is raising a religious family, and has made a

career of publishing seforim, all thanks to the utter commitment of a serious Rabbi in California.

Here is another example of Rabbi Levitansky's style that merits sharing: Someone rushed in breathlessly to join the evening prayer, but realized that he didn't have his *gartel*, the traditional belt worn during prayer. He asked the Rabbi if there were any spare gartlach. "Sure," said Rabbi Levitansky, taking one out of his pocket, "I have one right over here." And then the Rabbi walked over to the phone on the wall, detached the cord from the box and receiver, tied it around his own waist, and was ready to pray. (You can't do that anymore in this wireless age! But resourceful people will find solutions no matter what the world is up to.)

I came across a line that seemed made-to-order for this discussion:

"You can be serious and still have fun. Conversely, having fun does not mean you cannot be serious. Have some Serious Fun."

Here's my own two cents: You can't be *funny* unless you have *serious*. That's how opposites work – you can't be clean unless you have been dirty, full unless you have empty, and – you can't have Geulah unless you have galus.

II. Fear As a Path to True Joy

Fear is a lousy life-motivator. Imagine that we're cruising down the highway, but instead of looking ahead at the road, we are intent only on looking back to make sure we're not being tailgated.

The two opposing emotions of fear and joy expand and contract in direct relation to the presence of each other. This is why with true joy there is absence of worry, anxiety and fear.

Fear controls us, but we control joy. Which will have the final say? Our faith will vanquish the fear, and when we add the strength of joy, it will make the faith powerful and rock solid. Yield: the joy of faith.

Fear is a pipeline to true and constant joy

There's another kind of "fear." "Serve G-d with awe and *rejoice* with *trepidation.*" How do joy and trembling, two diametric opposites, co-exist?

Fear can be a destructive and negative emotion. But when we stand before an awesome person, like a King or a truly wise or holy man, awe is a constructive fear response. Serving G-d with fear and awe precedes all other steps in our Divine service, but it leads us to the greatest heights.

> **True and false:** There is *true* fear, and *false* fear. The former is awe and fear of G-d, the latter an anxiety-driven human fear that arises due to lack of faith.
>
> Likewise, *true* joy tells us there is a *false* joy. A joy based on eternal values is true. Ephemeral or materialistic sources are not true and enduring. When those sources are gone, the simcha is gone with them. Divine Joy is true and constant. It is not generated by prevailing conditions or circumstances or "causes." G-d is always with us, and therefore we can always enjoy *true* joy, free of fallacious fear and transient happiness.

"Rejoice with trepidation." In the place where there is rejoicing, there should also be trepidation.

The words in the psalm are *v'gilu be'r'ada.* There are several interpretations of this expression with its two opposing emotions. One version is that they should both reign equally; another is that the trembling should dominate the joy. According to my favorite interpretation, joy reigns: The word *gilu* – rejoice – is very similar to *gilui* which means 'revealed'. The message: Reveal the joy that is in the trembling, **gilu** be'r'ada![100] Joy should be the dominant quality, the vibrant foreground of life's canvas.

The Talmud recounts several incidents that relate to the theme of joyousness co-existing with trepidation: One example:

The Sage Rabbah noticed that his colleague, Abaye, was excessively cheerful. Rabbah reminded Abaye, "It is written, 'rejoice with trepidation.'" Abaye defended himself, "I am wearing tefillin" (proof that G-d's fear was upon him).[101] An explanation is offered: Abaye had been unable to don tefillin for a period of time due to an ailing stomach and was now full of joy that he was able to resume doing the mitzvah. Based on this, Rabbeinu Yonah concludes: Rejoicing which is performed for the sake of G-d rather than for our own pleasure does not run the risk of leading one away from mitzvahs; it is a mitzvah in and of itself.

The same conundrum comes up in our prayers. We are given two opposite instructions how to prepare for prayer. In one we're told to focus on the trembling awe; in another we're reminded to gird ourselves with joy.[102] Conclusion: There's both fear and love in our prayers. The *way* we do it, though, must be with simcha.

Davening (praying) is serious in that we take our joy – seriously!

I Love Love. Can't we skip the fear?

Love and fear are not conflicting, but rather, complementary entities. Through the former we are drawn to G-d; through the latter we resist anything that will separate us from Him.

Love alone is unstable. (We will read more about this in the next chapter.)

III. Joy Inflates and Humility Deflates ...and leads to Genuine Joy

Unimposing humility and the expansiveness of joy are two contrary concepts – and yet they go so well together. Self-effacement allows space for the expansiveness of the other. As the prophet Yeshayahu points out, "The meek will increase their joy in G-d."[103]

There's a difference between taking life seriously and taking yourself (too) seriously. (Joy-geniuses know this!) The first is laudable, the second is a ticket to unhappiness.

Humility doesn't demand that you put yourself down. Your self-esteem should be up and running. The only thing that should go down is your ego teleprompter that feeds you statements like, *"Look how I'm treated... What do they really think of me..."*

Are you humble? Here's a quick humility-checklist. If you're humble, you...

- are not a wimp, a spineless *shmateh* (rag) or doormat that everyone steps on.
- don't have an inflated ego, self-delusions, or unhealthy need for adulation.
- do have a strong inner core, emotional honesty, a realistic idea of your capabilities.

Are you humble? You are no doubt a gifted person with many wonderful talents and qualities. These talents are gifts. G-d could have given them to anyone, but He gave them to you. How privileged you are! You'll surely want to "give back" by making this world a better place.

And by the way, it's very possible that had He given these gifts to Mr. Ordinary down the block, he would have used those talents more fully. No need to get carried away.

Joy comes from trying to make G-d great and ourselves small. Humility clears the space.

Our Sages tell us that we should be happy with our lot.[104] There are two obstacles to being happy with one's (material) lot:

Our expectations: They interfere with being pleasantly surprised and grateful when good fortune comes our way. ("I had it all planned out...that's not how I envisioned life would be.")

A feeling of entitlement: Our belief that we deserve lots of good things. We've set ourselves up for disappointment and resentment when we don't get them. ("That's not how a wife, son, mother should greet me." "I work really hard so I deserve a nice, big house.")

Humility leads directly to full and unrestricted simcha. When we see our qualities as gratuitous gifts from Above, we are grateful for them. The gift is itself preferential treatment! So we're truly happy with life.

> **Every person is "entitled" to have the privilege of being humble.**

When everything is an undeserved gift, everything in our lives becomes something to sing about.

14

This Product is Made Of...

Let's analyze and dissect the "internal stuffing" of joy

The caliber of joy depends on how it is generated and what it stems from. Joy could be transient or eternal, internal or external, finite or infinite, material or spiritual. It could stem from external or internal sources. We begin with a brief preview of these joy subtypes.

Some companies (most notably a well-known soda company that promises a pick-me-up) keep their recipes secret. We will give you the joy ingredients so you can satisfy your insatiable craving for joy at any time! You will discover the sources, the depth and how to produce a pick-up anytime.

Transient or eternal

We know about tears of joy, but there are also tiers of joy. Simcha is typically a multi-tiered experience. There is relative joy based on the moment's good news and there is the enduring laughter that transcends the present moment. We can use transient triggers and harness them to enduring values.

Internal or external

Natural Springs… Jewish joy is organic. There is a place within every Jew that will always be free and joyous by virtue of the soul (*simchas hanefesh*). These joy-springs are constant. The sources are always available. In contrast, joy that stems from external sources fluctuates – the weather often determines our mood.

Internal and external are relative terms. There are many layers of Divine depth, each layer more internal, and at the same time external relative to the next deeper layer, reaching down all the way to the essence. The deeper in we go, the more powerfully the joy can break barriers and tangibly affect us.

Finite or infinite

Big league… A joy that is measured and is conceivable is called gvul, limited, as it is limited by the human mind. There is also a joy that we can achieve if we move beyond our own limited cognitive intake. Bli gvul means without limits. To do this, we need to break out of our safety net, our reliance on our own prowess and the limitations of our human logic. It is a transcendent joy. We are working with and through G-d's infinite powers.

Material or spiritual

Joy can be superficial (happiness) or can involve a deeper reality. We typically label matters related to corporeal pleasures as superficial relative to the inner, spiritual dimension of the person's neshama. Spiritual joy is enduring. It is not a "here today, gone tomorrow" type of experience. A new, fully-loaded car or a grand, new front door, the currency of the "real" world, excite us for a while, but then what? We can gain abiding spiritual pleasure by kindling a Chanukah menorah, doing an act of kindness, studying Torah.

> **Joy is the expression of the neshama. The neshama is always "up" because G-d is always in charge!**

Joy-opportunities present themselves in the most unexpected times and places. It's up to us to maximize those golden opportunities:

Pop-up joy... All types of "random" situations pop-up in our lives. When they resolve in a positive manner, they leave joy in their wake. The lost wallet that was miraculously found and returned; the good news from the lab report – thank G-d! I passed the driving test (the more times we fail, the higher the joy mercury rises when we pass). We finally got rid of the mouse that inhabited our house – what a relief to be able to become master of our domain and walk the floors freely.

Capitalism... Become a capitalist: Make the most out of those pop-up situations, large and small. Think back to the last time you were in pain. The amount of attention that was showered on the pain! You thought about it every move you made. The appreciation when the pain subsides and functioning returns to normal – there's where we need to be capitalists and get the most positive return on our "investment" (the pain and the disability).

The joy-capitalist version of no pain, no gain: There's pain? Gain!

I had paid the parking violation ticket but the city would not acknowledge my payment for a full year. It was a pain-in-the-neck, but now that the record was finally cleared, I was ready to celebrate. My family cooled me down, "What's the big deal? They should have credited the account long ago." Yes, but now that it happened, let's capitalize on the opportunity to generate joy and gratitude. *That's pain-in-the-neck gain!*

Recycling opportunity: "Recycled joy." The capitalist in me spots a profitable venture: We can recycle the "downs" by getting some good use out of them. The "bad" events provide us with the high that follows. *The advantage of sadness is the light that follows it; it shines even stronger than before.*

My neighbor Yafit told me, after a difficult and extended recovery from a postpartum ordeal when her health was jeopardized, "It's not the same *modeh ani* (morning thank-you prayer) as before."

Journaling... is a great capitalist ploy. Everyone should keep one! We go back and read them and are amazed by how many problems were successfully resolved. I was delighted to refresh my memory with several great miracles in my own life.

Writing about joy has proven to be a wonderfully effective way to preserve my good spirits, as everyone in my family can testify. Here's one sample of empirical evidence. One day, I discovered that my husband was cutting down the bushes that I had vigorously campaigned to keep intact. When I discovered what he was doing, I came outdoors and calmly said to him, "You're lucky I'm in middle of writing about joy!" and went back in to continue my work, surprisingly unruffled about it. (Will it last? Time will tell, and G-d will help.)

Should keeping a joy journal have been one of the 613 mitzvahs?

A New Joy is in the air

Pure Joy... is focused purely on the anticipation of the upcoming Geulah. The pure-joy concept was proposed by the Lubavitcher Rebbe just six months after the passing of his wife in 5748 (1988). It is a joy-concept that is focused purely on anticipation of the Geulah. In Hebrew, 5748 is *taf-shin-mem-ches* (using the numerical value of letters), or *Tismach*, "you shall rejoice." The year seemed to be anything but joyous, considering the momentous loss suffered by the Rebbe. However, there is more than meets the eye, especially regarding the life of a spiritual leader.[105]

The Rebbe bemoaned the fact that we've tried every trick to get out of the galus and yet we're still here. What more can be done? He proposed a strategy, a Divine service that *was never tried before:* Simcha! But not the simcha that is traditionally derived from doing a mitzvah. The Rebbe called it *simcha b'taharasa* – pure joy, a simcha that is focused solely on Geulah. This strategy, he asserted, will finally break the barriers of galus. "Try it and see," he urged, and spread this message everywhere – hence this book!

If simcha for Geulah is indeed that potent, why, asked the Rebbe, wasn't it proposed before? The answer is obvious. The pain and darkness of galus prevent a pure expression of simcha. But, being so close to Geulah, **the potential is granted from Above**. We can tap into that joy by bringing to mind the imminence of Moshiach's arrival.

Leaders of world Jewry have aired similar themes.

"Because Moshiach is almost here," said Rabbi Aharon Leib Shteinman z"l, "G-d has created a special desire [a new potential from Above] among people who are not yet *frum* to become baalei teshuva."[106]

As the sun casts its rays before its appearance, the imminent Geulah already illuminates the world. The new light in the dawning sky awakens new potentials embedded in our future.

15

Tiers of Joy
The many levels of joy

Next time you cut into an onion, look at it carefully. You know what onions and joy have in common, don't you? They both make you cry. They share another similarity: they both have layers. Everything in life has layers. The earth, the trees, even the fashion world had a trend called "the layered look." Every day as we recite the Shema prayer, we are reminded that there are seven heavens. Have you ever seen those heavens? Yet we know they're there. Who knows, maybe each is another heavenly layer of joy...Joy, too, has lots of layers, some of which we've never seen. Let's take a closer look:

Tier #1: Seriousness

The bottom layer

The foundation on which we build our joy is – seriousness.

The text on this page is on a white background because that makes the words easier to read.

Joy too needs a suitable background to offset it. That background is *seriousness.*

A core prerequisite to joy is fear of Heaven, *yira'as shamayim.* Truly satisfying joy is built on a deeply earnest reverence for an awesome G-d. We enlist G-d's participation – we're looking to get closer, not farther. It's a joy-of-content we seek rather than empty amusement.

Joy artists: Use seriousness and earnestness for your back-drop and paint joy lavishly over it.

How sober and majestic joy can be! Here is one man's report of a Purim celebration with a Rebbe and his followers: "...*The room was furnished with a décor of majesty and solemnity. Indeed, there was joy, but a most elevated and refined joy that stemmed from the true celebration of the holiday. I felt the paradoxical mix of happiness and seriousness all at one time. I found myself dancing, sucked in by the multitudes of men in ecstasy and transcendence. The entire world was transformed before my eyes; my perception would never be the same after being exposed to this bright light!*"[107]

Love or Fear?

Joy can be accessed through either of two paths, two options completely contrary to each other:

1. Through love of G-d.
2. Through fear of G-d.

Most people assume love is the logical medium to joy. It makes perfect sense. Love inflates the heart with joy. It's a natural outgrowth. A love-ly route with a happy ending.

But there is another route that leads to that same ending, and the sources tell us that it is even more effective and successful. Surprisingly, that route is fear, specifically "fear of Heaven."

Accessing joy through fear does seem counterintuitive. Fear usually implies "I want to get away from here," while joy is about *wanting* to be here and present. Love implies connection and relationship. Love does seem to be the right path to joy.

Surprising as it may be, the fear (and humility) route provides a more stable foundation than love. A commitment based solely on love is unstable. It could easily end up being self-serving. For example, I love chocolate, so there goes my diet. Love alone is unreliable and does not endure. It is a great conduit for things we like, but when we encounter the things we don't like, our emotional response is likely to be biased.

Love needs to be laced with awe to keep us on our joy track.

Tier #2: Rational Joy

The mind is the most powerful ally in our journeys to joy.

Once the basic foundation is laid, it's time to get the mind involved. Oh, and what a mind it is. The human reigns supreme over the three kingdoms (inanimate, plant and animal), and the brain is the sovereign of the human kingdom. The brain, a soft hold-in-your-hand-size mass of grayish matter, controls the emotions, operates the sense organs and directs the hands and feet. It is a supercomputer operated by a spiritual power. A neurosurgeon commented once, "I have seen many brains. I know what does not belong there and has to be removed. But I do not understand what I left in there."

The mind is a gatekeeper. It can reject ideas that will sully the emotions and select the ones that will purify the system. We need merely to keep arranging those thoughts until we find simcha. The Hebrew word for thought, *machshava*, has the same letters as *b'simcha*, with joy, just arranged differently.

Mindful *machshava* maintains a healthy ecology within the brain. A Rabbi counseled his disciple: "I would advise you to stop thinking foolish and sad thoughts and that your mind should rule your heart and make it happy, not your heart making your mind sad."

The brain is the Grand Conductor. It sifts and expands selected thoughts; it vivifies concepts. Texts, lectures, audio recordings can fill our beings with positive thoughts and ideas. We want to keep the spaces of the mind filled with beautiful thoughts so that unbidden negative ones have no room left to squeeze in.

The mind is the most powerful ally in our journeys to joy. To "serve G-d with simcha" is an invitation to the intellect: Make joy come to life by dwelling on the many aspects of G-d's loving and awesome relationship with us. Toss the idea about, the way you swill a sip of wine in your mouth. Savor it; consider the many nuances in it. And let the idea "go to your head," until you are heady with joy and it spills over into the heart.

And, on top of all that, the mind aspires to go higher, to soar to the maximum heights possible, until the point where our "knowing" encounters the not-knowable, until it throws up its hands in submission, "*Que sais-je*" – what do I know?

A mind that is filled with concepts of joy wishes to expand, like air molecules that have been warmed by the sunshine. The *goings on* of the mind stretch into the *growing* beyond, to explore and delight in the truths that lie beyond the limiting human system. The human race has an unquenchable thirst to know the planets and explore the galaxies; the Jewish mind has an insatiable drive to know and connect to its Source.

Each tier will bring us a step closer...We ascend to the next rung.

Tier #3: The Joy of Surrender

Put your mind aside!

For a full-scale appreciation of joy, go to the pinnacle of joy. Tourists trek along snaking mountain trails for a view of breathtaking vistas. The thrill of the exclusive perspective can be akin to a religious experience, an encounter with G-dliness.

One of the greatest outpourings of joy in Jewish history was during the Sukkos festival. "Whoever has not seen Simchas Beis Hashoeva, the Festive Water Drawing, has not witnessed true joy."[108] It was the pinnacle of joy for the Jewish nation during the times of the Holy

Temple. Any other joy, when compared to this joy, is superficial. We can't even begin to fathom the full extent of what genuine joy is unless we take in this joy first.

The water was drawn each evening of the festival with great jubilance and fanfare. It was used for libations to accompany the daily sacrifices – a Sukkos-exclusive (wine libations were done throughout the year). It generated a week-long pageant, complete with jugglers and gymnastic feats. The performers were illustrious scholars expressing their unbridled spiritual joy. Sages, heads of the Sanhedrin, chassidim and elders would dance before the assemblage, accompanied by songs and praise to G-d.

The fountainhead for year-round joy:

Each category of *avoda*, divine service, is empowered by a specific holiday. What is pumping Divine joy into the hours and minutes of our time-bound world?

Initially, the empowerment to fulfill mitzvahs with joy throughout the year came through Simchas Beis Hashoeva. Nowadays we lack the full dose of that intense joy. We need a more accessible feeding supply, something more in sync with our galus existence.

These days, joy 'round the year is powered by both Sukkos and Purim. Purim is a festival born in galus. Weekday activities are permitted on Purim, making it analogous to the galus, which has a weekday flavor relative to the holy era of the Beis Hamikdash (Holy Temple).

The power to fulfill mitzvahs with simcha is sourced in Sukkos but is channeled via Purim.[109]

What relevance does this have to us during the galus? We cannot witness it, so how can we appreciate genuine joy today?[110]

As we examine the root of that extraordinary joy, we will reveal the spiritual underpinnings of authentic joy and its relevance during the galus.

Sukkos gives us the power to reach our spiritual potential through joy exceeding our intellectual limitations. The transcendent joy of Simchas Beis Hashoeva is mined from kabolas ol. We will see how *kabolas ol* serves as a solid base for joy.

But first, what is "kabolas ol"? Kabolas ol is a mode of Divine service in which we put aside our own rationale, pleasure and personal opinion; we serve G-d by surrendering ourselves to Him.

Kabolas ol – A Mind-free Service

Oxen don't do much thinking – and it's not a bad thing. They stoically submit to the yoke placed on them and obediently plod back and forth across the farmland, so that the farmer can plow, plant and harvest. The yoked oxen typify the Divine service called *kabolas ol* (literally – accepting the yoke). It embraces acceptance of the yoke of heaven. It ennobles submission, commitment, loyalty – "G-d, I'm with you all the way."

This is a stable foundation, not subject to the whims of man and the winds of fate. Kabolas ol is incorruptible. There are times when we're not in the frame of mind to emote enthusiasm, but kabolas ol does not operate via emotion; it just soldiers on, deferring humbly to authority. In truth, kabolas ol leads to a more actualized way of living and a more highly developed connection with our Creator.

In the Future, the soul level that motivates a Jew to do mitzvahs with absolute kabolas ol will be revealed, a level rooted more deeply in the soul than is intellect. Why is this? Because the inclination to obey without question – without understanding the logic behind it – comes from the essence of the Jewish soul's connection to its Divine Source. It is a level of unity nonpareil.[111]

Kabolas ol today?

Call it subordination to authority, obedience, compliance – kabolas ol is a dying art. We're lucky it's still in vogue in the military forces! We bemoan the dearth of kabolas ol in our children. Maybe we should dress them in military fatigues and drill them daily. Ah, how much easier it would be to raise children if they were naturally equipped with kabolas ol.

When, oh when, will my little *refuse'niks* and *nud'niks* grow into mature *"kabolas ol'niks"*?

We don't like to do things that some authority imposed on us – and neither do our children. They resist blind obedience to a superior's orders. They want to know "why" and they argue and challenge every step.

Is it possible to raise children today to be compliant and yet feel the pleasure of *Yiddishkeit*? Won't kabolas ol turn them off? Shouldn't we just make sure to fill them with the pleasure of it all? Kabolas ol is possible as an educational method, even in our times. Kabolas ol may be suffering a popularity dip, but for the Jewish people, it's always in. We are called the legions of G-d, and G-d is our loving Father, Master and King.

How do we transmit kabolas ol in a "feel good" generation, where "they've got to enjoy it or they won't do it"? We simply have to team the kabolas ol with joy and pleasure, as we train them in the habits and mitzvahs we want them to retain through adulthood.

Children pick up on tone of voice and body language. They can detect whether we view activities as something desirable or burdensome. They build theories for their own lives based on these emotional subtleties. The practice of mitzvahs is not enough; we have to *think* joyfully. Feelings are contagious and our unspoken words will make the loudest noise.

Rav Shalom Schwadron, zt"l, the "Maggid of Jerusalem," known for his fiery inspirational sermons, would often spice those talks with humor. People didn't think the humor was proper. They protested his humorous interjections. Rav Shalom consulted with the Chazon Ish[112] who told him: "In Vilna there was Torah and fear of Heaven, but joy was practiced only by the non-religious Jews. That is what caused the spiritual decline there."[113]

Children need to see joy integrated into their Torah and mitzvahs.

Lack of kabolas ol is not just a child's malady – we adults have plenty of occasions to work on ours as well. Like getting up every morning without hitting snooze.

Hershel's physician put him on a salt-free diet. He is complying obediently with the diet, albeit not so willingly. He's "doing it with kabolas ol," so to speak. But kabolas ol *can* be done willingly, like the soldiers who voluntarily enlist because they are passionate about serving their country. Rather than grumble, if Hershel manages to generate a happier perspective, he is going to be more successful in sticking with the diet. It certainly beats doing it resentfully for the rest of his life. Surrender is a not-so-simple formula for happier and healthier living.

You've never heard of oxen staging a rebellion, have you? ("We've had enough of being pushed around.") Probably because they don't think about things much. They're so matter-of-fact, it's a pleasure to deal with them. No lobbying for better pay, no personal agendas. And no inner voices challenging them one way or another.

Sometimes we need a little kabolas ol to save the day. We experience so much mental resistance to what we encounter during our day. *This is wasting my time... A "little" favor? – not again!... It's all your fault!... If we had done it my way... How did I get stuck in this?... Can't you wait?...*
Do oxen have to deal with this? Maybe we should oxen-ate our thinking and embrace life as it unfolds. How serene we could be.
Embrace... Therein lies the difference between the kabolas ol of an ox and a Jew: Our wondrous wisdom helps us generate enthusiasm for the kabolas ol so that we get to love what we have to do.

Kabolas Ol as a Conduit to Simcha

How does kabolas ol morph into simcha? Let's examine the following two verses related to simcha and pay attention to the unusual verb choice.

"Due to the fact that you did not serve G-d with simcha..." Moshe rebukes the nation.

King David uses the same word, **"Serve** G-d with joy,*"* he urges.

Serve and service (*ivdu* and *avoda*) share a word-root with "servant" (*eved*). Something has to get done and the servant does it. The master-servant relationship is characterized by fear of Heaven and kabolas ol.

Fear of Heaven is the bedrock on which kabolas ol is built. Fear of Heaven means to be in awe of a Higher Power. And kabolas ol means to be dedicated to something beyond ourselves.

In kabolas ol mode...

- we do things although we may not derive personal pleasure.
- we may even do the very *opposite* of what would give us pleasure.
- we accept what may seem irrational and contrary to logic.

And here true joy can enter.

The seemingly constrained modality of kabolas ol is an ideal stepping stone to expansive joy...

What's Better than a Bottle of Wine? A Metaphorical Journey to Joy

Wine and Water Ways to joy: A lofty excursion into Pleasure and Acceptance

(No, this is not an invitation to an exotic wine-boutique in France, nor an enchanting gondola ride down the canals of Venice, but a far more elevating excursion awaits us.)

No one has to convince us to pursue pleasurable experiences. If anything, we have to exercise restraint to desist at some point. What would motivate anyone to pursue "pleasureless" joys? In this armchair tour we explore two genres of joy – a rational, pleasurable one, and the *kabolas ol* brand of joy – metaphorically captured in the Wine and Water libations on Sukkos in the Holy Temple. The outcome may surprise you.

A little background is needed on this fascinating ritual. After all, none of us have ever seen it, and even the eldest ancestor in our family will not recollect it – we've been in galus a long time...

Generally, wine accompanied specific sacrifices. The kohanim (priests) would pour wine libations into an aperture in the altar to accompany these sacrifices. On Sukkos they would pour an additional water libation into a specially designated aperture on the altar, used only during this festival.[114]

Although the Simchas Beis Hashoeva celebration can only take place during the glorious era of the Holy Temple, its luminous joy can be imported into our galus situation – duty free! It takes up no shelf space, adds no weight to our baggage – but *will* add substance to our lives.

Compare wine and water. Wine is a pleasure to the palate and warms up our insides, while water is tasteless – we don't hear anyone raving about its wonderful bouquet. Paradoxically, our extra jubilation at the Simchas Beis Hashoeva was precipitated not by pleasurable wine, but by tasteless water.

These beverages, besides being functional and flavorful, also have an import on a soul level. No need to import them though! They're native and innate to everyone's soul. Wine and Water are metaphors for two paths to serve G-d. We can serve G-d the Wine way or the Water way.

> **"I'm savoring the delicate bouquet in this water. It has an earthy undertone..."**
> **"I think you had too much wine. Let me help you up from the ground and into bed."**

Wine naturally leads to joy. We usher in the joy of Shabbos and yomtov with a cup of wine. It has a *ta'am* as we say in Hebrew and Yiddish. The word *ta'am* has a double meaning – *taste* and *reason*. *Taste* and *reason* are a luscious blend, used to describe the enjoyable, rational way of connecting to G-d.

Many mitzvahs are comparable to wine. They have a ta'am, an enjoyable *taste*, especially when we invest the performance with kavana, which is about appreciating the light and delight of the mitzvah. Or, there is a logical *reason* – they make sense. *Thou shalt not covet* makes moral sense. Holidays that commemorate historic events have a definite ta'am – we enjoy their *flavor* and appreciate their *reasons*. They are self-rewarding.

Customer: Sir, these wines are very expensive. Do you have more "reasonable" ones?

The joy of the water ceremony had no physical pleasure basis. Its joy was completely spiritual, due only to G-d's command to "draw water with joy."

There are mitzvahs that we do without knowing why. G-d did not offer any rationale for separating milk and meat. We do it without knowing the *reason*. When we do a mitzvah with kabolas ol we are doing it like soldiers in the army, no questions asked. It seems to be an impoverished, dry action.

What joy is there in that? Isn't joy associated with pleasure, passion and intellectual stimulation?

Admittedly, it's more exciting to do things when we know just what we're excited about. Imagine celebrating a holiday like Passover just because "G-d said so." Where's the fun in that?

The kabolas ol route seems counterintuitive, and yet, we are getting more bang for the buck. "Mindless" joy provides entry into Divine joy. It taps into the limitless reservoirs of the Commander-in-chief. G-d is infinite. Therefore, His joy is boundless. It is a supra-intellectual joy.[115]

The water-drawing ceremony is G-d's way of saying "Serve me via kabolas ol with joy. Selflessly. We redirect our pleasure center, from self-centered to G-d centered. And G-dliness is sublime!

We give up of ourselves to access something greater.

Not to tamper with altruism, but ultimately whatever we do for G-d we're doing for ourselves. Kabolas ol with joy, because it is the purest, truest manner of doing Hashem's will, arouses Supernal joy, breaks through boundaries of creation and culminates in Geulah – and that's a pleasure in which all parties will revel.

A way of life…
Beis Hashoeva's waters produced a unique brand of joy that can be applied to our mitzvah performance all year.
The wine libations were performed only during the daytime. But the water libations were halachically acceptable at night. This guides our attitude to life. Serving G-d with a comprehension-based approach works well for the "daytime." When life conditions shine brightly as the day and life make sense to us, it's as enjoyable as a good wine. But when we draw close to G-d in the darkness of the night, unconditionally and joyfully, the prophet Yeshayahu assures us the drawn waters will become wells of salvation.
We serve G-d when it's dark and when it's light. When we know the reason – we enjoy our l'chaim. When G-d owns the reason, we rejoice even with water – mayim.

The Mind, Ltd. – "Sensible and Senseless"

We fuse independent thinking with kabolas ol.
We thank G-d daily in our prayers for the gift of wisdom and

understanding, and then we turn around and advocate a mind-less, submissive relationship. How do we make sense of this "sensible senselessness"?

Mindlessness can be an asset – when used mindfully! We don't relinquish the mind – there is something useful about having *ah bissel sechel*, some sound sense. But even a sound mind needs a stable foundation. With kabolas ol, we're not giving up our independent thinking. We're gaining – G-d's assistance.[116] We need G-d's help every step of the way. Despite our freedom to choose "good from evil," it is only due to G-d's help that we succeed, even in spiritual matters.[117] Kabolas ol is a form of spiritual alignment.

How many times a day do we ward off that little wise-guy inside us – the impulses we give in to, the guilt that follows in its wake, the destructive behavior patterns? We all know how vital His support is.

If not for the spiritual alignment we achieve with our kabolas ol, we would not own our minds either.

With my own mind I ally with myself. With kabolas ol I ally with Him.

A delicate dance is often necessary to preserve a balance between the mind-mode and kabolas ol. Each on its own is powerful but incomplete, and therefore imperfect. Of course, we want to serve G-d with the very best that we have and what is more precious than our minds? What is more *geshmak* (enjoyable) than engaging the brain in thinking and learning (especially about joy)?

Intellect is our greatest strength but also our limitation. We can't rely only on the mind, ingenious as it may be.

There are several drawbacks to rational-based joy:

- It has limited duration. The fact that it is based on a particular reason means the joy will stay alive only as long as the reason exists.
- It is subjective. Our innate anxieties, preconceptions and former experiences have a way of distorting, exaggerating

and embellishing the facts.

- It is confined to the parameters of the person's intelligence. "A person is praised according to his intellect."[118] The mind is like a changing landscape. What excites us today may not evoke the same delight tomorrow. Did you notice that when you take a course to learn a new subject, art or skill, the concepts that were so exciting those first lessons become banal, relative to the exciting intricacies subsequently discovered as newer theories are explored and more exciting frontiers are forged?

Today, we outgrew yesterday's source of joy. Tomorrow, today's joy may no longer work for us, because our intellect, as much as we develop it, has far more potential buried in its system.

True and authentic simcha cannot be limited and bound by the information in the brain.

> We address G-d in our prayers with what seems to be unnecessary verbiage: *Elokeinu... v'elokei avoseinu*: Our G-d and the G-d of our forefathers. Conviction based on faith is unshakeable because it is not dependent on our own logic. But it lacks the fire and initiative produced by our own understanding and knowledge. We need both: mind (*our* G-d) and above mind (the faith we inherited from our forefathers).

Conclusion: A rational approach gets in the way of true, deep and unlimited joy.

Leave the limits of your mind and bind yourself to G-d, and then you can enjoy genuine joy.

Of course, our minds should be filled with joy, but it should not end there. It should penetrate our deepest recesses. It should be so entrenched, that neither hail nor hurricane can uproot it. To live like this, we need to rise to the next level.

Tier #4: Be Irrational! The Joy of Faith

In our quest to taste authentic joy, we must learn how to go beyond the finite and to take the leap into the infinite. Our soul makes it possible

There is a vast gap between what I, a finite human, can grasp, and the infinite possibilities available to G-d. Our finiteness limits the way we process personal and global events. We can remain boxed in by our limitations – or we can dig deep into the wells within us, unearth the soul's infinite potential and move beyond natural limits.

Though we are finite beings, our life force is sustained by our infinite souls.

The neshama is an optimist. It suffers no fears and no doubts. We sometimes forget G-d is in charge but our neshama knows it "intimately, absolutely and constantly," as Rabbi Yossi Paltiel, master Chassidus teacher, put it. That means that we can reach into our inner joy reservoir *at any time* and bring out its courage and strength. Although the simcha supply itself is unlimited and infinite, we don't usually unleash its full depth and power.

Joy can be accessed on different levels. Joy based on finite factors will be just that – limited. The deeper we go, the more transformative.

We connect to infinity...

- when we rise nobly above difficulties to unite with joy's incredible powers. Rather than allow our joy to be diminished we seek the joyous embrace of the One Above.

- when we give deeply of ourselves to others by going beyond our comfort level, as in raising a family or energetic community involvement.

- through the sanctified union of marriage, with the intention of bringing more souls in bodies into the world. (Surprisingly, the lofty Supernal unions which produce angels are in the cat-

Gvul, limited human thinking, and *bli gvul*, unlimited-ness, each has its particular style. Each has its own way of running the business of life and joy.

Gvul is cautious, practical, logical, the voice of reason – qualities that are often necessary.

It is also anxious, worried, fretting – qualities that are (almost) never necessary. If *gvul¬*-thinking doesn't see a solution, it doesn't exist – a perspective that curbs our connections with the supernatural realms.

The voice of *gvul*:

It's not possible…

It can't be done…

I can't possibly do more…

I can't possibly *give* more (oh, yes, you can…you would be surprised how elastic time and money can be).

There's not enough to go around – that includes money, apartments and houses in your neighborhood, marriage mates. "There are one hundred eligible boys in the yeshiva. If we don't snatch one of them real quick our daughter is doomed."

I need to have it all figured out; I need to be in control.

This is taking me too far out of my comfort zone.

Gvul is running a business called "My Life, Ltd." It is a human-centered approach.

When *we're* the one running the business, we need things to make sense to us.

The pitfalls of sense and logic: *King Shaul was instructed to decimate every member of Amalek as well as their livestock. His innate sense of mercy could not stomach this wholesale destruction. He decided that*

Bli gvul (without boundaries), on the other hand, doesn't limit its enterprise by its assessment of the situation. "Why pin G-d down to a narrowed world view? I will "let go and let G-d," because there's always another route to the desired salvation. This is a G-d-centered perspective. This is the way people who "trust in G-d" live. There is joy in this faith, of knowing it's not up to us to figure things out, because it is simply beyond us.

Nonprofit organizations, yeshivas and those Chabad Houses that dot the globe, each one will attest that they could not exist without manifest G-dly intervention. Each one insists their organization or building came to be "only with a miracle!"

It all started with Avraham our Forefather. When G-d told him he would have a son from whom a great nation will emerge, Avraham pleaded with G-d to build the promised great nation through Yishmael, the son he already had. But G-d wanted the Jewish nation to be built specifically through Yitzchak. His supernatural birth was a suitable precursor for a nation whose existence is supernatural.

An Unlimited G-d with Supernatural Solutions...

G-d has the most creative solutions. When our ancestors followed Moshe into the desert they had no idea how they would survive. Would any of them have conceived of bread falling from the sky, not once, but daily for forty years?

G-d has His ways of arranging miracles so they look natural, so keep an eye out for them. Here's one example: *It was late Friday afternoon. I couldn't find the salad greens that I distinctly remember throwing into my cart at the supermarket. With a few hours left until Shabbos, I got dressed quickly to make a run to a store. Too late. The store was roll-*

ing down its gates as I rounded the corner, but – I met someone on the way home, and as a result – I found a cleaning lady, just in time for the Pesach season! And she turned out to be the best one I've had yet. I knew G-d would take care of me!

> We thank G-d three times daily for those daily miracles. I thank G-d that I have become more mindful of that prayer with the passing years.

The Jewish version of "my way or the highway": "My way *is* the higher (G-d's) way."

Avraham our Forefather would not have risen to greatness if he had taken the rational view. G-d's request to sacrifice his only son was completely illogical. Avraham Avinu was able to proceed with alacrity and joy because his infinite love for G-d was more powerful than his finite mind.[121] And because he blazed the way we are now empowered Jews – we can do it, too. We are eternally endowed to rise above our own logical limitations.

> *"Every Jew has a G-dly soul that is connected with the infinite Creator Who is above nature. By fulfilling Torah and mitzvahs, a person…is raised up above nature and accomplishes acts that are considered wondrous and supernatural.*
> **"What remains to be seen is to what degree the person will bring this potential ability to fruition."**[122]

G-d can lift the limitations anytime. But we have to lift ourselves above the limitations. Two suggestions:

1. **Stop worrying. Trade *doubt* for *confidence*.** Which is how the cleaning lady sequel developed:

   My great "find" of the previous Pesach season had to resign due to a health issue. By the next Pesach season I needed another miracle. This time I met a very nice lady passing by right in front of my house. Miraculously, two days a week had just opened in her schedule. Once again, my "find" was superb!

Not every situation resolves so smoothly but a trusting, confident mindset boosts our chance for success. Not only won't we waste precious energy worrying, we will come out ahead. Worrying implies that it's my problem, so there's no need for G-d to get involved. But when I remain serene because I trust in G-d to look out for me, it becomes His responsibility.

2. Think BIG! Be expansive.

A philanthropist, George Rohr, was addressing one thousand participants at a national learning retreat. He recalled that when the visionary organizer of the program approached him to seek support for a learning initiative targeting college students, the organizer had candidly confessed that people thought the proposal was "a crazy idea!"

"That's how I knew it was a good one," said the philanthropist, and he threw his support behind it. (The project, Sinai Scholars Society, has grown by leaps and bounds.)

Not everyone is created equal. We need the cautious, practical ones as well as the visionaries and trailblazers. An encouraging note... the one who has to sweat harder to st-r-e-t-ch past his prudent nature gets more credit from Above.

Nevertheless, it's nice to know *bli-gvul* thinking comes naturally to us. It's in our makeup. Crumbs of *bli-gvul* talk often pop out without our noticing.

Anything's possible...

I hope and pray...

Unbelievable, but true...

The impossible happened...

A miracle!

Those who do not believe in miracles are not realistic!
Miracles have the ability to lift a person above the stark
physicality of daily life and reconnect to our soul exis-
tence.[123] *There's "reality" – the physical surroundings, and*
there's the "true reality" – the infinite hand from Above.

Admittedly, it's hard to let go with nothing to hold on to but a concept called trust. Don't be deterred if it's hard for you – Einstein found it hard, too.

Einstein had a hard time letting go of the accepted notion of "determinism" (that everything is predetermined) and replacing it with the theory of uncertainty. (The Heisenberg uncertainty principle states that we cannot get true measurements of our observations. It's not that we lack the ability to measure, it's that there's a fundamental uncertainty in the world.) Einstein protested, "G-d does not play dice with the universe"; there cannot be that kind of uncertainty in the world. Neils Bohr, another Jewish physicist, argued with Einstein: "It is not our business to tell G-d how to run the universe."

"Who was right?" was the question Dr. Naftali Berg, a noted Orthodox scientist, posed to the Lubavitcher Rebbe at a private audience many years ago. The Rebbe told him that Einstein was wrong, because G-d is above the laws of physics. He created those laws and can do whatever he wants. There is no uncertainty as far as G-d is concerned. On the other hand, the uncertainty principle is also incorrect, and the Rebbe proceeded to explain his reasons.[124]

The seventh day, Shabbos, and the seventh year, called *shemita* (sabbatical), are bona fide bitachon-testers. How will the man who decided to become shomer Shabbos survive if he loses his job due to Shabbos observance? How will farmers in Israel survive if they do not plow, seed or harvest their fields during the shemita year? Does G-d have enough in His storage houses so that even if, according to the natural order, succor doesn't seem possible, we *will* manage? Do we *truly* believe G-d is unlimited?

Inexplicably, those that observe the shemita laws are more prosperous. But it's not so "inexplicable" – G-d promises He will ordain His blessing in the sixth year and the earth will yield a crop sufficient for up to three years.[125] There are documented reports of crops producing triple the non-shemita-observant farmers' yield. A farmer in Israel tells his tale…

> *One shemita year the Agriculture Department offered him free vegetable seeds that he had to refuse, tempting though it was. As the shemita year came to an end, he called the government office and asked if they had any seeds left. They did – lots of celery seeds. So he planted lots of celery. His nonreligious neighbors laughed and dubbed him Mr. Celery. The next winter many European countries suffered a harsh cold spell and their celery crops were destroyed. "Mr. Celery" sold his crop and made a nice fortune.[126] How they all wished they were in Mr. Celery's shoes.*

Having the guts to stick with a decision is the first part of trust. But more important is: **How** will we approach the challenge? With what spirit and frame of mind will we weather the "opportunity"?

If I were in a farmer's situation would I bite my nails, or would I be utterly relaxed?

My joy declares my trust in Him.

> *A man lamented to Rav Moshe Feinstein that his children had dropped their Jewish observance. He lived during a time when it was practically impossible for a Shomer Shabbos Jew to keep a job. He was fired as soon as he notified his boss that he could not work on Shabbos. There were two kinds of yidden. One kind lived with oys and worry all Shabbos – as this man did. No wonder the children left his path – who wants*

to be part of a joyless venture? But the children of those who were b'simcha each Shabbos, fueled by their trust in G-d, were more likely to stay on their father's path.

Simcha provides the fuel for trust; conversely, where you see trust you know that there is simcha.

And where there's simcha and trust, there is a brisk readiness to act, as befits a descendant of Avraham Avinu:

A young scholar, disciple of the Maggid of Mezritch, spent a night at a roadside inn run by an elderly, G-d-fearing Jew. The innkeeper told the disciple that this inn has been his livelihood source for almost fifty years.

"What do you do on Shabbos and yomtov?"

"Unfortunately, we have to make do without a minyan (quorum). Only for the High Holidays do we close our inn and travel to the city so we can daven in a shul."

"But how can you live this way?" exclaimed the visitor. "How can a Jew live without hearing kaddish or krias haTorah (public reading of the Torah) throughout the year?"

"But what can I do? This is how I earn a living..."

"How many Jewish households are there in the city?"

"About a hundred."

"So for one hundred families G-d provides. Don't you think He could find a way to provide for one more?"

Shortly after the scholar was shown to his room and retired for the night, he heard a commotion outside. He looked out the window and saw the innkeeper and his family piling a wagon with household items, bundles and furniture. "What's going on?" he asked them.

"We're moving to the city," the innkeeper told him, "where we will be able to pray with a minyan."

"But where will you stay? And what about a job?"

"Didn't you say, if G-d can take care of a hundred families, He can provide for a few more souls?"[127]

Such is the potential of faith and trust in G-d of a Jew. **The sky is not the limit.**

The next level will advance our pursuit of authentic joy.

Tier #5: Joy Out of its Box

What is real, full-blown joy?

Are you out of your mind? It may be a good thing.

We're supposed to be happy every day, but we do have high-points along the way. Our engagement party is going to elicit more joy-waves than our twenty-second birthday party. A reunion with friends we haven't seen for ten years is going to register higher intensity than one with friends we saw only last week.

Did anyone try to come up with a Richter-type scale to measure joy? Unlike with earthquakes, I'd always want it registering higher on the scale. And, I'd want to know how to stir up more of the same.

There is a way to measure our joy-waves: by our body response, by the way we are shaken out of our standard composure. Something predictable or possible will elicit a pleased but composed reaction. A joy that jumps into our lives by total surprise leaves our minds behind, hence the temporary lapse of composure. It is a kind of volcanic spillover that floods our bodies with the lava of joy.

What makes people "high"? Most of the time, the source of our excitement is about an anticipated event. We get excited in advance, and we are excited when it actually takes place. Or maybe we didn't actually expect it, but it's something that *can* happen; it is conceivable and possible. This is rational joy.

More rarely, a completely unanticipated, out-of-the-ordinary event materializes. It "blows our minds." It has no rational or logical basis – the mind did not conceptualize it and the mind cannot contain it.

Joy is proportionate to its cause. Unlimited causes elicit unlimited responses.

Have you ever experienced the kind of event that precipitates full-blown joy, the kind that spills over and bursts out, that because of its intensity cannot be cerebrally contained? Everyone has their favorite stories and memories.

One day, my doorbell rang and in response to my "Who's there?" I heard a male voice on the intercom asking for *tzedaka*. I went to the door and there, instead of the *tzedaka* collector, stood my dear twenty-year-old son who was supposedly in a yeshiva in Russia, his hand on his carry-on bag and a smile on his face. What a shockingly delightful surprise! (No, he was not expelled. The yeshiva had allowed a few students to return for a special celebration.)

I can't recall exactly how I reacted. I may have clapped my hands to my head, stamped my foot in disbelief, done a half twirl. Frankly when you get blown away you don't quite keep track of what you do. People who are rattled will hug people, utter disconnected verbal exclamations, maybe even grab someone and dance a jig with them.

Emotional responses of great magnitude make us lose our composure. That's probably why people love making surprises. They gather the family for a milestone birthday or anniversary and don't tell the celebrants in advance. It's all worth it for the reaction they get.

But what registers highest on the joy-Richter scale is when a person gets something that seemed beyond his reach. When it materializes suddenly, the body reacts with a real loss of inhibition, totally out-of-the-box, as for example, a pregnancy after having given up. Our matriarch Sarah laughed when she heard the news that she would bear a child at the advanced age of ninety years. These kinds of things don't generally happen.

Laughter, like joy, is caused by an unexpected and surprising turn of events. That's why our laughter will be uncontained when the Geulah arrives. We declare our belief in its coming every day, but after so many years of knowing, the actuality will be inconceivably delightful.

How's this for the unimaginable coming to pass...
Some Polish businessmen were returning from an annual business trip
into Russia. They were slowed down by a bout of Russian early-winter

weather and forced to stop and seek a place for Shabbos. After knocking on many doors hoping to find a Jewish family, they gave up and at the next house, asked only for sleeping accommodations. The elderly woman who opened the door agreed to take them in.

As nightfall approached, they noticed the woman holding two matches together and murmuring a prayer. It aroused their curiosity but they said nothing. Eventually, she engaged them in fluent Polish. Where were they from, she wanted to know. She seemed familiar with the town they were from. Suddenly she asked them, "Do you by any chance know Avraham Chaim the Dairy Man?"

"Yes, I do," answered one of the travelers in surprise. "That was my grandfather. He passed away and left one son – my father. My grandfather had a difficult life. His young wife had disappeared without a trace and he raised his son singlehandedly."

And then the lady told them the unimaginable: "I am Avraham Chaim's lost wife. I am your grandmother!"

She filled them in on her side of the story: She was abducted by a Russian officer who brought her back with him, forced her to adopt his religion, and married her. They had a few children – one of whom still lived in the house with her – and then the husband was killed in a battle. But she had no way of returning to Poland.

As the woman relived these painful memories she began to cry over the years she had been estranged from her heritage. She cried and cried, until she expired – that very Shabbos!

The Jewish travelers, fortuitously, were on hand to give her a Jewish burial.[128]

This bittersweet galus mix of good and bad presents an opportunity to assess how we view life's various events. Certainly, we feel sorrow for this and the many severed families throughout our galus – but do we also celebrate the Divine Providence that arranged a proper burial for a lost Jew?

Although joy in-the-box is nice, joy out-of-the-box is the authentic brand of joy. "Often you must do something out-of-the-box in order to make yourself happy."[129] advises Rabbi Nachman of Breslov.

Granted, it's not easy to get "out of the box."

For me, the *awareness* that I am "in a box" is a great first step.

Crisis Intervention

Life is capricious. We hear of tragedies that we can only describe as senseless. (Let's not forget, though, the many worrisome, frightening circumstances that are happily resolved.)

What should we do when we are faced by a bleak situation?

What we should *not* do: surrender to despair. We do not have to be bound by circumstances that stare us in the face.

Don't settle for passive acceptance. We have the power to tap into the infinite and actually change events. Don't get trapped in the box!

We *are* finite humans, after all. How do we free ourselves from a constricting realism and shift to an expansive optimism? How do we move from limited thinking to the liberating no-limits-to-what-He-can-do?

We take on the demeanor of a projected positive outcome *before* it actually takes place. A man with a worrisome state of health wrote to the Lubavitcher Rebbe to request his blessing. The Rebbe's response completely upended the expected rational approach to a crisis:

> *"...It would seem that the state of openly revealed joy should be delayed until after you're actually healed... But the joy itself will be a catalyst to hasten your healing. This is in keeping with the saying, 'Think positively, and you will see positive results.' Most assuredly this will be effective when you transfer these positive thoughts into **joyous words and deeds**..."[130]*

This is a classic example of not being fazed by the rationalism of *gvul*. Take note: To be effective we must transfer these thoughts into *words* and *deeds*. Joy is a spiritual phenomenon with an energy that has real powers, but the joy has to enter our lives in a very real way.

Enter the world of G-d and you enter the world of joy; enter the world of joy and you enter the world of G-d.

Joy loosens the emotional noose

Joy is a powerful crisis intervention tool. Being in the eye of the storm can be overwhelming and it may be up to friends or relatives to introduce joy's life-changing energy. I was privileged to witness joy's pivotal role firsthand when I passed on some useful advice to someone in crisis:

> *Bella was being harassed at her workplace by a hostile co-worker and it was paralyzing her ability to function. To make matters worse, other co-workers had joined the ringleader. Bella asked me how she should respond when the perpetrator would start in with her abusive tongue lashings. "When you answer you are stepping down to her level and inviting more abuse," I warned her.*
>
> *"What then should I do then to defend myself?" she asked in desperation.*
>
> *I didn't have any ideas how to reform her co-workers. Instead, I focused on empowering Bella. "Don't answer; ignore her and power dance instead," was my advice. I advised her to seek out a private area to dance for a few minutes; some back and forth steps, some twirling 'round with extended arms. I trusted that joy would give her the power to break this obstacle. I could think of no other solution.*
>
> *Two days later, I got a call from Bella. She had unbelievable results to report. She decided to take the advice and dance. She describes how it went. "I had become so constricted that my arms were just clenched against my body. I began to dance in the evening, in the privacy of my bedroom, expanding my arms upward as I danced. My feeling of being intimidated dissipated when I opened my arms. I became powerful. I was not in a personal prison but making a choice to be expansive. That opened the way, allowing the feelings of simcha to enter.* **It literally unchained me.**
>
> *"I never thought much into the morning blessing, 'He who loosens bonds.' The mere actions, the physical dance move-*

ments, release and expand you. The success of this story opened my eyes. I saw in a very clear way that the link between simcha and Geulah is not far-fetched and unrealistic... When you do something simcha'dik, and dance when you are crushed by a problem, you move from constriction to liberation. You are like a balloon that had been tied down, and then someone cut the string. Unchained it can soar upward.

"The next day one of the hostile co-workers in the 'enemy camp' was actually friendly – a complete turnaround from the previous days. The simcha did it! And the chief instigator did not intimidate me. Something about me was different. I had become internally powerful. Simcha could unshackle me any time."

Like the gases of a helium balloon, joy carries us above the stratosphere of our normal existence and allow us to soar into a realm above and beyond.

Notice that this strategy is typically practiced even though you are not in the mood, a perfect example of kabolas ol. You have to talk to yourself about it, empower yourself: *I'm faced with a situation that will weigh me down but I'm not going to allow myself to surrender to it.* You're not fighting it. Fighting it is hard – and unnecessary. You're transcending it.

Bella concluded by reiterating her newfound wisdom with ardor. *"I had always heard that simcha had the power to achieve Geulah. Now I believe it; I experienced it firsthand. It has a powerful potential."*

Do not be fazed by barriers. Barriers were built with the intention of being broken. That was G-d's original intent and plan – to bring the supernatural down into nature.[131]

Transcendent joy

There are five levels of the soul, discussed in Kabbalah, and each has a corresponding form of joy – the intellectual dimension, the emotional one, and so on. The highest level of the soul, *yechida*, has no fixed border or definition. It transcends all lower levels and at the same time, permeates them all with its elevated joy, similar to oil, which rises to the top while saturating all substances. When the yechida-level is revealed, no form or barrier stands in its way. It is a joy connected to the soul's very essence. This is the joy-level that unifies all the other levels of the soul, and it is the joy-level that unites all Jews.

This transcendent joy is revealed on Simchas Torah. It has moved Jews to dance and rejoice in the face of the most daunting dangers. Whether the Jews facing the furnaces in the Nazi extermination camps were Torah-observant or Jews in name only, Simchas Torah sparked their inner core.

And, finally, this joy-level is the taste of Geulah-joy.[132]

Tier #6: Pure, Unconditional Joy, No Strings Attached

The more we strip away, the more pure the joy

Joy-triggers wash up constantly on the shores of our lives. It could be the sense of relief after some stress, or an unexpected boon that came along and spiced up our lives.

Samples from my "unexpected-boon" journal:
- "Can you take on a new student, a child in ---'s nursery class, until the end of the school year?" the caller from the agency asked me. Can I? You bet. My adorable granddaughter is in that class. What a treat!

A guest at our Shabbos table who had joined us unexpectedly shared fascinating success stories from her clinical psychology practice. She attributed her successes – in cases where others had failed – to methodology she had learned in a book written by a Dr. Yaakov Frankel from Israel. Well, that was my husband's Uncle Yaakov! (Sadly, he passed away in the prime of his life, so we were especially gratified that his theories live on.) That was a lovely surprise for both guest and hosts.

No matter what the basis, all our joys are contingent joys, hinged on various factors.

In our spiritual service, as well, our joy is built on contributing factors. Our enthusiasm may be based on the reasons behind the mitzvah. And that's not a bad thing – knowing the deeper meanings behind the actions or prayers will invest kavana, joyful mindfulness, into our acts.

These are admirable motives, and I humbly aspire to serve G-d in any of these truly mindful ways. And yet, there are limitations to the joy that is achieved by anticipating benefits, whether material or intangible. *When a motive is involved, our joy is not pure.* The more we strip away, the purer the joy is.

Perfect joy is unconditional. No strings attached. It is not dependent on anything. Therefore, it can endure.

The servant-master relationship describes a model in which all personal gain is stripped away. The servant is committed to the master. It's pure altruism. Paula, a housekeeper at a friend's house, insists on ironing the children's pajamas and underwear. My friend reminds her, "We don't need to iron these things. Go to sleep." But she continues to do it, at the expense of her own sleep time.

Altruism seems to be a rare quality. Is it possible to serve G-d with the purest of motives? And what's wrong with doing mitzvahs in order to go to Heaven? Nothing – it's a worthy ambition, and Heaven is a good place. And there is nothing wrong with striving to elevate our souls or refine our characters.

While these all are fine motives for doing mitzvahs, they aren't the real reason. We do mitzvahs because that's what G-d wants.

> *Rebbe Elimelech of Lizhensk had offered a visitor some fruits. Rebbe Elimelech took an apple from the bowl, cut off a piece and ate it. The guest, too, took an apple and ate. He then asked Rebbe Elimelech, "With all due respect, Rebbe, what's the difference between us? I made a blessing and ate a piece of apple, and the Rebbe made a blessing and ate a piece of apple. Rebbe Elimelech said, "The difference is, you are making a*

blessing in order to eat the apple; I am eating the apple in order to make the blessing."

In the pure-motive way of serving G-d, the Jew's mind is not focused on his own benefit, not even a spiritual one. We can learn this selflessness from a simple mountain whose name we all recognize – Mount Sinai. Mount Sinai had no distinguishing qualities, only a simple desire to be the site for the giving of the Torah. And G-d chose this simple mountain for that very reason: He wanted no external distracters. If Mount Sinai had outstanding features we'd remember it for those features and not for the fact that the Torah was given on it.

Is it possible to serve G-d with the purest of motives? It's hard to always be doing good things for the right reasons. So, do whatever it takes to motivate yourself. But remember to always keep one part sacred, dedicated to the grandeur of the cause and mission, even if no one but G-d and you know about it.

The way in which the Torah was given can also be a guide for the way G-d would like us to fulfill His commands. Not to become great, elevated, or receive a reward, whether physical or spiritual. At the forefront of our mitzvah observance is our relationship with G-d. Everything else is secondary.[133] When we understand this relationship, we can proceed to serve Him for His sake, and then our simcha in serving Him is pure. Purely for G-d.

This true joy derives from a deep source, from the very essence of one's soul, called *etzem hanefesh* in Chassidic philosophy. *Etzem,* or essence, is a term for the most inner aspect that we can't see or define – it is beyond our conceptual grasp. We can tap into our *etzem hanefesh* and find the joy to serve G-d, no matter what is going on in our lives.

Let's take a peek from up above and try to see things from the Divine perspective.

Every time we do a mitzvah, we evoke G-d's *nachas ruach*, pleasure and delight, as He sees that His coveted project is succeeding – that Man has invited Him into the world amongst the challenges. Despite the challenges, our invitation stands!

How's the penthouse view? **Divine!**

"Rejoice with His joy as He rejoices in His dwelling place in the lowest world."[134]

Stop and rejoice now. G-d picked us...
- to be His chosen nation.
- for a special assignment, the particulars of which are richly arrayed in a magnificent guide book – the Torah.

A note about *pleasure* (*oneg* or *taanug*)...

Our many deeds elicit spiritual taanug on levels Above. Each level of Divine *oneg*, Supernal Pleasure, is a separate reservoir, a self-contained limpid pool of pristine pleasure. The difference between *oneg* and *simcha* is this: Oneg is quiet and self-contained and has many levels. We cannot see the *taanug* that results when a Jew does a mitzvah for His sake, as it is hidden within His Essence. Simcha plays the role of revealer and is all-inclusive. It reveals the oneg and stimulates its flow. Simcha is like a flowing spring. It has an active quality and begs to be heard as it gurgles and gushes determinedly along its energetic path. Nothing can stand in its way. If we want to elicit G-d's **joy**, we will have to employ a special trick, because the individual taanug levels we aroused Above through our Torah and mitzvahs will not reveal the innermost Supernal taanug. Only the current of simcha can reveal the *taanug atzmi* (His Essential Pleasure).[135]

It works the same way with people. A person's pleasure is hidden within him. Oneg is an internal elevation, serene and calm. A radiant countenance may testify to its presence, but it cannot be compared to the swelling personality of simcha. Simcha manifests itself actively, with vocal or other physical expressions. When we express delight, such as a personal celebration, we call it simcha. For example, we may experience delight at some great personal achievement, but the feast we make, that is the simcha!

Our simcha down here activates a chain reaction, a "circular joy route." It stimulates and reveals that simcha from Above. When we do His Will in the purest, truest manner – kabolas ol with joy – we reveal the purest level of His essential innermost simcha.

The Geulah brand of joy will be a pure essential joy that will exist, independent even of simcha shel mitzvah. Because we are so close, we can tap in to the purity of essential joy now by rejoicing for the Geulah, a joy "**purely** for the Geulah."

A note about "pureness":

Most experiences of simcha are based on external factors, music, a beautiful idea, completing a major project. The joy is a composite, based on that factor. It's not "pure." It comes from outside of our essence and is therefore a "limited" genre of joy. In the deepest part of self is a simcha that is pure, that comes from our essence, rather than a relationship with the world.

Here's a short version of the above: We are doing His will because He has pleasure when His will is done. There is joy in our submission to our King. G-d has pleasure from this, but it is hidden and remote. The only thing that can reveal it is simcha.

Our simcha here in this world reveals simcha Above, as whatever we do here in the world below is echoed by G-d in the worlds Above. Our **pure** simcha releases and reveals G-d's essential, **pure** Simcha.

This pure simcha is the key to breaking barriers and constraints of nature. And with nothing to bar the way, we invite our redemption.

Every Jew has within him the capacity to connect with G-d on a pure level, even if the simcha is hidden deep in his soul:

Just Because

During the closing days of Israel's 1982 "Peace in Galilee" campaign in Lebanon, Tuvia Bolton was one of ten volunteers who obtained authorization from the army to enter Beirut to cheer up the soldiers and assist them with their religious needs.

Walking around, Tuvia happened upon a line of open-roofed jeeps, motors running, with two soldiers seated in each. He approached a soldier in one jeep and asked whether he wanted to don tefillin.

In response the soldier shot back, "Get out of my sight!"

At that moment the driver of the next jeep in line suddenly called out, "Rabbi! Could you come here? I want to put on tefillin." Happy to escape, Tuvia walked toward him. "Tell me, rabbi," the soldier asked, "If I put on tefillin, will G d protect me?"

Tuvia assured him, "G d will protect you whether you put on the tefillin or not. He loves you unconditionally. But if G d protects you for free, why not do something for Him for free, and put on tefillin?"

After a while, the soldier who had lashed into him called him back and started rolling up his sleeve.

"What happened?" asked Tuvia incredulously.

"I want to put on the tefillin, too."

"For real?"

"Listen, my friend. To put on tefillin in order to go to Heaven, that's not for me. But to put on tefillin for no reason...that I'm willing to do!"[126]

Tier 7: The Ultimate Level: Sheer Joy

The joy and laughter we will experience when Moshiach comes

The simcha of the future will be of a quality we have never before experienced. We will be totally enveloped in a delirious mound of perfect joy. Any spiritual bliss experienced during galus is trifling in the face of that Geulah joy. Our mouths will be filled with a most fulfilling kind of laughter.

According to our galus perception, the laughter will be a natural result of the indescribably wonderful conditions of life. But more than that, joy will have an independent existence of its own.[127]

Do you keep a tablecloth on your dining room table? Some tables have tablecloths, some don't. We can actually muddle through life without joy, just as tables can remain standing without cloths on them. But can you imagine a tablecloth without a table? The tablecloth would slink into a shapeless heap. Our joy-in-glaus, like that tablecloth, needs to be constantly propped up.

In galus we need to keep shining a light to keep our spirits up. In the future, the light will be on all the time; joy will become a stable enduring element. It will not need to be propped up; it will be a stand-alone entity. We can't imagine that state of being from our galus vantage point. It's as hard to imagine joy having an independent existence of its own, as it is to imagine a tablecloth suspended in the air with nothing to support it.

Who knows, maybe the table and tablecloth will switch roles then, too.

We don't know yet what the bliss of the hereafter will feel like, but this letter, written by the Baal Shem Tov, offers us a rare preview of sublime joy.[128]

"And there I saw Great Joy"

"To my beloved brother-in-law, who is dear to me and my soul friend, the wondrous Rabbi and famous Chassid in Torah and fear of Heaven...
"On Rosh Hashana of the year 5507, I performed, by means

of oath, an aliyas neshama (elevation of soul), as is known to you, and saw wondrous things I had never seen before. That which I saw and learned there is impossible to convey in words, even face to face.

"When I returned to the lower Garden of Eden, I saw innumerable souls, both of the living and the dead, some of whom I knew and others whom I did not. They were flitting back and forth, going from one universe to another through the Column that is known to those who delve into mysteries. Their state of joy was so great that lips cannot express it, and the physical ear is too coarse to hear it.

"There were also souls of many formerly wicked people who had repented; their sins were forgiven, as this was a special time of grace. Even to my eyes, it was wondrous how many were accepted as penitents, many of whom you know. There was great joy among them too, and they also ascended in the manner described above.

"All of them beseeched and petitioned me unceasingly: 'To the glory of your Torah, G-d granted you greater understanding to perceive and know these things. Ascend with us, so that you can be our help and support.'

"Because of the great joy I saw among them, I decided to ascend with them... I rose up level after level until I entered the chamber of Moshiach, where Moshiach learns Torah with all the sages Tanaim, Talmudic Sages, and tzaddikim, including the Seven Shepherds.

"And there I saw exceedingly great joy, but I did not know the reason for it. At first, I thought that the reason for this joy was because I had passed away from the physical world, Heaven forbid. Later, they told me that my time had not yet come to die, since they have great pleasure On High when I bring about unifications through their holy teachings down below. To this very day, I do not know the reason for that joy..."

It seems we have indeed come up with seven levels, seven layers of heavenly joy. Each layer has taken us up a level, until it seems – behold! We have indeed accessed the very heavens! No wonder "seventh heaven" is used to describe sublime delight.

Section III

The Joy Production Center

Practical ways to enter a new joy era

If you want to learn how to paint, you must work on your canvas. If you want to learn how to play piano, you must sit at the keyboard. If you want to learn how to teach, being in a classroom provides the best form of teaching experience.

We don't need a canvas, a keyboard or a classroom to practice joy. No matter where we are, no matter what we're doing, we're at it, practicing away in the laboratory called life.

Just wondering...If experience is supposed to be the best teacher, why do I still have so much to learn? I have been practicing joy 24/7 for as long as I can remember, and I still have not mastered the art.
*If experience qualifies, joy should not be a struggle. Joy should be a cinch. Joy should be – **a joy.***

Of all the many talents which G-d has implanted in us – be it the ability to draw, sculpt, sing, act or dance, the most valuable is the talent to be joyous under all conditions – to be joy artists and joy-geniuses.

Some people have a natural inner well of joy. The French call it *joy d'vivre*. In Hebrew it's called *simchas hachaim*. The joy wells up just like that, "just because," like the hot springs that spurt out in random geographic locations around the globe.

Is *simchas hachaim* a genetic predisposition? Or is it a conscious, determined decision to face each day with relish, inspired perhaps by a remarkable role model?

Do you have a good recipe for relish?
I've got the best recipe for relish you ever tasted.
I need a recipe for living with relish. I already eat with relish.

Joy-geniuses *relish* life.

For those of us who haven't inherited or internalized the amazing talent – gift – of invincible joy, could we, too, dredge up and manufacture joy as a daily act?

"Sometimes it is the artist's task to find out how much music you can make with what you have left." So said Yitzhak Perlman, world-class violinist. The musical genius was stricken with polio as a child, which left him with a lifelong mobility impairment. But nothing stopped this master player. Once, he had just begun playing a composition at a major concert and a string snapped. It was too difficult to make his labored way across the large stage floor. He decid-

ed, after a brief pause, to continue the performance, rearranging his notes to compensate for the missing string. It was, arguably, his finest moment. His standing ovation was well-earned.

Sometimes we have to make our music with the strings we have... Even when we have a missing string we can still play the music.

The more difficult the task the more exquisite the music.

How To...

The objective of this book is to increase joy. The big question is *how*. We'll have to work on that together. I'm learning, too, and hopefully getting better at it every day. The *ins* and *outs* of joy can be learned and developed at any stage in life.

The *ins* and *outs* of joy production: How to get more joy to flow *out* of us, and how to get more joy from the outside *into* us.

Look at all the personal wealth opportunities you can enjoy tax-free. Joyous living offers:
- An import-export business: import joy, export your own native joy.
- A quick-and-easy export commodity: the smile. ("If you have nothing more than a smile to give you are rich enough to give the greatest gift.")
- We're "rich" in daily opportunities to practice joy.

Not every artist makes it financially. But a joy-artist is enviably rich. After all, who is rich – he who rejoices in his lot. Even in what he has not. No matter what, there's a spark of joy in every moment!

16

There's Something I Need to Change

How does one change the bad habits of a lifetime?

S habbos is absolutely delightful. It definitely deserves space in a book about simcha. The moment we light the candles we enter a blissful new world. Here is a whiff of the recommended Friday night atmosphere, according to our codifiers:

> "*Kabbolas Shabbos (the Friday night prayer) is recited with joy, just as if we are greeting the Shechina, the Divine Presence. We should greet the Shabbos with a hearty voice; the Arizal would daven extra loud in honor of Shabbos. We should strive to recite Kabbolas Shabbos with a minyan, since greeting Shabbos is similar to the blessing for choson and kallah, which is done with a minyan.*"[139]

Yes, Shabbos is blissful. But something needs to change: the prelude to Shabbos.

I can handle the serenity and joyousness of Shabbos. It's my erev-Shabbos style I'm working on. It doesn't make sense that Shabbos, the most serene island of time, is preceded by considerable tension and stress. It's one of the great oxymorons of life.

My mother was the erev Shabbos queen. She sat, five-foot-tall and stately, with Tehillim in her lap, everything ready for the upcoming holy day, making her way through the innumerable chapters on her list. Even in her earlier years when she would close the family restaurant late Friday, everything was organized in advance. She heartily disapproved of my erev-Shabbos hustling and bustling with food production oozing out of every corner until the last hours before Shabbos. Baking a cake on Friday afternoon was a no-no! Her delectable *mandelbroit* variations (an adapted recipe that no one could replicate) were cut and tucked away in her signature containers by Wednesday.

My father would sound gentle but urgent alerts, updating us as candle-lighting time neared. "Candle-lighting time is 5:46 today... Two hours left... Candle-lighting in an hour..."

Everything *always* takes more time than we had allotted in the idealistic chambers of our mind. How do a puny few items on the to-do list burgeon into a beat-the-clock marathon? But we didn't figure in the smoking oven due to an inadvertent spill. Or little Nosson smearing black marker all over his baby brother's face and linen while I was rushing around the kitchen (one art project would have been enough, but generously he manages two). Preparing the house in time for Shabbos can be a draining ordeal.

Except for the delightful aromas. Nothing beats the "sniff" of a house on erev Shabbos. And where there's aroma – there's food. The brightest spot of our erev Shabbos experience is the assorted delicacies being whisked out of ovens and food processors and temptingly arrayed on the counter. The smells tease our taste buds so that we're *forced* to try a piece of kugel, then another bite of that second one, okay just one more slice of the first one again.

It's okay. Help yourself. Our sages taught us that those who sample the Shabbos delicacies on Friday afternoon will merit extra blessings.[140]

What needs to improve, first and foremost, I decided, was the erev Shabbos atmosphere in my home. The one thing I've changed is that it's not just the kitchen that is humming with activity, but that we are humming through it. The hustle and bustle reflects and resonates with what's coming. My mother would be so proud of the singing (as those who read *Okay to Laugh* know). A Jew needs to be happy and needs to show it.

> *Many happy days are coming now so just listen to me,*
> *We will be singing, dancing, laughing everybody just you*
> *wait and see,*
> *Miracles, amazing wonders, like no one's ever seen before,*
> *It's finally that magic moment we have all been waiting for!!*
> *(Lyrics by Mordechai ben David)*

"Shabbos is coming...only one hour left!" now sounds like a lilting song of joy that ends on a high note of excitement as in "Can't-wait-to-see-you." Rather than focus on Friday's turmoil I focus on the anticipation of Shabbos. (Nice shift, hey?)

The brightest part of our pre-Shabbos is the joy of anticipation (that's what all the good food is for, right?). But hear this: There's a Shabbos coming soon that won't have us scrambling with the last-minute preparations. I'm referring to the everlasting Shabbos, the Geulah.

"Shabbos is a taste of the World to Come" say the Sages.[141] The seventh millennium, the era of Geulah, will offer a most delightful delicacy – genuine, full-bodied, perfect joy. **Joy is our pre-Geulah kugel!**

The delicacies of the seventh millennium are already available for tasting. Just as the Shabbos foods are actually available on erev Shabbos, temptingly so, the Moshiach joy is already available in this pre-redemption time. And just like erev Shabbos when there's more stress and tension just before the holy day enters, there's plenty of darkness and *tzores* everywhere we look.

So how can we "sing"?

Darkness is inverted light. A Jew is going to turn darkness into light. Knowing this adds to the joy.

A secret of our success in dark moments of history has been the "Miriams," the heroines of yesterday and today. They lead the way, in the deepest darkness. Miriam, whose name actually means "bitterness" was able to remain fixed on the future salvation, to anticipate it by preparing tambourines for the expected salvation, and to lead the women...

In song...

We sing to soothe our sorrow over what we have no more. We sing to express yearning for things we wish for. The Miriams, the forward thinkers, sing in joyous anticipation as they stretch their hands forth to catch the light of the bright future, and bring it in to light up the present, inverting darkness to light. Shabbat Shalom! Good Shabbos!

And in dance...

I am scaling even greater heights now, having learned something new from a little child in a playgroup. It was Friday, and the teacher had dumped a huge bucket of play dishes, pretend food and Shabbos table accoutrements on the rug. A delightful children's CD was playing traditional Shabbos songs. Little three-year-old Zlatie was busily "cooking" in the kitchen corner, clanging around pots, slamming cabinet doors as she busied herself moving kitchen utensils about. Suddenly the chubby little tyke stopped her busywork and started to sway and wiggle to the music. I looked at her and thought, "Dancing in the kitchen in middle of the erev Shabbos hubbub, I haven't tried that yet!" I was truly tickled by the notion and couldn't wait to share the idea with my family. Is it possible to stop and dance in the thick of things? We won't know until we try.

*Women were "blessed" with atzvus, sorrow, as a conse-
quence of eating the forbidden fruit. Their tikun, correction,
is simcha. The woman can change the atmosphere beginning
in her home and then, like a ripple effect, the simcha fans
out further and further.*[142]

Our heroines, the balabustes who prepare their food and sing their way through it, deserve a tribute. Thanks to them we have our delicacies ready for sampling before Shabbos and create an atmosphere that "ups" the excitement in anticipation of the eternal Shabbos – the *yom shekulo Shabbos*, the Shabbos millennium that is approaching. Rabbis worldwide who have linked an increase in joy to speeding up the Geulah are certainly blessing our unsung singing heroines for rolling out the welcome mat.

Change can take a lifetime – as I am discovering. Don't be hard on yourself. Pat yourself on the back for the smallest shifts. Celebrate them. Once your system sees how welcoming you are to those small, even miniscule changes, it will invite more change.

Fellow Jews, let's welcome change! Change in ourselves, change in the world.

17

Joy-fusion!

A New Joy Cocktail

Suppose we had a so-so-week and now we're in a so-so-mood. Shabbos is approaching, and we need to rise to the occasion, ante up the Shabbos atmosphere. How would we go about it? How does spiritual joy "work"? Many people assume that there are two distinct modes: a regular, weekday joy and a holy kind of joy, right? Wrong!

Here's good news: We don't have to choose one or the other. We can merge the two.

Simcha is not some airy, spiritual experience. The simcha has to be brought into the concrete physical realm. That is the uniqueness of the Divine soul: "Though it is sheer ethereal spirituality, it impacts physicality at its most palpable."[143]

How is that possible? Don't the needs and tastes of the animal soul differ from those of the spiritual soul? One wants to be fed, pampered and satiated on a purely physical level. The other subsists on Torah study and good deeds. When one is full, the other may be hungry. They are two contrary drives.

Surprisingly, we already co-join the two appetites.

For example, on yomtov, which is all about a joyful reunion with G-d, we are actually required to indulge the body. After all, didn't we just herald

– ingest! – the upcoming Shabbos joy with a slice of kugel? Every yomtov has its specialties as well. The physical body is a partner in the spiritual festival joy.

On yomtov we are expressly commanded to increase in simcha.[144] How do we implement it on a practical level? With new clothing, jewelry, treats.[145] The actual mitzvah in the times of the Beis Hamikdash was to eat the sacrificial meat.[146] Interesting, isn't it, that the obligation for simcha was not resolved by the spiritual aspect of the sacrifice, but by *eating its meat*. (While the sanctity of the holy sacrifices was absorbed through the tangible consumption of the sacrificial meat, the focus, obviously, was on the joy of the mitzvah, not merely on the physical feast.[147])

Aren't festivals spiritual occasions? Why then are meat, wine and other goodies prescribed?

As a wick needs fuel to burn, the body achieves its mission using the fuel of corporeal provisions.

Our soul can achieve only through its host – the body. We engage the physical world, and we ally the body with the soul. Rather than "drown out" the physical desires, we welcome them in to provide relish and draft them into our holy affairs. We get the enemy to become our ally.

We are not capable of understanding spirituality without physical form. Judaism is a spiritual religion but our service depends on very physical acts. Even a tzaddik who loves G-d with all his heart must perform physical mitzvahs with all their details. It's not enough to rejoice only with one's heart and soul. The physical body must participate in the joy.

The physical act is a valuable part of Yiddishkeit, and not merely as a means to arouse the emotions. The mitzvahs of a festival have two aspects: (1) the aspect that is done with the heart and (2) the aspect that is done with our bodies. In this way we connect to Him with both our bodies and souls.

We've covered Shabbos and yomtov but there's one festival we haven't included – because it hasn't happened yet.

We are gearing up for a new festival – the upcoming Redemption. And we'll make this next one happen too – we'll invite it in with our joy.

"The thing that was not done yet to bring Moshiach is the proper avoda of simchah, joy...through increasing pure joy that will bring Moshiach." (Lubavitcher Rebbe 14 Elul, 5748)[148]

We get credit for making some of the holidays "happen," most famously Chanukah and Purim.

Short summary of every Jewish holiday
They tried to kill us.
We won.
Let's eat.

As quantum physics scientists explain, we literally "change" atoms through our involvement with them. We can change the world through our anticipation, our joyous observation of the future.

There are two kinds of Shabbos: the weekly Shabbos and an everlasting Shabbos.
And there are two kinds of joy. There's joy-in-galus and there's joy-for-Geulah.

But how can we realistically be expected to increase our joy in this deep, dark galus place when we've had a so-so week and we're in a so-so mood?

We need to craft a special blend of joy that will coax and move our world to where we want it. We're not talking about a futuristic activity but something we can do right now. We will fuse the body-joy and spiritual-joy to form a unique formula, a concoction that will make Geulah atoms dance. Introducing... Joy-fusion!

It's a solid, legitimate strategy. Fuse the physical to the spiritual in order to infuse physical pleasure with holy intent. Combine interests. When all forces combine efforts, we have a joy superpower that can break the barrier of galus.

So, how do we generate "Joy-fusion"? Simple...we partake of a physical pleasure and bear in mind that it is for the sake of generating extra joy, joy for the sake of inviting Geulah. Profound spiritual achievements can be attained with the ease and speed that we can access information in the electronic age. (It's the age of pure whizdom!) Just as clicking on a link brings us to a site, we can link the pleasure with a "click" of the mind to a spiritual "site" called Joy-of-anticipation-of-the-everlasting-Shabbos.

All it needs is our intention.

The fact that we're spicing the joy with corporeal delights and galus vernacular is not taking away from its authenticity. We've got to be practical if we want the joy to take off. Here's a sample suggestion:

On an ordinary Monday night, have a "popcorn party for Moshiach." The popcorn party is the trigger to draw the family into a happier mode. If no one else is available, do it by yourself. Once we've sparked the joy we can hook up to the higher spiritual element and make the G-d-Geulah link.

A woman asked me, "My family members are not interested in this stuff. How can I get them excited?"

Try this:

1. Hang an exciting quote about the Geulah on the wall. Quotes are offered throughout the book. My favorite, the pure-joy quote that hung on my own wall is in the introduction. Now that you've got happy walls (or fridges) you're ready for the next step.

2. One humdrum afternoon hand your son a ten-dollar bill and send him out to buy some treats for the family. "Ma, what got you going?" he's likely to ask. You don't have to say a word. Just point to the quote on your wall. You could designate special treat days every third Monday, or as you desire. Have a rotation system for who's next to choose the treat. Who can resist a treat? If you live by yourself, invite a friend, or treat yourself.

"No one will be left behind!" when Moshiach comes[149] and so no one should be left out of the opportunity to beckon him in.

3. Anyone enterprising out there? Someone should start a franchise: Muffins for Moshiach. It may be an incongruous combination but remember that the physical body's taste is different from that of the spiritual soul. By appealing to its taste buds we entice it to work for the same Boss.

(We need YOU to join our company.)

Trending: Moshiach Muffin Mania fueled by Jewish consumer's expectancy of anticipated new world order...

Don't they say to start your day with a healthy breakfast? What could be more healthful for a body than joy! The joy of anticipation in particular is highly vitalizing.

Think of fun muffin fillings – get your family's creative juice flowing: Clouds-of-glory whipped cream (Get the healthy whipped cream, available in health shops. It's important to have a nutritious breakfast!), jolly beans...what can your family come up with?

If kugel could be our pre-Shabbos treat, why can't muffins be our pre-Moshiach breakfast delight?

> Of course, we don't need to rely on food to spark our enthusiasm. We could take a moment anytime to meditate on the excitement of the upcoming Geulah. Isn't that treat enough?

Where in the Body Systems is Joy?

Joy is not just a spiritual idea. It must enter the body systems.

Imagine someone gave you a gift – a new engineering marvel. It has buttons, levers, lots of mysterious parts. But you don't know how to use it.

Our body is a joy engine. Somewhere in there we have a precious element (App!) called Joy. In which parts of our body is joy stashed and available? Where are the tabs and levers that operate it?

Joy is as close to us as the curve is to the lips, but we may need some hints on how to access it. We know where we keep our lips but we don't readily know where else in our body joy is stored and available.

How many "joy-activators" can you come up with from within your body-system? (Test yourself before reading on.)

1. The centerpiece: the **soul**. Joy is the natural state of the soul, but life gradually saps us of natural that state.

    Before Adam and Chava ate from the Tree of Knowledge, joy was a constant state. After that, life became a mix of good and bad. Every burden drops another stone into our heart. To access our joy, we have to reach under the sorrows and expose the soul's powers. Hidden under the deepest apathy is a constant and faithful joy that never dims. Children remind us of that original state of joy – that is their mission! They are uninhibitedly joyous. They drop their grievances and bounce back quickly. Watching their free spirits can help us get in touch with our own natural states.

    The joyous soul has no hands or feet but it has three means of expression: thought, speech and action.

2. The **mind**: We have a fraction of a second before we choose our reaction, the psychologists tell us. Which thought will we pick from, a positive one or a negative one?

    ...Or a humorous one? A sense of humor is a wonderful mind-gift. Some people are naturals, others don't use it often enough, and yet others are straight arrows. If your funny brain is rusty, you can turn it on – or "grow" one – by hanging around humorous people. Even if you can't come up with a joke, just laugh. Laughter defuses the tension and lightens things up. Whatever your humor aptitude, remember to laugh at yourself.

    Joy-genius strategy: Hang some fun reminders around your house to get into the habit.

3. The **eyes**: How we "look at life." Eyes can be awe-inspiring reporters, when we know (or learn!) how to put a positive slant on what we see and experience.

4. The **heart**: The straightest route to continuous joy is filling the heart with gratitude. Learn to sincerely thank G-d for all the daily blessings we have, so that there is a bodily sensation...

    "that the very flesh of the heart actually feels [the emotion of love or fear or joy] just as, for example, when one meets a truly devoted friend...he...forgets all his troubles...[150]

5. The **body**: It is not anti-spiritual, and we're not meant to shun it. G-d provides the fire – the joy, and our bodies provide the fuel.

6. The **lips**: Celebrated for the **smile**, the good-feelings-spreader. One person's smile can change a person's world – the person you meet may not have a smile but you can give him one of yours.

7. The power of **speech**: When we use it to bring expression to the goodness and beauty in the people, world, and events around us, we can rightfully call it "the *gift*" of speech. **Laughter** and **song** are wonderful gifts of speech!

    Laughter deserves honorable mention in this joy-fusion discussion. People think that joy is an abstract emotion. Not so. Fully expressed joy is a thoroughly corporeal event. Laughter, joy's voice, is a real body-shaker.

8. The **feet**: When we break into joyful dance, we've spread joy to its furthest extent, and to its fullest expression in the world of action.

The experience of joy is not confined to a head, heart or any other body part. It's the "inner you" and whole of you – but it manifests in these body parts when it is stoked and developed.

18

Changing the Molecules
of the Mind

Success tiptoes in subtly, one molecule at a time

I t was a very hot day. A lady came into the variety store, looking for a fan. After examining fan after fan, she finally settled on the cheapest fan of the lot.

The next day the lady was back. "The fan didn't last even one day," she complained.

"How did you use the fan?" asked the seller.

"What do you mean, how did I use it? I waved it in front of my face."

"Lady, that's what you do with the better fans. With this fan, you hold it still in front of your face and wave your head!"

Sometimes we try to get away with the least possible investment. We may be cheating ourselves out of a better quality of life. We need to invest more of ourselves and in ourselves.

Don't look for the easiest, cheapest ride. Invest in your joy. These pointers may be helpful to maximize the investment return:

- **Joy often has to be worked at.**

Joy has to be nurtured along to become a mindset. It is important to know this so that:

1. We don't feel like failures in case we're not "naturals."
2. We realize it's "normal" to make joy an ongoing project.

Is it possible to change a mind that's accustomed to its old ways of thinking?

Here's proof that we can: Not so long ago, doctors followed the firmly established policy that infants should avoid common allergen foods for the babies' first year. The American Academy of Pediatrics has since changed its mind. Based on new studies, it decided that it is actually beneficial to introduce these foods earlier. Very quickly, the old way of thinking was overturned and replaced with the new theory.

- **Knowing is not enough. We need to implement the knowledge.**

> Aron studied day and night. He was what you call a real masmid, assiduous student. A man who was looking for a scholarly son-in-law inquired in the yeshiva about him.
> "I've heard about this amazing masmid," he told the rosh yeshiva. "He must be a real talmid chochom (scholar)."
> "The Rabbi responded, "I will tell you the truth. Frankly, the boy studies so much he just doesn't have the time to really know!"

Having the thinking equipment is not success yet! We may know all the right answers, but when a situation comes up that requires that very strategy that we had ably rattled off to someone just a few days or even minutes ago, we fail to "connect the dots." We've got to *use* the information.

- **Everyone can change.**

Every one of us has a mind, no matter how much we complain

about our faulty memories. And, the one common feature of all our minds is: we think. So, what do we think about? The majority of our thoughts – up to eighty percent! – are said to be negatively based. Am I hearing a clamor of protests? Go ahead and test it. Chart the meanderings of your mind for several hours (it's harder than you think, but you could do a few minutes here and there). Becoming more aware of your thought processes is in itself is a potent harbinger of change.

Granted, eighty percent is a daunting percentage to consider changing. But let's take a positive view. The good news is that we *have* the mind. Fortunately, we're good to go, right away!

How often do you…
- Feel sorry for yourself? Resentful?
- See what went wrong rather than what went right?
- Think about what you lack rather than what you have?
- Read negative intentions into a person's words or actions?
- Project negative outcomes for a given situation?

The mind is perpetually rehashing, brooding, fretting and distressing over recent occurrences, future *potentially*-negative interactions that may take place (*what ifs*), or something that *could have* taken place (but didn't, so why stew when we could be singing!)

How long does it take to develop a habit? According to halacha, after ninety repetitions we consider ourselves habituated to a new mode.[151] In my work with challenged children, after three months of seeing a desired new behavior, I feel confident that the change has taken root. After six months I consider the new behavioral achievement cemented. Self-motivated adults may be easier to change than children, but then again, habits that have formed over many years may take longer to change. Note: recovering from addictive behaviors is never considered habituated; a recovered addict must always be vigilant to avoid relapsing.

How to Change Your Mind

"Ma, I want to go to Camp Fun-and-Play"
"I thought you wanted to go to Camp Angel-kid."
"Well, I changed my mind."

Nothing will prevail on this child to go to Camp Angel-kid now that she changed her mind. Nothing really changed – only her mind. But the mind is a hugely powerful machine that can paint the world any color it decides. It can fell mighty forests, move mountains, recoil in fear at fancied attack and envision the most intense events that will never happen except in the mighty arenas of its imagination.

- **To change your mind – replace your thoughts.**

There is no need to change our (entire!) mind; we merely have to *replace its thoughts.* The negative thoughts enter unbidden, like waves that perpetually cascade up on the shore, no effort or invitation necessary. To change the mind's content, we have to *displace* it by choosing productive content.

This dawned on me recently as I was mulling over ideas for a talk, during a visit to a seaside community. I strolled over to the ocean, and as I was watching the waves breaking onto the shore, rolling on, never ceasing, I realized how much the ocean and the mind have in common. They both never stop churning. Thoughts, like endless waves, come in on their own, many of them from the ego and animal soul. It's up to us to introduce constructive thoughts into that continuous random flow.

An added benefit of shifting from a preoccupation with negative thoughts to happy ones: It is a great anti-*loshon hora* (speaking negatively about others) strategy. Abstaining from loshon hora is a common struggle. But the negative speech is merely the crystallization of negative thought tracks.

Loshon hora strategies typically focus on what we should *not* say – or think. However, these strategies have the opposite effect. A stutterer who tries to stutter less stutters more. A person who thinks "I must not think how angry I am at my neighbor" is not going to become less angry. Like the pink elephants, the more you try to minimize them, the bigger they get.

If only we could unfailingly view people, and their actions (and life!) in a positive light. At least, when a person's actions are distasteful to us, we should see past them to the untarnished inner core of every Jew. Our Sages teach that every person is as full of good deeds as a pomegranate.

"Imagine you could open your eyes, see only the good in every person, the positive in every circumstance, and the opportunity in every challenge."
The Lubavitcher Rebbe

So what will we think about? Instead of getting worked up about things that don't please us, we can get *enthusiastically* worked up about things that *do* please us. Gratitude is the antidote for negative thinking.

- **No one can do it for you.**

A burglar was caught red-handed, a bag of incriminating loot still in his hand. He was hauled into court and faced a grim-looking judge.
Did you have an accomplice?" asked the judge.
"What's an accomplice?"
"A partner. In other words, did you commit this crime by yourself, or with another person?"
"Myself, of course!" asserted the culprit. "Who can get reliable help these days?"

If we want to succeed, we can't depend on someone else to do our positive thinking for us. Imagine a person you share your space with says, "I'm miserable, and I'll continue to be miserable unless you make me happy." We've got to do it ourselves, with our own minds. It requires inner resolve and stick-to-it-ive'ness.

We don't have to be very smart to serve G-d with simcha. After all, we didn't have to be so smart to let the bad thoughts enter! We just have to be determined.

"Appreciation" for example, is a foolproof way to create molecules of joy – but no one can fill our being with feelings of gratitude. The deep appreciation has to emerge from within our own systems.

Whether we were straight-A students or brought home report cards with F's circled in red ink, whether we use our minds or our feet to get around in life, each of us is capable of finding evidence of G-d's kindness daily. Appreciation can be achieved by pondering just one detail such as the brilliant design of our skin.

> **A phenomenon called *skin*...** Where is that deep cut you got from that new kitchen knife? Or those other cuts you sustained over the years? Imagine the grand total of appreciation we should be feeling now for each healed cut. How wondrous a material the skin is. It heals itself from a multitude of cuts, sheds all stains, is waterproof, grows with us, stretches to accommodate new bulges and shrinks back when we shed them. And it lasts a lifetime. Show me a fabric that can do any of these.

- **Steep to reap.**

On a visit to a famous art museum, wanting to cover as much ground as possible, our group raced through exhibit after exhibit. At one point, we realized that we were not really absorbing anything. So, we slowed down and focused more intently on several paintings. We were able to appreciate the talent, technique and message, and become more intimately connected with the picture and its creator. Imagine the world as a giant art gallery. We can race through our lives and emerge completely unaffected, or we can spend time studying G-d's artistic magnitude. His many exhibits are arrayed in our morning prayers, reminding us to "gaze" mindfully at each blessing.

Change seeps in gradually – those reflections *will* penetrate. I speak from personal experience. After rubbing noses with joy for several years my thought patterns have evolved. More and more, I am learning to extract a spark of joy from every moment.

> (R-r-ring...) As I was typing these words the phone rang and brought this very point to life. (G-d must have intended for me to share it with you.) "Hi, this is G.G. I was wondering if anyone might be coming in to Brooklyn from M--- this Shabbos. I am looking for a ride for my son." She had already left a message about it earlier in the week, but I did not yet return the call as I had no leads.
>
> Now that we were on the phone, I invested a few minutes to brainstorm for possible solutions with her. About five minutes into the conversation, I suddenly clapped my hand to my forehead. I was having a couple for the Shabbos meal, and they would be driving in from M--- on Friday!
>
> *I noticed that I had to really steep myself in the subject matter in order to reap results. I had to think a bit harder and longer. The life lesson I came away with was: we have to steep to reap!*

- **Seek out a mentor.**

   If you truly want change, follow the sage advice we read in Ethics of our Fathers[152] to consult with a wise guide or *chaver*, buddy. Someone else can help you be honest and objective about your needs and progress. A mentor is not a substitute for self-investment but can help maintain the momentum.

   When we team up with someone, we have a better chance of success because we have two against one. Here's how it works: Every person has two souls, a Divine soul and an animal soul. Because Divine souls are altruistic, the two Divine souls unite for the same cause. They genuinely want to help each other. The animal soul, on the other hand, is self-serving, motivated by its self-interests. It cannot be relied on to work honestly on behalf of another. With two G-dly souls working on our behalf, we outnumber the one animal soul, and our self-improvement efforts are more likely to succeed.

Change How You See It: "Vision" Exercises

Let's keep it simple. There is no need to battle the mighty mind. Instead, we offer a repertoire of replacement thoughts and subtle shifts in perspectives that can produce mighty changes.

Perspectives, how we "see" things, influence our mindset. We can translate an event as good or bad. The brain can only think one thought. *If you think happy, you can't think sad.* How can we become "happy" thinkers?

Sometimes we think something bad happened to us. But then we get new information and the bad thing turns into a pretty good thing. Let's say someone was going to be very late for work. Bad news, right? What if they were fired? Terrible, right? But what if this happened just in time to avoid being in the Twin Towers on the morning of September 11, 2011? In retrospect, those untoward events were Divine munificence.

Visualization: When things don't go as planned, we could direct our mind to envision how G-d is doing us a favor and there is absolute munificence hidden in it.

Pleasant mind-scene scripts: The same mind that can act like a monster when it overwhelms us with fears and anxiety has the power to take us to calm, serene places. *What a gifted and graphic designer the mind can be!* Do you know the type of person that, when her husband or child is late, already "sees" in her mind, with great clarity and vividness, several dreadful possibilities? *That person should be able to arrive as quickly to a state of joy!*

> "The wise man's eyes are in his head" says the wise King Solomon.[153] This metaphoric observation also refers to the powers of visualization.

Rabbi Levi Yitzchak of Berditchev was found one morning dancing away in his room. What was the reason for all that simcha so early in the morning, he was asked. Reb Levi Yitzchak explained, "I was saying my morning blessings, and when I came to the blessing 'You did not make me gentile' I thought, how lucky I am to be a Jew." Imagine it had been otherwise, a life bereft of all its Jewish joys. Apparently, he had gazed with his mind's eye and the concept had become very real for him.[154]

It doesn't cost a dime to:
- Relish a bright memory from our childhood. (Have a few prepared to fall back on.)
- Relive the highlights of an enjoyable trip.
- Anticipate an upcoming event, such as a lunch date with a friend. Or, start planning one.
- Imagine the glorious feeling we will experience when the world will be a perfect place and we all sit together and bask in the glory of G-d.

• New Forward-facing Solutions for Old Ways

There are three negative thinking patterns that seem to be very popular, as evidenced by their large following. They have stubbornly resisted being washed away with the tides of change for countless generations:

What was: Holding onto ancient grudges. People can get stuck in the misery of their past traumas and be quite resistant to change.

☹ Worrying drains us. *"Worrying does not empty tomorrow of its troubles. It empties today of its strength."*[155]

What will be: Many of us are "wedded" to worries about the future, the *what if* scenarios.

☹ Grudges divide us. *"The first to apologize is the bravest. The first to forgive is the strongest. And the first to forget is the happiest."*

What is: We are wont to walk through life thinking about what we lack rather than what we have. Many don't even realize there's a better way.

☹ Feeling deprived drives a wedge into our relationship with G-d. Our "poverty" stems from an appreciation deficiency of G-d's extensive bounty. Here's a reminder that may help us snap back when we slip into the deprived mode: *You may be unhappy with what you have now – but you'd go to pieces if you lost any part of it!*[156]

(I have not included *guilt* in this list. Should I feel guilty? NO! I won't give in to worry, to grudges, to feeling deprived – or to guilt!)

Each of these thought patterns erodes our ability to enjoy life Our joy-status is allergic to these thinking patterns! It's time to replace them with forward-facing solutions.

☺ **Erase the grudges:** *Don't live in the past.* Look ahead. Become a forward-thinker. Like the radically different perspectives of the two fellows that met at the edge of the city, we can focus on distasteful views, or we can face the beckoning vistas of the future.

In our glorious future, past negative records will become irrelevant; negative memories will lose their emotional sting. Rather than waste precious life-energy being stuck in the past, let's look forward now!

☺ **Eliminate the worrying:** Rather than *worry* about what *might* be, we can *revel* over the anticipation of what *will* be: our glorious future that is practically here.

☺ **Restitution for the "deprived":** People who focus on what they *don't have* rather than on what they *do have* (an area in which I excel!) will benefit from gratitude – the joy-of-*now*, a powerful strategy discussed in "The Gift of Grateful Vision."

The mind is a skeptic. Why should it change the way it's been doing business all these years? Here's a sales pitch that will convince even the most resistant mind.

When we think positively:

- *We enjoy others more freely.*
- *We enjoy ourselves.*
- *People enjoy us;.*
- *G-d enjoys us.*

> *Gratitude, besides improving our vision of life here-and-now, can be forward-looking as well. The Jewish nation sang their gratitude to G-d after crossing the Red Sea, but G-d is looking forward to an improvement on this final pre-Geulah era. Then we will sing before the miracles happen.[157] We're singing now; can you hear us, dear Father in Heaven?*

• The Gift of Grateful Vision

A chassid complained that his mind was being assailed with foreign thoughts. The Alter Rebbe told him, "They gather in empty space."[158] The trick is to fill the empty spaces with good thoughts. How can we create good thoughts? One way is with gratitude.

Gratitude is a gifted way of seeing things. It is a great magnifier, but it is selective. It only magnifies what's going right in our lives – not what's wrong.

Our days are a succession of gratitude opportunities: *I tried a new recipe and everyone loved it. The cream that the doctor prescribed this time finally alleviated my skin condition. I found out about a new place to buy clothing. I got in and out of the shoe store quickly!* Gratitude is a great joy-fusion strategy. We can gloat over everyday issues and get spiritual credit when we verbally acknowledge G-d as the source for our gifts.

Two important elements to "cementing" gratitude, or any positive-thinking habit:

1. **Make it corporeal.** Filling our heads with gratefulness turns our minds and hearts to a happy place, but the objective is to make the joy as corporeal as possible. Thoughts are intangible but words bring the gratitude down to earth and into the world. When we verbalize, the gratitude-habit becomes part of the fabric of our lives.

   Gratitude that is thought but not expressed is like a gift that is wrapped and not delivered.[159]

2. **Formulate a plan to give it time to "gel."** We can do this

by incorporating regular opportunities for gratitude recognition with family members or friends. It can be in the form of lists, charts, games and sharing in a common forum over the course of several months. This will give the new way of thinking time to form positive pathways in the brain.

"We can't always bring ourselves to a place of joy, but we can bring ourselves to a place of gratitude." Genuine gratitude makes the heart sing – not the distracted, lip-service kind of gratitude but the kind that engages your entire heart. If that's not joy, what is? (A glimpse behind the scenes: Chana from Melbourne happened to offer the quote above as I was formulating this chapter. It offers an opportunity to express my gratitude to the One Above for His continuing input. That's part of the trick: becoming an expert at finding those opportunities.)

Now is an opportune time to deliver my "gift." I thank G-d...
- for all the things that could be going wrong and are going right.
- that He has led me to pursue the deeper meaning of joy.
- that gratitude is becoming a "heart-felt" experience.

And my joy-genius grandfather's overflowing gratitude levels continue to beckon... I will keep at it until my heart is brimming with joy!

Suggested family activities:

- A gratitude contest. The winner is the one who can come up with the most gratitude entries. A more elaborate version: Participants take turns reading their lists, and everyone crosses off duplicate entries. The person left with the most original entries wins.
- Original gratitude *grammen* (rhymes) composed by family members, featured at family meetings.

A creative mother turned a disappointing event into a growth opportunity.

As ten-year-old Mendel explained, "I was very upset when I couldn't go to my friend's house for Shabbos. Mommy made a special Shabbos for me right at home instead, with many fun activities with my brothers and sister. One of the activities was to prepare a list of things we thank Hashem for. This is my list:"

I am thankful that I have a book to read.

I am thankful that I have a mommy and tatty who take care of me.

I am thankful that I have a lamp / and seforim.

I am thankful that I have a MP3 player / and that I have food.

I am thankful that I have a place to live / and a place to sleep.

I am thankful that I have a warm place in the winter and cool place in the summer.

I am thankful that I have a shul to daven / that I have cutlery.

I am thankful that I have a piano and keyboard to play with / and that I have games.

I am thankful that I have a yard to play in / balls to play with.

I am thankful I have a basketball hoop / and that I have a phone to call.

Each child came up with their own impressive list, even the young non-writers who dictated theirs to mommy.

Gratitude bonus: Parents will find their children complaining less and appreciating more as they learn to celebrate things that are going right. (Now you're hooked! I may just have made the most convincing statement in this book.)

• Joy-ish Talk

Do you enjoy public speaking? Many people shy away from it. Remember those speeches we had to give in class? Each word and pause was meticulously planned. Well, the assignments are safely behind us, but the speaking podium is a portable one. It accompanies us through life. We could be standing at the entry of our living room and discover with horror that the worker put the tiles in all wrong. Or, at the threshold of the messiest room in our house, aghast at the chaos that confronts us. Or, on the side of the road, looking at the damage our car just sustained from the tailgater behind us.

What are the epithets these scenarios would evoke? Just remember that every word that comes out of our mouths becomes public property – "real" estate. Talk gives substance to thought. It carries power to fulfill the reality of those words whether their orator intended it or not.

Every word comes back to haunt or help us sooner or later.

> *A patient complained to her doctor: "I've been having terrible obsessions for years, and no one has ever been able to help me."*
> *"Who's been treating you until now?"*
> *"Dr. Mead."*
> *"Oy, what advice could that unqualified man have given you?"*
> *"He recommended I see you."*

Our Sages warned us not to tempt the Satan with negative comments.[160] My father would not allow us to use dire predictions like "You're going to fall off the chair!" "We *could* fall off," he would gently prompt, or better yet, *"Be careful."* Why think negative? On the positive side, if you point out a desirable quality, such as patience, even if it is not that person's strong point and you noticed just a wee bit of it, his positive self-regard will surely surge. We are literally coaxing it out of him with our positive declaration.

Many of us think in "Oy!" language, and the next thing we know, we're talking this way. Thoughts become words, and words shape our destiny.

Oys take many forms.

☹ *Oy vey...* it's going to rain the whole time and ruin our plans.

☹ *It's hopeless...*"I'll never" lose all that weight...find...get married.

☹ *I messed up...* how will I get out of this hole I'm in?

☹ *Bad news... my plans were disrupted.* Flight canceled!

☹ *Uh-oh! I don't have...* a proper cleaning lady and Pesach is approaching. I'm doomed.

The right thoughts become the right words. Maintaining a joyous trust, appropriately attired in the right words, enables limitless possibilities.

☺ Hurray… It's a great day, no matter what. And the weather will not determine my mood.

☺ I *can* do it… and it *can* happen. Not only do I believe in G-d – He believes in me!

☺ I *trust* G-d can get me out of this unsolvable predicament in infinitely creative ways.

☺ Good news! I got a voucher for a free trip due to the canceled flight. Now I can come back for my cousin's wedding. (This is working out better than expected.)

☺ I *know* (I'm confident) G-d will help me… I'll have my house ready for Pesach, wait and see.

Words have weight, though they emerge freely, effortlessly and weightlessly.

Pessimistic words will make the future heavier. Optimistic forecasts will make our future lighter.

And when everything is going well, why not voice our jubilation over that? A regular good day deserves its moment in the spotlight too, along with those hair-raisers with the happy endings!

19

When the Battery is Low

Joy Ports and Charging Stations

You wake up in the morning and you're groggy, paying the price for having gone to sleep too late. Hopefully a cup of coffee will offer the pick-up you need to start the day. With your eyes half-closed, you head to the kitchen to get the coffee going.

Everyone has times in life when their spirit flags. We want to ensure the power sources for that needed lift are readily accessible (unlike some outlets in my home that are in the most inaccessible places – I have to bend myself into a pretzel to plug in the cord.)

We also want those sources to be reliable.

Remember how exciting it was when solar energy-powered devices came onto the market? I bought little solar-powered lanterns to flank my walkway. They were supposed to recharge automatically but there was one problem – the cloudy days! On the days when the sun didn't shine, the fixtures emitted a feeble light or none at all. Luckily, we had spotlights with automatic sensors that turned on at twilight, no matter what the weather.

Notice how closely our spirits mirror the relationship between the sun and those lanterns. When the sun shines, we shine. But when twilight falls we compensate with some auxiliary lighting. When there's utter darkness, the light has to be powerful and reliable.

So, who is turning on those lights?

Hopefully, we are. Joy can be passively imbibed, but a proactive person squarely and solidly shapes his destiny. That's the difference between fate and destiny: Fate means we are the passive recipients of life circumstances; destiny means we take control of life. Proactivists continue to shine their joy. No matter what's going on.

A Closer Look at Charging Stations: Passive and Active

Where can we plug-in for our joy? There are benefits in both passive and proactive practices though the second is preferable.

- *Passive joy'ers:* People whose joy levels ebb and flow in response to events. It's a win some, lose some, subsistence.
- *Proactive joy'ers:* People who are proactively joyous are helping G-d effect positive changes in their own lives, as well as in the world around them. Everyone gains.

There are many ways joy can be activated, whether passively or proactively.

Passive:

When a short-lived joy is triggered by some joy-inducing event in our lives. For example, Rosa couldn't find her cell phone, and she was frantic. She was involved in a project and it was essential that she find her phone. Everyone in the house was searching for it. A few hours later it was discovered – a child had been playing with it and left it on Rosa's bed. How overjoyed Rosa was when the cell phone was found. But, how long will that joy last? It may not even be able to provide enough joy momentum to offset her chagrin when the soup burns later that day.

Notice how many of life's joys are created in response to a previous void. The lost phone or ring that was found, the couple that waited for years for their first child, the absent parent that returns home from a trip or military duty... Without darkness we can't explain light. In the words of writer Yanky Tauber: *"According to the mystics, darkness is the stuff out of which light is made."* First comes darkness, then comes light, says the Talmud regarding the order of Creation. In halacha as well, night precedes day. First goes challenge, followed by achievement. It's an optimistic track. If things are dark now, they are bound to brighten up.

Proactive:

Intentionally lifting our spirits with **material-based** objects or activities, such as the famous or infamous shopping spree, a spa treatment, treating ourselves to a lunch date or our favorite snack. Music, singing, a walk in the park are mood enhancers, as are exercise, social time, or an interesting lecture. A dose of humor and laughter can be active or passive, depending on our participation (laugh-producer or "laughee"). Though these are more superficial activities, they are invested with worthiness when linked to goals of substance. They refresh and invigorate us for the next bout of purposeful activity or relieve tension when we need to lighten up.

- **Helping** people and **volunteering** does wonders to make a person feel good. Giving is getting... *Who is happy? He who helps others to be happy!*
- Proactive, but destructive: People take **drugs** or **alcohol** because they're looking for a high. They're missing joy, connection and meaning. They haven't found the path to genuine fulfillment. If only we could demonstrate to them how satisfying and fulfilling genuine joy is. *"If there is no joy from true sources, happiness will be sought from other sources."*[161]
- **Love** is a superhighway to joy. Love G-d, not the way you think He should be loved, which means when He fulfills your terms and conditions, but love Him anyway. That, actually, is the way He would like to be loved – unconditionally. Love your spouse, your child, your mother, not necessarily the way you want to love, but consider the way they would appreciate being loved. Love your child not to become the fantasy of your ideal, but the way he or she was meant to be loved, based on his or her unique

makeup. If you could love that way, everyone would be happy.

- Use your **mind** to migrate to a happier place and meander through pastures of pleasant thoughts and notions. When you lay in bed at night, don't dissipate your last moments of the day on negative thoughts. Instead, think Love. "G-d I *love* you" (add a virtual hug), "G-d *loves* me." Think how good He is. (Remember how he saves me a parking spot every day? That's just a dot on the huge list of what He does for me throughout a lifetime.) It's okay to repeat many times. Your default of negative thoughts will magically switch to positive ones.

- Doing a **mitzvah** generates simcha shel mitzvah. Because it is a G-dly source of joy, it endures. It is spiritual, internal and eternal.

- A **smile**. This deserves special attention. It is active, but requires the least energy output, certainly less than other items on this list. When we pass a person in the street or elsewhere, being the first to smile is proactive. Expecting them to smile first is taking the passive route. Not smiling at them and then frowning inwardly because they are acting snobby or like "cold fish" is going the negative route. But, smiling at them even though they didn't smile back at us last time and maybe even eliciting a smile this time around is a noble act that can really light us up. It's an amazing power we all have – to be the reason someone smiled today.

A smile is a laughably cheap commodity and brings immeasurable joy into the world. Here is an irresistible story:

> *Rivkah, a wonderful human being, would visit a nursing home periodically. On her first visit to the home she noticed three seniors sitting together with the glummest looks imaginable. Their sour expressions were daunting. It wasn't surprising; the place they were in was quite bleak. Rivkah thought, "There must be a smile in there somewhere. Everyone has something to smile about. Let me walk over to them and try." What she said was simply brilliant. "You have the*

most beautiful smiles!" Suddenly – rusty smiles appeared! On her next visit she said the same thing, and again the hazy sun peered out from their scowling faces. After a few visits, they were "conditioned." As soon as they saw her, the smiles broke out. Rivkah, by the way, is an artist whose paintings exude joyfulness. I wonder if she realized that she was "painting" smiles on these people's faces and producing a most exquisite form of art. (I called her to share this thought and she loved it! Joy-artists, too, benefit from smiles.)

A simple smile can thaw an iceberg, build bridges and change the climate on any continent, even if you speak not a word of the native language. It also lights up the world around you.

And of course, you've got a case of double success. You're happy, and you made others happy.

No matter what you leave behind on your various trips and travels, you'll never leave your smile behind. You might occasionally forget to *use* it but it's always there, ready and available for immediate use.

Joy, like the smile, is always there. We just have to tune into the joy frequency, just as Rivkah tuned the gloomy seniors into the smile frequency. We each have the most beautiful joy inside us.

20

Why?! When Life "Surprises" Us

Crisis! Practical perspectives to pull out in a pinch

When we own a valuable gem we do our best to safeguard it. Simcha is the cherished link to our future. We don't want to lose it – every moment counts! True, crises are an inevitable aspect of life but a kindly mental interpretation can make a dramatic difference.

What are "bad" experiences? They are constrictions of Divine light, sparks of G-dliness that were scattered and severed from their origin as a result of the shattering of Tohu. At the beginning of creation, the world was in a spiritual condition called Tohu, chaos, which "collapsed" as it lacked order and balance. This was followed by the breaking of the vessels, and the light departed from them. This "break" was planned; G-d made a world that was designed to fall apart—so that we could recreate a better, more harmonious, self-sustaining world.[162]

How do we reattach the fallen sparks to their origin? Through simcha, said the Baal ShemTov. By celebrating with G-d in life's downers, we redeem the Divine sparks and reconnect them to their origin.

Here's the point: Simcha is the key to Geulah. With simcha we're not fixing, we're fixing *up*. The world will be better than it was originally. Seen in this light, our "crisis" tools take on a more glorified role. We must appreciate that every crisis, and therefore, every damage repair tool, is an instrument to repair the world. Simcha is redemptive! Through it we achieve our global mission of *tikkun olam*.

Pain? Gain!

Every moment has a redemptive spark. Hopefully this chapter will sharpen our skills to recognize, reveal and redeem those sparks (the three R's – they should teach them in primary school!)

We offer some useful lines to have in our repertoire, a kind of emergency toolkit for when these joy-blocker events surface. Hopefully we can teach the mind to come up with these positive responses as its standard default setting.

☺ Finding meaning and purpose

There's a reason for whatever happened – and a good one – we just don't know it. When life mystifies us, the one question we might as well eliminate from the running commentary in our mind, is "Why?" No one is going to tell us, and we don't often uncover an objective.

When the Jewish heart is struck by tragedy, the Jewish mind has to know that G-d's decrees are not arbitrary... *"We cannot know the reasons behind a tragedy, but we have to know that they are there."*[163]

But we can ask a different, useful question.

☺ **What for?** Let's take a cue from our favorite queen. Esther, before approaching the throne room of King Achashverosh, unbidden, cries out to G-d, *"Keili, keili, lamah azavtoni*, G-d why did you abandon me and my people?"[164] *Lamah*, why?, could be read as *L'mah*, to what purpose? We look for meaning, and even more important – we look for purpose. If Divine Providence guides our lives at all times, it is surely planning this moment of challenge. We must be on the look out to find the opportunity lurking in it, like a gift waiting to be unwrapped.

Keep looking until you find one – **"one should never let a good crisis go to waste."**[165]

L'mah – what-for – thoughts-to-think:
- G-d has a plan. Let's stay positive.
- There's something good in it. A liability can become an asset.
- G-d is sending me a message. I'll be listening for it.
- It's definitely for my benefit. I may discover how.
- Every descent is for the sake of a subsequent ascent.

☺ Rather than getting stuck in a rut we seek to find a redemptive quality.

- *When my neighbor was advised by his doctors to have a tracheotomy to help with his breathing, his children were unhappy about it. They worried, "How will our father look?" "Everyone will make fun of him!" The parents called for a family meeting and their mother, Toby, told them – on the contrary, "We're so fortunate to have this possibility available to us. Look at the relief it's giving him."*
- *Dina developed a problem with her eyes and had to hire a driver for the lengthy daily commute from school every day. Besides the extra expense, she resented the invasion to her treasured private time with her kids. And then she discovered a redemptive value: she began to use the travel time to do her children's homework*

with them. No more prodding, motivating and nagging once they came home; life became so much smoother. A deficiency had become an asset.

- *Mrs. S. schlepped into the city for her special-needs daughter's eye appointment, only to discover that the appointment was canceled and no one had called her to tell her. "It was doubly irritating; I had canceled my daughter's all-important therapy session for nothing. Thank G-d, I managed to keep my cool. As I waited for my child near the restroom I heard the receptionist comment, "She didn't raise a ruckus?" When I was rescheduling, she asked how I managed to maintain my composure. I explained that there is a G-d and He runs the world."*

Was it a waste of time and energy? Bad luck? Mrs. S. reported afterward that showing the people in the doctor's office how a Jew's relationship with G-d manifests in real life was rewarding in itself. She concluded that her trip was not "for nothing."

Nothing happens by accident. Every footstep is according to G-d's plan – and every step we *don't* take, as well! When a foot injury grounded me, I wondered, what can be the redemptive aspect of this? There must be something I can do now that I'm usually too busy to do. (Remember? We have everything we need, to do what we are needed for – right now.) Sure enough, I was fortunate to carry through a project by phone that is possibly one of the most valuable achievements in my life.

Sometimes we don't get to see any redemptive value...We often contrive exciting plans that don't work as intended. I once set up a plan so efficient that it made life sing. I streamlined a work-related appointment, a mega-sale, a meeting with an old friend, and some additional errands, all in the same neighborhood. I was feeling so good about my well-oiled plans – and then the car stalled and my carefully stacked deck of cards came tumbling down.

Sometimes the timing turns a midsize misfortune into a world-class crisis. *Shoshana was making a sheva brachos for a close friend right after returning home from an extended trip. She had cooked as much as she could before leaving. "I prepared chicken cutlets, cake, made my challahs, bought my cholent meat, fish rolls, and... guess whose freezer broke* ☹" she texted. "*It was a bummer*," she admitted. "*I did feel a need to tell my Mom to get empathy, but now I'm taking it in stride.*"

Valuables left behind in hotel rooms, refrigerators konking out at the wrong time... Surprises of all kind define our lives – from "bummers" to catastrophes. And yet we sing!

What's the redemptive quality in these stories? That we sing even if plans nose-dive! There's a redemptive value even when don't see it – because G-d does. The fifteen *Shir Hamaalos*, fifteen songs of the ascent[166] in King David's Psalms are an apt metaphor for climbing the challenges of life. Climbing involves exertion; each ascending step demands new effort. Nevertheless, we do it with a song, with joy, knowing that our exertions bring a special pleasure to our Father in Heaven and Redemption to the world.[167]

> G-d designs intricate plans – loyalty tests – that throw us off guard. When we're alert – we ascend to the next level simply – by singing.

☺ "We think we know what will make us happy, but *often it is the very things that we consider negative that become gateways to something wonderful.*"**[168]**

> *Benny and Aliza missed a very important doctor's appointment for their eating-disabled child because they were ten minutes late. At that moment, it was nothing less than a tragedy. But the loss turned into a gain. Aliza discovered a new eating therapy that averted the need for the planned G-tube insertion, all because of the appointment they had "missed."*

☺ **Even a bad day is a good day. If only we knew!**

My daughter finally found a dress for her friend's wedding, but somehow, came home with the wrong size. There had been only one piece left in the size she needed and the sales-girl had to hunt for quite a while to locate it. "Think positive," I suggested gently. "There must be good in it." She travelled back to the store the next day. Sure enough, everything was on sale. The dress was waiting for her, and she found several more outfits, all for the amount she had paid the day before.

"Bad news" is in reality "good news." Having a positive outlook on a challenge can actually transform the challenge into something good. When we focus our mind on the Goodness behind it, the manifest reality will change for us. It is Good all the time, but we can make it appreciably good.[169]

When bad news is viewed as good news, we coax it into that state.

The next time something goes awry, try to "sing" the follow-ing see-bad-news-as-good-news "song":
"The bad news is... *I came home with the wrong size.*
The good news is... *I came home with the wrong size!"*
Try it for small and large mishaps. The bad news/good news is: I missed the bus... didn't get into the program... This is a powerful tool. When we change how we see the "reality" of the situation, the situation can change accordingly.

Sing it out loud – even to yourself! Songs create a flow to get us places and generate the proper frame of mind – as the soldiers who serenade their courage with rousing songs of victory. Verbalizing it will provide an extra boost for the good within the mishap to be re-vealed.

Our awareness of a positive potential induces it. As quantum physicists noted, observation of electrons influences their movement. "Many successful people credit their success to their positive thoughts," says Val Kinjerski, PhD,[170] a leading authority in the field of employee motivation and productivity. "When we think positively and visualize a positive future, we tend to have positive experiences."

The way we look at ourselves, G-d looks at us. The way we look at G-d's ability to help us, He does. We are partners in the endeavor.

☺ What seems like a calamity in the physical world is actually quite good.

Chana lost her beautiful diamond ring at a women's convention. She was frantic, mostly with feeling badly about the money her husband of only two years had invested. A sympathetic acquaintance tried to assuage her angst. She took Chana's hand in hers and told her, "G-d is going to bless you with your true diamonds." Several months later, on Lag B'omer, Chana prayed at the gravesite of the Lubavitcher Rebbe, asking that she merit double blessings to compensate for her two miscarriages." A year after the diamond was lost she was blessed with her first children – twins, a girl and a boy. "Diamonds," just as the lady had said! To make the connection crystal clear, the boy's bris was on the exact Hebrew date that she had lost the ring and received the blessing. Chana was 39 years old.

Looking back, Chana notes that despite just wanting to succumb to her misery, she pushed herself to join the women as they danced joyfully after the desserts. Although she shed tears again during her drive home, she credits the dancing and moments of joy as the catalyst and vessel for the blessings to descend.

The Magid of Kuzhnitz was in failing health. He summoned his son and told him that Reb Levi Yitzchak of Berditchev had appeared to him and told him, "In a short while you will be with us and here, Above, you will see everything clearly. When your eyes are not limited as they are in the physical world, you will see that what seemed like a calamity in the physical world is actually quite good in the world of truth."[171]

Probably my favorite eye-opener of the goodness lurking within a calamitous event is the Breaking of the *Luchos* (the Tablets containing the Ten Commandments).

Imagine coming down from Heaven with a piece of Divine handiwork in your hands, sapphire stones etched with the fiery words of His holy Torah and discovering the intended recipients have abandoned G-d in favor of a Golden Calf.

Their leader Moshe Rabbeinu is faced with an unenviable quandary. To whom does he owe his supreme loyalty? He chose his nation. As their leader, his love and allegiance to them were indissoluble.[172]

The Tablets were like the betrothal contract between G-d and His nation. By breaking them, Moshe spared the nation from judgment. They could no longer be prosecuted as an unfaithful wife. He broke the Tablets "for everyone to see," a public display that his love for his people was shatterproof. Nothing can sever the deep, essential love of this leader for his nation.

Ever since my eyes were opened to this underlying reality of one of the greatest calamities to befall our nation, I have lived with a new level of love. If this is the magnitude of His servant's devotion, how infinite is G-d's love to us!

I call this love to mind very often as I lay in bed at night, waiting for sleep to take me. After racing all day, navigating life's limitations, the mind needs a change of focus. How fortifying to shift into a positive space of the limitless love of our leadership (every generation has its "Moshe Rabbeinu"). How comforting to melt into the reciprocal embrace of a child with its Father in Heaven.

> What a warm way to end the day.
> No matter how great the calamity, there's love behind it.

☺ Thank G-d it's this and not worse.

- A container of juice spilled all over the freshly washed floor. That's annoying, but think about it this way – it could have been oil!
- I discovered I was incurring eighty dollars interest per month because I had erroneously checked the 'minimum monthly payment' box. Thank G-d I discovered it after four months, not a year!

☺ A 'T' in a road leads to a new – and better – one.

Rabbi L. had to give up his teaching position because he developed a problem with his vocal cords. What a calamity! How will he provide for his family? He became involved with selling Judaic items, and, thank G-d, business prospered. He was in a far better position to provide amply for his growing family's needs as they married and established their own homes.

☺ Every delay is for the good.[173]

Blessings are likely to await us as a result of those irritating delays. But don't just sit back and practice optimistic thinking. There's opportunity in it. See what you could do in the interim to maximize the time-opportunity you were granted. I was introduced to this phrase when the order for my new kitchen windows was not properly processed so they would not be ready on time. I used the opportunity to rethink my options and make an upgrade. I enlarged the window opening, giving the kitchen an airy openness. Oh, was I happy for the delay.

Trying to reach someone by phone or playing "phone tag" can often "ruin" our day's plans. We can't go on to step B before we speak to person A. Actually, whenever we reach them *is* the best time, some-how or other.

Our lives abound with delays. Plane schedules, hospital proce-dures, marriage plans. I guess that means there are so many opportu-nities for blessings in our lives.

☺ A Pleasant Surprise

Not every surprise is a negative one, of course. There are pleasant surprises as well.

Three of my grandchildren were sleeping over for Shabbos. As they were dropped off, I heard my granddaughter petulantly demand-ing something that her mother was not willing to give.

Children's needs-lists are longish, and the more parents try to shorten them by giving in, the longer they seem to get. I thought: Here I am, writing and preaching about joy to the world; could I con-vince one young lady in my house to change? How could I convey the negative effects of "expectations" and feelings of "entitlement" to a child growing up in a have-everything culture?

After empathizing with my granddaughter's disappointed feel-ings, I began to unfold the concept that in truth, all a person is en-titled to is food, clothing and shelter. Everything else is a gift. Imagine if we would instead feel... I was stuck – what is the antonym of disap-pointment? We came up with an excellent one... *pleasantly surprised* with every item we got above that! Why, we'd be happy all day. My granddaughter was intrigued by the notion! We generated all sorts of examples and followed up with a "pleasantly surprised" campaign. Whatever we did for the next hour generated delighted *ohs.*

Bedtime came. I told them they'd each find a treat under their pillow when they awoke in the morning. "It's a one-time event. It's a pleasant surprise, right?" I told them, to ensure we didn't create expectations for future sleepovers. Some politics ensued when both boys wanted to sleep on the same bed. A solution was worked out; I would transfer little Yossi to another bed after he fell asleep. Everyone was happy. Five minutes later my granddaughter walked up to me in the kitchen. She had come out of bed to tell me, "Yossi will be *pleasantly surprised* when he wakes up and finds he is sleeping in the other bed!" And she pitter-pattered back to bed.

Kids are great learners. She had mastered the lesson and had adroitly and wittily made the switch from disappointment to *pleasant surprise*.

When everything is an undeserved gift, everything in our lives becomes something to sing about.

> The ultimate surprise, not that it will take us totally by surprise, will be us singing *and* laughing... *then our mouths will fill with laughter...*

Section IV

The Jewish Joy Imperative

The Why-to

In the previous sections we focused on *How* to produce joy. This section will address *Why* we need to live with joy – the joy-imperative.

How imperative is it for a Jew in particular to pursue joy? Can't I be a perfectly good Jew without the joy? Is joy just a nice – or optimum – way of living, or is it an actual "obligation" of Torah?

Obligation is not a popular word. Certainly not joy-inducing. For many, Torah laws are equated with "obligation." Pretty cut and dried. Doing something based solely on a sense of obligation leeches all the exciting drive out of it. So why are we so eager to seek out the Torah-requirement of joy?

Imagine if joy were strictly an obligation. What a killjoy!

Why ruin the fun and talk about obligations? We can just talk about the many advantages of joyous living and leave it at that. But then one might get the impression that joy was merely an option – albeit a wonderful one. We'll give you the best of both worlds – the authority of Torah-status and the delight of desire.

> When *must* turned into *want*: A history about Jewish "imperatives."
>
> The Talmud[174] tells that, when we encamped at Mount Sinai, G-d threatened to topple Mount Sinai over our heads unless we would accept the Torah and its laws.[175]
>
> During the reign of Achashverosh, the Jewish people *willingly* re-accepted the Torah that had been given some 900 years earlier.[176] We *chose* to accept it.
>
> We do what we need to do. But it's nice when we want to do it as well.

Duty or desire?

There are two ways to serve G-d: because we *have* to, or because we *want* to. That's what's so unique about joy. It is a sacred duty, but also a *desirable objective*. Duty and desire can travel side by side.

> **Need or Want?**
> Which way would you like to perform these activities?
> - I need/want to go to shul on Yom Kippur.
> - I need/want to be well.
> - I need/want to thank G-d for the meal.
> - I need/want to buy my devoted brother a birthday gift.

21

Optional or Mandatory

The more we prove that joy is mandatory, the more compelling the joy message will be

would love to find that sixth grade English teacher who scandalized us by telling us that the only two things people have to do are "die and pay taxes." (Funny thing about that order, once a person does the first, isn't he exempt from the second?) Years later I discovered that the teacher didn't make it up – it was Benjamin Franklin.[177]

We were shocked at the baldness of her statement. Young as we were, we had already learned to distinguish between *mandatory* and *optional* aspects of Jewish life. We learned that there are three cardinal sins for which a Jew is required to give his life rather than transgress[178] – paying taxes was not on that list! Fasting on Yom Kippur is an example of a mandatory mitzvah. Feasting on unlimited doughnuts on Chanuka is optional.

Optional or mandatory?
Life presents an array of options every step of the way. Here's a sampling.

- For dessert we are offered a triple-layer Rosemarie torte with hazelnut cream. Don't forget – a minute on the lips, a lifetime on the hips. Maybe I should skip it?
- The office is on the third floor. Should I take the elevator or walk the stairs?
- Should I pursue higher learning after high school? I will go further in life if I do, but I don't have to.

Is joy a pleasurable extra, like dessert?

Is joy yet another thing to do that demands energy, like climbing stairs?

If I'm content with a simpler life, why invest all the effort?

Is joy just an optional perk in our lives, or is it a must-have, must-do? *Is it an actual mitzvah?*

Despite the assertion in the Tehillim to "Serve G-d with joy"[179] and despite the popular proclamation by Rabbi Nachman of Breslov that – "It's a great mitzvah to be joyous always!"[180] ...**year-round-simcha is *not* one of the 613 mitzvahs.**

Simcha plays a central role in mitzvah performance. And yet, the closest hint in the Torah regarding the practice of joy is presented in a roundabout way:

> **"Because you did not serve G-d with joy...***when you had an abundance of everything. So you will serve your enemies... in hunger, thirst, destitution, and while lacking everything..."* (Devarim 28:47-48)

The simple meaning of this verse is they did not serve G-d properly despite prosperous conditions.[181] But according to the Rambam (and the Arizal as well), Moshe is censuring the Jews because they did not serve G-d **with joy**. Yes, they fulfilled the mitzvahs, but the joy was lacking.

Notice that the wording is oddly indirect, *"Because you did not serve G-d with joy."* There is no overt command ("Be joyous!"), not even a recommendation. Only: You didn't experience joy as you went about doing your Jewish thing.

We get it... G-d is not pleased with an unhappy Jew. But if joy is that important, why not come out and tell us so outright? This reminds me of a line from a Rebbe who was chiding a downcast Jew: "Knowing that you have a Divine soul – how could you not be b'simcha!" Knowing that we have been selected to receive G-d's precious Torah and the mitzvahs, how could we *not* be b'simcha? We are missing the entire point.

It's as if someone were marketing gems but people had no idea of their value. Would it be worth the effort of cutting and polishing diamonds if no one appreciated them? The Torah is often compared to precious stones. Our joy is very important to G-d. It makes His creative endeavor, the world, worthwhile.

Another unusual feature about this "un-command" is its peculiar setting. This one and only pro-joy assertion is tucked amidst the curses that will befall the Jewish people if they stray from the path of Torah (G-d forbid), like one perfect little rose blooming in a bed of thorns.

Though it is not mandatory, serving G-d with joy is so important that failure to do so can lead to severe consequences.

> "Because you did not serve G-d with joy... **you will serve your enemies**" (Devarim 28:48)

The Rambam, the quintessential halachic codifier,[182] takes a stringent stand on the obligation of simcha, supporting his position with this very verse from Devarim. "**Whoever refrains from this joy [in their mitzvah performance] is worthy of retribution**, as spelled out in Devarim 28:48."[183]

We wonder at this extreme stand. Give the Yidden a break! Life is tough.

What's so Bad about Joylessness?

This passage from the Torah, also quoted by the Rambam, has baffled many people – why be punished for lack of joy?

Really, what's so bad about doing the mitzvahs without simcha? Why focus on the process? Isn't the product – the actual doing – the important thing? We all agree that joy is a life-enhancer nonpareil. But why should we be *punished for lack of joy,* as long as we're doing the right things? It's just one missing element!

Let's consider how the one missing article affected the following situations:

Not all circumstances are equal. A missing item at a party is disappointing but the show goes on, and its absence is soon forgotten (unless desserts are your sole sustenance). Imagine though if the caterer was a complete no-show. That would be a lot worse. What's a party with no food? An even worse-case scenario would be every guest showing up in a bad mood and nothing the host does succeeds in cheering them up. They may have had valid excuses. Maybe they were distracted by things going on in their lives, or maybe they didn't want to be there. But they didn't even put in the effort to pretend, to act *as if* they were happy to be invited. What a washout of a party.

> Henny was throwing a dinner party. The caterer had delivered all the food, but she noted with consternation that the desserts had been left behind!

When the joy is missing, it is more than a missing detail or feature. G-d invites us in to be exclusive guests of His Inner Circle – and we show up – but sometimes we're aloof, detached, distracted. A bunch of sour grapes. Well, I wonder what our Grand Host must be thinking.[184]

Imagine...
a house without windows,
a class without a teacher,
a belt without a buckle,
an egg without a yolk,
a safe without a lock,
a president without a cabinet,
a life without joy.

It was Jake's first mountain climbing expedition. He had climbed for a bit when he realized he was missing his climbing rope. He had to backtrack. A rope is the lifeline of a mountain climber as it secures him to a climbing partner.

There are times when a missing detail, like mountain climbing without a rope, can be downright dangerous. Lack of joy can put people at personal risk as well. That's because simcha has the ability to save a person from undesirable consequences. Simcha can sweeten judgments and nullify decrees.[185] Even if the Jews deserved galus, even if they were guilty of real transgressions, the simcha could have rallied to their defense and saved them from the harsh decrees outlined in these verses.

Simcha is essential. Sadness is dangerous for our spiritual, emotional and physical health.

> Enemies continue to pursue us... in the form of financial and health issues, concerns about children, and the list winds on wearily. The Alter Rebbe would command those who had problems to pray with song and simcha. This would sweeten the judgments and chase away all the adversaries.[186]

Rabbi Aharon of Karlin would warn his followers, "Sadness is not an actual sin, but the damage that sadness and depression can cause is worse than the damage that any sin can cause. Conversely, joy is not a mitzvah, but serving G-d with joy is greater than a mitzvah (because of its beneficial outcome)."[187]

"Be determined to keep away from depression and aim to be happy constantly. Simcha is the remedy for all kinds of diseases because many illnesses are caused by depression," said Rabbi Nachman.[188]

Sadness feeds into anti-holy forces. Despondency encroaches on the legs of the *Shechina*, the Divine Presence that wants to come down to rest in this world. Unhappiness drives a chasm between G-d and us.

Anger, a violent form of unhappiness, is equated with idol worship.

Unhappiness takes us away from G-d; joy brings us closer. The Divine Presence doesn't rest except in a place of joy.[189]

Two of the most effective tools in the evil inclination's toolkit are sadness and depression. When it succeeds in getting us "down," we become vulnerable and easy to vanquish. The objective of the internal evil inclination is to make the person disconnect from G-d.

As soon as we're unplugged from joy, we lose the connection. Then we experience:

☹ Doubt: *I wonder if I'm really accomplishing anything – so why bother.*

☹ Lethargy: *This is too hard... I won't succeed.*

☹ Poor self-image: *I'm not good enough.*

☹ Defeat and resignation: *It's no use.*

Sadness resembles a black hole, a star whose gravitational pull is so strong that nothing can escape from it, including light. If the sun were just a smoldering black hole it would not be of any use to the world.

Happiness flows out; sadness sucks the energy inward.

Sadness disrupts our connection with people as well. Depressed people become self-absorbed black holes. They sap everyone else's positivity along with their own. Giving and helping others make us feel better and happier. We are meant to be suns, to shine and radiate good vibes, not energy sappers.

Americans are big on the right to happiness. **For a Jew, happiness (joy) is not a right; it's a religious obligation.**[190]

Joy is clearly a Jewish imperative.

Joy is imperative for daily life, and also to ensure our future. "Because you did not serve G-d with joy...you will serve your enemies." If absence of joy can result in exile, a positive mindset will surely lead to Redemption. "Simcha has a unique potential to bring about the Redemption."[191]

"Oh, you're writing about simcha! A worthy endeavor," an acquaintance cheered me on. Then she challenged me, "So, is there a mitzvah to be b'simcha?

"No, there is no actual mitzvah," I responded confidently. (After all my research, I knew my stuff by now!)

"There are 613 mitzvahs to be happy!" she countered. I was momentarily thrown. Then it registered. Simcha is an integral part of every mitzvah!

Torah Tunes – into Joy

Education is compulsory, and school is notoriously the Kingdom of Rules. No standing up during class, no speaking up without raising your hand, no eating during class, no laughing...

But recess was ours. We poured all our exuberance into those fifteen-minute oases of freedom. When we weren't punching balls outdoors, my classmates and I would unwind by spending our recess break sprawled on the worn marble steps outside our classroom in our old, solidly-built school building in Brownsville, lustily singing popular songs like *Mitzva gedola l'hiyos b'simcha tamid* (it's a great mitzvah to be happy all the time),[192] *Ivdu es Hashem b'simcha* (serve G-d with joy), *Ki v'simcha sei'tsai'yu*[193] (you will go out with joy). At the time, we focused more on beautiful melodies and harmonies than thinking deeply into their meanings, innocent of how soon we'd need these fortifying words to prop up our spirits in the real world. I must say (humbly), we did produce some brilliant sound – some of my classmates had magnificent voices – and the rest of us didn't ruin it by singing too loudly!

Tuning into their content now, so many years later, I'm noticing some interesting ideas. Take, for example, two of the songs we sang: **"Serve G-d with joy"** and **"Then our mouths will fill with laughter"** Both verses are from Psalms[194] and both address joy, but they make contrasting points. Ivdu means "serve" or "work." **"Serve** G-d with joy" reminds us that our relationship with G-d requires effort – as does the joy that drives it. In contrast, the second

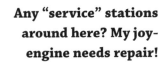 **Any "service" stations around here? My joy-engine needs repair!**

verse is joyous and carefree, describing the times of Moshiach, when serving G-d will come naturally, and our mouths will be filled – *effortlessly* – with abundant laughter.

The first verse directs us how to handle galus challenges, and the second describes the wondrous joy of Geulah. It is history in a nutshell. When we succeed in the first assignment of *serving* G-d with joy, we will *earn* the effortless joy. These two verses could have been merged into one song...the before and the after. The efforts and the results. The investment and its profit.

Serve G-d with joy – everyday!

Pulling out joy on the day we lose our job requires honorable exertion. We may need some recovery time! (But don't take too long.) "It isn't easy," we complain. Joy requires effort. I think that even the Creator agreed. After all, if joy were so accessible, why would G-d have created **laughter and humor** for us? Joy needs nurturing, so G-d provided us with ingenious tools – the auxiliary gifts of humor and laughter. They are wonderful recovery tools to help us rebound from a crisis and they help surround us with the sounds of joy.

The eternity of Jewish song...Back in our school days we sang with the naiveté of youth. But we continue to sing. We will never cease to sing.

The Psalmist, after enticing us with the notion of abundant laughter, goes on to describe a scenario of the future: *"When G-d will return the exiles of Zion... the nations of the world will express their wonder at the great things G-d will do for...us; and [as a result] we will be joyful."*[195]

A novel interpretation of this verse credits our being joyful as the *cause* of the extraordinary wonders rather than the outcome:

What have we done to merit these great miracles, the nations will ask in wonderment? We will tell them that the reason we merited this dazzling display of G-d's love is **because** *we were joyful* – no matter what happened to us in galus, we responded with joy. No matter how difficult the circumstances, our response didn't falter – we remained resolutely joyful.[196]

Joy is the investment as well as the profit.

22

Big, as in Big Bucks

There are two intensity levels, two settings for ideal joy: High and Medium-Low. Each has its time – and reason – to shine.

J oy can be elusive. We're grateful for every scrap and we figure the more the merrier, right? Yet, the halacha has opinions that govern how much or how little joy befits the occasion. The Rambam describes two power levels of joy. Sometimes an extra powerful surge of energy is required. Sometimes a smaller surge is enough. It reminds me of the 220-voltage line we installed to accommodate a larger air conditioner in our living room. What a difference that extra power made.

Setting One: High

When I set out to research Torah sources for joy, I was told that the Rambam expounded on the halachic status of joy in his halacha compendium, Mishneh Torah, in – not one but two – different sections. What a find!

I opened to the first source,[187] and there I found two key words that seemed to hold the answer. Joy is an *"avoda gedola."* It was a somewhat cryptic phrase, though. How does one translate these two words? If you know a smattering of Hebrew, you may know that the definition of *avoda* is "service" or "work," and *gedola* means "big". But, is it a "big" service as in "big bucks," or is its big-ness intimidating, as in "we saw a big bear emerge from the woods"? And pairing *gedola* with *avoda* may indicate that joy is a big job, possibly a difficult one. Not a very encouraging message, if that is the case.

An English translation of the Rambam translated *avoda gedola* as "a great service." Hmm, a tsunami wave is great too. So was the Great Depression. I finally got my answer in a collection of talks and letters by the Lubavitcher Rebbe called *Simcha u'Bitachon L'Hashem* (Joy and Trust in G-d).[198] Yes, it's true, that simcha is "big work" and often challenging, but the work is done with simcha born from love of G-d. The love provides the relish to appreciate the great value inherent in it. This changes everything, don't you think?

"Big" also means "important." People will invest intense labor into projects that are important to them. One loves to build, another loves to cook up a storm. Many people will push themselves beyond their endurance to build body stamina, and marathon running has mushroomed. What's a little work to produce some joy, a self-rewarding accomplishment? Among chassidim *avoda* is a coveted, internal process held in high regard. It describes the ongoing self-development practiced by those who strive to progress in their spiritual quality of life. The endeavor requires no less resolve than do the physical tasks.

The ultimate simcha is gained through *avoda gedola*, hard work. "It is the toil of the heart and soul that generates within us a happiness that is never-ending." The more you sweat to achieve your goal, the greater your joy will be.[199]

Joy is Work; the Work is a Joy. Ahh, after all that work, joy feels wonderful.

> *Guy 1: Work? Oy, I hate work.*
> *Guy 2: You like joy?*
> *Guy 1: Yeah, I love joy. I'd do joy all day – if I didn't have to*

work.

Guy 2: Join me. I'm working my way to joy – all day. It's so enjoyable, I feel like I haven't worked a day in my life.

To make ideas come alive you have to work.

The joy of achievement… Everyone wants to live "on top of a mountain," to be on top of his world. But the growth and satisfaction derived occurs while we're climbing. The child born on top of the mountain – what does he know about the thrill of accomplishment that is achieved patiently and painstakingly step after careful step? There is no meaningful gain without pain in this galus world of ours. But, with the struggle left behind, the joy of triumph will be ours to enjoy forever.

So how does "*great service*" translate into life? The Rambam tells us how, by citing an exemplar: "David was

Horse to horse: What a lot of fresh, nice hay I'm chewing through. Oy, pleasure is such work…

cavorting merrily before G-d"[200] as he escorted the Holy Ark to Jerusalem after an extended absence and captivity by the Philistines. By citing the intensely animated joy of King David, the Rambam is conveying the intense joyfulness we should strive for in our mitzvah performance.

Caution: High voltage area!

That is the message the Rambam wants us to hear: Our *simcha shel mitzvah* should be hearty and real. We should not merely go through the motions. Even moderate is not "great" yet. It should be so sweepingly intense that it can't be contained. It should spill over and make us *move*.

Joy is a moving experience!

We should be so caught up that we forget to be self-conscious, *because in remembering G-d we forget ourselves.* When you see a person singing, dancing, clapping, looking like he temporarily "lost his lid," you may be seeing a joy-genius in action, experiencing true simcha shel mitzvah!

Our joy should be an authentic experience. It should spill over its banks and be palpable and conspicuous. It should be boundless and – may it flow ceaselessly.

Is this type of joy only for those joy-geniuses?
"This work is addressed to all people, to the great and to the small," says the Rambam in his introduction. Every Jew – even the great and important ones among us – must constantly pursue greater heights of joy. No one is excused.

If we serve G-d the way the Rambam prescribes, our avoda will be "big" – important and valuable, as in "big bucks" or the "Big Day" which is almost here. (Beyond that Big Day marked on your calendar, there's the one we're collectively anticipating.)

Setting Two: Medium-Low

In a different section of the Mishneh Torah,[201] the Rambam paints a mellower image of the joy experience, one that seems inconsistent with the first source. He seems to be turning it down a notch. (Note: Explanatory commentary is interpolated by the Translator, in brackets.)

"He should not be overly elated and laugh [excessively] – nor be sad and depressed in spirit. [Such expressive "happiness" is often a sign of inner discontent and suffering]. Rather, he should be quietly happy at all times, with a friendly countenance [and his joy should be a composed sense of satisfaction]."

Again, further on: "One should neither be constantly laughing and a jester, nor sad and depressed, but happy. Our Sages declared: 'Jesting and lightheadedness accustom one to lewdness.' They also directed that a man should not laugh without control, nor be sad and mournful, [but always happy in a composed way, *b'nachas*], and receive everyone in a friendly manner. [If he's too sad he won't be able to greet people pleasantly]."[202]

The recommended simcha-level seems to have toned down quite a bit. Were the neighbors complaining about the noise?

These two simcha levels refer to two different situations:

1. The first level addresses a Jew actively involved in performance of a mitzvah, such as shaking the lulav on Sukkos. The best simcha shel mitzvah scenario is when simcha *is* the mitzvah, such as enlivening a groom and bride at a wedding or dancing with the Torah. (220 volts!)

2. The second discussion on joy describes the way a person should carry himself when he walks in the street or goes about his daily activities. We should have enough joy in us so that our smile and greeting will positively affect the people in our passing encounters. This is the lower setting, the composed, celebrate-G-d-all-the-time mode. This mellower joy is for all-purpose use. (120 volts.)

Everytime and Everywhere

If joy is imperative, we need it all the time, and in every place. Truly, each day offers so many opportunities for often-overlapping, joyous living. It's like spreading luscious frosting on every inch of cake.

- Joy *before* doing a mitzvah
- Joy *while* doing a mitzvah
- Joy *after* the mitzvah
- Joy in gratitude for the kindness G-d has done for us *until now*
- Joy for the upcoming *future*
- Joy for *everyday* living.

Look how much we manage to pack into twenty-four hours! How blessed we are to have our days filled with multi-hued joy.

Before. The simcha provides impetus. It gets us to do more mitzvahs more often.

During. During the actual mitzvah performance there is joy but the joy is not pure. Serving G-d is an awesome affair, so there's a co-mingling of joy and trepidation.

After. It's only after the mitzvah is done that we can enjoy pure joyfulness over our privileged connection.

For the past. As King David states so eloquently in Psalm 116:12, *"How can I repay G-d for all the kindness He has done for me?"* My list is too long to fit in any book. How about yours?

Speaking of after... The Ramah concludes his Shulchan Aruch[203] (Code of Jewish Law) with four important words, a parting message: *Tov lev mishteh tamid*, a good-hearted person is *always* celebrating.[204] What a flourish of a finish. This is not the joy of doing the mitzvah, but the afterglow. Not the main course but the after-dinner mints.

After the mitzvah deed is done, after the day is done, after our service in galus is complete, we (will) feel a rush of joy for having had these opportunities to unite with G-d.

For the future. In preparation for Moshiach...

> *"Simcha needs preparation. We must become accustomed to that state now, to be in tune with the ethos that will prevail when Moshiach comes. We must learn to dance, to sing, in preparation of Moshiach's arrival. These preparations must begin in earnest."*[205]

At all times. No matter what we do, as it's all part of serving G-d. We're never out of the joy loop.

Our everyday activities are part of our overarching purpose *to know G-d*. Eating, sleeping, and exercising, we are "serving G-d"[206] – 'round the clock.

King Solomon and the Sages are of the same mind: *"Know Him in all your ways,"* says King Solomon;[207] *"All your deeds should be for the sake of Heaven,"* say the Sages.[208]

"When we are spiritually mature enough to feel pleasure and joy in the revelation of G-dliness, we look to bring awareness of G-d into all facets of our lives, not only in the ways expressly required by the Torah."[209]

From morning coffee through late night snacks, during daily commutes or haircuts, our life journey is an ongoing chronicle of Joyous Purpose.

My board of directors is gonna love this. I'm reaping profit for every breathing moment, day and night, awake or asleep.

Joy should pervade every nook and cranny of our lives. Every time and...

Everywhere (even home)

Don't you look forward to coming home and kicking off your shoes (who cares if the socks have a hole or two), scrounging for goodies in your cabinets and fishing pickles out of the pickle jar with your fingers? In my own haven I should feel free to let my guard down. I want my home to be a happy place, of course, but do I always have to be "on"?

What if I want to sulk?

At work I have to maintain a professional demeanor, choose my words carefully, be tactful, patient and keep my voice even, like those ever-smiling, unfailingly polite flight attendants.

But at home I should feel "at home" – free to stew, snap and mope, be forthright and "tell it like it is," raise my voice as needed (my kids call it yelling, but they must be exaggerating). Of course, when a neighbor knocks at the door, I snap to professional attention.

I'll bet our families would love us to keep our professional mode on at all times.

> A father came to a counselor to seek help for poor self-control. He would become enraged and smack his children and then feel bad about it later. His counselor asked him, "What if your neighbor rang the bell as you were about to hit your child?" He admitted he would answer the door and greet him pleasantly, though he was "uncontrollably" enraged a half-minute ago.

It's nice to be home, but we're not scot-free. We have an interesting rental agreement with our "Land-L-rd." G-d allows each our own little domain, but we need to turn it into a G-dly space in which He can feel "at home." At the same time, He respects our privacy. He does not intrude. Although He is omnipresent, He waits politely outside our doors, so to speak. "G-d is in every place we allow Him to come in." We need to invite Him in.

Good hosts, before their expected guests arrive, inquire about their visitors' preferences, their diet and whether they will want the cooling system on a higher or lower setting. They want their guests to feel comfortable. What makes G-d feel comfortable, at home? G-d's celestial headquarters features a year-round climate of unlimited joy.

"In His place there is...joy." When we make our domain a happy place, G-d comes home.

We've got you fully covered!

Section V

It's Jewish to be Joyous

Spiritual advantages of joyous living

What's so Jewish about being joyous? Isn't joy a universal quality?

What special relationship do Jews and joy have with each other? Jews and joy certainly have ample reasons not to be on talking terms!

What is Jewish joy?

A basis for Jewish joy is our relationship with G-d, usually expressed through mitzvahs. Of course, the act is the main thing. But how we do a mitzvah is a key indicator about the relationship. Do we go about it like someone forced into a contract (we have to daven everyday) or joy in the privilege (we get to daven everyday)?

And, why are mitzvahs a source for simcha?

23

The Joy of Relationship

Doing it joyfully means we are doing it willingly. Loving the person helps accept his terms and conditions.

unning marathons has been gaining popularity. Grueling as it
is to push oneself for mile after mile, most runners are in the
race again next year. People run marathons or climb mountains
to challenge themselves. They feel good about proving their commitment. And nothing rivals the thrill of achievement.

A marathon is an example of a self-imposed commitment. But
when someone imposes the commitments or inconveniences on us,
we may be resentful. It depends on who imposed them.

- *Our children made quite a bit of noise playing outdoors
  on Shabbos afternoons in the spring and summer. Our
  elderly neighbor remarked: "If you love the people, you
  love the noise."*
- *The first-year teachers were exchanging strategies in the
  teacher's room, "You can't be too nice to the kids or they*

*won't listen to you." Veteran teachers know that when students love their teacher they'll do anything the teacher asks of them. Those students are experiencing the **joy of relationship.***

Loving the person helps accept the conditions he makes. That's when obligation meets pleasure.

Yes, there is a religious imperative to be joyous, but there is also a joy born of love and loyalty to our Creator and to our mission. Joy is the *how* we go about running our lives, and *how* we do our Jewish thing.

They say that joy is not a destination; it is a journey. It's true; joy must be an integral part of our journey. But joy is waiting at the end, just wait and see.

How we do it can outweigh *what* we do: When G-d asked Avraham our Patriarch to sacrifice his only son, Avraham rose early the next morning to do what G-d asked of him. This model is held up through the ages as our ideal. Now, wouldn't anyone do G-d's bidding if he were *personally* asked? Avraham made it momentous because of *how* he did it. We've all come up against situations in which the *how* altered the entire nature of an experience. For example:

- *Avigail, a single mom, asked Miriam to accompany her to the hospital. Miriam agreed readily, and actually made Avigail feel as if she were doing her a favor by asking her to come along. Avigail asked her to accompany her on several more occasions, and each time Miriam responded in the same gracious manner. Avigail summed it up gratefully. "It's not just what you did; how you did it made all the difference."*
- *A woman confided to Simcha that she was struggling financially and did not have the money to buy her son a sorely-needed suit. Simcha took money she had received as a bonus, tucked it into a gift card with a warm note, drove over to the woman's house and hand-delivered the*

envelope, along with treat packages for the kids to deflect
attention from the purpose of her visit.

Of course, it could go the other way:

Mom didn't allow her son to join his friends because he had
not finished his homework. Even though he knew she was
right, he got into a funk. It wasn't much fun being a mother
until Pinny snapped into his usual self.

We can't coerce relationship. We can invite and encourage relationship and hope for it. Parents and teachers know all about this.
They cannot expect the child to understand and happily agree with
all they're doing. Every decision is made for child's benefit but is not
always seen as such by the child.

They hope, though, that their long-term relationship remains intact, unmarred by resentment and animosity (– and pray that their
daily interactions remain positive!). Deep down the child senses the
caring. *"Pinny sulked for three days. But tonight I finally got a good-night*
hug and kiss."

G-d constantly gives us growth opportunities. Who likes the
School of Hard Knocks! That may be why there is no explicit command
to be joyous. You can't force joy, just as you can't force love and relationship – especially if you are in the unappealing position of having
to censure the person from time to time.

Serving G-d joylessly is a symptom of a relationship gone off
course. Doing a mitzvah – G-d's command! – without joy is not one
localized short-circuit. The entire motherboard is malfunctioning. An
overhaul is needed!

The absence of simcha may be a way of registering a silent protest,
or a passive-aggressive response... *The Creator is the cause of my suffer-*
ing. He should not expect service with a smile.

That's why we need to hook up duty and desire. On an "up" day,
desire comes readily. But whether we're up or down, joy is too essential to be discretionary.

Is joy optional? Only if connection and faith and loyalty are.

The Purpose of Challenge: Loyalty

It was Purim. Margalit hurried about her kitchen, eager to finish her work so she could get outdoors and enjoy the festive atmosphere. The weather was beautiful and she looked forward to airing out from those long workdays. A young lady who was passing by when Margalit opened the door of her apartment asked if she could come in to charge her dying phone. "With pleasure!" It fit right in to the open-door spirit of the day. The girl left and, shortly after, Margalit was ready to leave the house. She went to get her keys, but they seemed to have somersaulted out of sight. She checked every possible place she could think of – even the refrigerator and freezer, in case they had inadvertently been dragged along with some food, but no keys. Margalit was stuck in her apartment that overlooked back windows, missing all the Purim fun, until her husband returned home for the Purim meal.

The mystery cleared up that evening. It turned out that "in return for the favor," the phone-charging visitor had mistakenly walked off with Margalit's housekeys, as they were similar to her own. "Why would something like this happen?" Margalit wondered, pondering the mysteries of life as we drove home from work the next day.

Why did G-d foil her Purim fun? Honestly, I don't know why. Maybe G-d wanted to test her loyalty to joy. Would she still retain the joy of her relationship with Him? Margalit aced the test: She had firmly decided, when she realized she was stranded, that she was not going to allow the situation to dampen her spirits.

We can buy into the joy of purpose; but what is the purpose of challenge? No human, even the wisest King Solomon, could plumb the intricacies of G-d's designs. The most we can do is offer perspectives to ease the journey.

We do know that a purpose of challenge is to test our commitment and love. "The main purpose of man's creation is to test him with the trials and physical tribulation, to ascertain what's in his heart."[210]

The Dance of Loyalty

*In the course of his travels before his greatness was revealed, the Baal Shem Tov passed through an agricultural town that was suffering a severe drought. A travelling maggid, preacher, came to town and addressed the residents. He berated them for their errant ways, which were certainly the cause of G-d withholding the rain. The holy Baal Shem Tov was in the audience and called out in protest. "Who gave you the right to attribute the famine to the low level of people? Their simple but pure avoda is precious to G-d. **The drought may just be a test from Above to see if they maintain their faith in Him and continue to serve Him with joy."***

The Baal Shem Tov then invited the people to dance with him. Were they capable of dancing with true joy, or was their faith and simcha diminished by the drought?

They danced, with pure, simple simcha. And then it rained. Their simcha prevailed over the drought.

Real Facts of Life:

- Nothing is random. Everything is part of a Divine plan.
- The world is not spinning out of control. G-d remains in full control at all times.
- No evil can emanate from G-d. He is entirely good.

Remember these facts. Thou shalt not forget! (Yes indeed, the tricky thing is to remember them when we're in a tight spot!)

As loyal as we wish to be, it is hard to handle nasty surprises – and harder still if we keep it all to ourselves. A sharing-strategy for burdened hearts was offered by King Solomon.[211]

"If there is worry in the heart, *yashchenah* - he should minimize it." Our Sages interpret the key verb *yashchenah* in two ways.[212] (1) He should remove the troubles from his mind. (2) He should *share* the troubles. By talking it over he actually distributes the burden and reduces the load. A likely outcome, the Maharsha's commentary predicts, is that his friends will give him useful advice.[213]

Lena lives by herself. When she discovered she might have a new complex health problem on top of her already existing ones, she was shattered. She reached out to friends for support. And just as King Solomon had predicted, they helped her see the picture was not as black as she had imagined. That same week, a doctor's office called to cancel an appointment she had booked to get some sorely needed advice. Deflated, she called her friend again. Her friend assured her, "You'll see, things will work out very well – even better." She was grateful to be reminded to look for a redemptive quality rather than get stuck in a rut. And sure enough, she was rescheduled for a closer date and got an even bigger time slot to discuss her issues with the doctor.

Good news reminder: If you stick with G-d and truly believe it's all good (your cheerful disposition will attest to your faith!) **the goodness becomes palpably visible** as a result of a kabbalistic "chemical" interaction powered by your emunah.

There have been too many tragic experiences while I was writing about joy. Friends who know I am writing about this topic ask me what I have to say in response to the latest tragedy. I have to concede, "the One Above is putting me in a difficult position" when a tragic event takes place. How can we preach simcha when a family has just been handed a great test or suffered fresh and deep personal loss? G-d, have mercy on your children.

While the salvation is brewing, G-d continues to send me some philosophy to chew on. A visitor at my house today shared a wise saying, just when I was particularly distressed at some recent news. "What doesn't kill us builds us."

Nevertheless, dear G-d, we beg of you to make life good for each of our fellow Jews. May they enjoy life so they can truly – and easily – serve you with joy...

When G-d considers how faithful we remain to Him despite our troubles, His love for us is reawakened and rekindled - a love that will ultimately be consummated with the Final Redemption.

24

The Joy of Judaism (Yiddishkeit)

Twelve Reasons to be Joyful Always

A Jew is joyous. But why? On what basis is a Jew joyous *at all times* and *in all conditions*?

"What's there to be happy about?" a downcast Jew asked the Lubavitcher Rebbe. The Rebbe's response to him, brimming with fervor, was "You're a Jew, aren't you?"

Happiness pros tell us to be "happy for no reason." A Jew *always* has multiple reasons to be happy.[214] Knowing the source of our joy can only enhance our appreciation of who we are and why we ought to be in a state of constant joy.

So what's there to be happy about? We have identified twelve reasons. You may come up with more.

1. "It's good to be a Jew," or, in the words of an old-time Yiddish jingle – *oy vee gut es iz tzu zein ah yid*!

2. G-d is everywhere, and where He is there is joy and gladness.
3. We were personally crafted by Him.
4. Our neshama is literally part of G-d.
5. We have a special relationship with G-d. Notice, we address Him in our blessings and prayers as *You* and *I*.
6. He is always with us. We're celebrating that we're never alone.
7. We are connected to the light source. Joy is compared to light, and light lends clarity.
8. G-d gave us the Torah and mitzvahs. His statutes gladden the heart.[215]
9. Knowing we have a G-d-given purpose and mission.
10. We have the ability to connect to Him at all times. We're connected to truth and eternality.
11. G-d has given us many gifts, some of which are enumerated in the morning blessings.
12. We live with joy-of-anticipation as we head towards a perfect world.

> **"Because He is but good all the time… so a person should be happy and joyous at every time and hour and live by his faith."[216]**

In 1961 a young student, Bentzion Bernstein, visiting from England was preparing for his first private audience with the Lubavitcher Rebbe. He sought advice from a spiritual mentor at a local yeshiva. "What should I ask for in those precious few minutes?" The mentor suggested he should base his request on a personality trait that challenged him. And so he did. "How is it possible to be b'simcha?" he asked the Rebbe during his yechidus.

*The Rebbe told him, "If you know that the soul of a Jew is a part of G-d above, how is it possible **not** to be b'simcha? And," he added, "I see that you are by nature a 'mara sh'choro'nik'*

– a morose type of fellow, but if you bear this in mind at all times, you will be joyful."

The Rebbe had deftly flipped the question completely around. Let unhappiness bear the burden of justifying its right to exist!

And in case Mr. Bernstein could ever forget this memorable exchange, every time he came to visit the Rebbe would remind him, "So what is with the simcha?"[217]

I never met Mr. Bernstein, but I got a chance to meet him "secondhand" in an interesting postscript to this story. I once related this story to a group, and a woman in the audience commented excitedly, "This man you mentioned, Mr. Bernstein, lives next door to my family in London! We know him very well. He is a *very* lively man, always smiling and happy." She was surprised by this piece of history, as she couldn't imagine him ever being anything but happy, while I was astounded at how he had succeeded in reshaping his personality.

The Rebbe liked to see Jews brimming with joy.

Looking Back: History of Joyous Jewry

The Sages warn that it is prohibited for a person to fill his mouth with laughter in this world[218] unless it is connected to the performance of mitzvahs. Until the Baal Shem Tov came along and established simcha as a cardinal principle in the path to serving G-d, Judaism was defined by somberness, and joy was perceived as sacrilegious frivolity. His new ways of relating to prayer and life scandalized the Orthodox Jewish world and created strife and rifts that lasted generations.[219]

Chassidim were originally known as "the freiliche" – the happy, lively ones. Chassidim take their joy very seriously. A perpetual state of joy is necessary to generate the passion and motivation that bring us closer to G-d and His Torah. As the Baal Shem Tov said: "The ability to be joyous, by discerning the good and joyous within every experience, is considered by chassidim as a biblical command!"[220]

This, of course, doesn't rule out fear of G-d, and feeling repentant. The "joy-mix" proportions changed, though. Originally, the desirable route to serving G-d was dominated by berating one's shortcomings, and fear of G-d's wrath. The joy was cloaked within the trepidation. Chassidic teachings, such as the seminal Tanya, written two generations after the Baal Shem Tov, direct followers to limit feelings of contrite bitterness over their lowly state to specific, appointed times, but with a major proviso: the low should lead directly to a greater high than before the spiritual reckoning, like the sun after a rainy day.[221]

Sad feelings need not displace the happy ones. Two emotions can exist concurrently. A broken-hearted Jew can feel deep regret for his mistakes and lost opportunities, and at the same time, joy in the opportunities that are available and awaiting him.[222] The process of teshuva, though defined as regret, offers a powerful occasion to rejoice. No matter how badly we messed up, no matter how far we strayed, teshuva helps us restore our relationship with our Creator. Can there be a better cause for rejoicing than that?[223]

Joy can be experienced on many quality levels and "depths." There are profound explanations in Chassidic literature about the nature of the ultimate "pure" joy that trace joy to its most sublime origins. These are intricate studies, even to the initiated scholar.

Breslov derives joy from emunah. The Breslov approach places great emphasis on serving G-d with joy and living life with intense vitality. Depression makes it difficult to direct the mind; a person must do his utmost to move out of his constrictions that hamper his ability to function as a Jew. Through joy a person is liberated from his or her own personal exile to the realm of freedom, "for through joy you will go out" (Isaiah 55:12). When a person is in a state of joy, he can direct his mind as he pleases and attain yishuv ha'daas, clarity of mind.

Breslover chassidim see being joyful as the way to live a Torah life, with an inner process that is very personalized and emotional. Joy is itself an essential part of serving G-d and being a Jew, hence Rabbi Nachman's advice, "It's a great mitzvah to always be happy." Handclapping, singing, and dancing are some of the ways of serving G-d. In the most difficult conditions such as the Nazi concentration camps, the Breslover chassidim strove to find joy in life.

Looking Forward: Future of Joyous Jewry

Selda was moving to Israel and the shipping truck was coming to in less than a week. I said, sympathetically, "Plenty of work, huh?"
"It's fun," she corrected me," especially when I think of where we're going to be when we unpack."

It's *exciting* (a "fun" word) to think about the outcome of all our purposeful activity and to contemplate where we all are headed. We're just about at the end of our journey now.

> *Having fun* was not a trendy notion in the shtetl. But *fun* has become a central drive in the time and country in which I live, so why not harness its energy to add appeal to Yiddishkeit? (It's a Joy-fusion strategy!)

Because we are so close, we have access to a channel of joy that was not previously available to us. We can tap in to this Divine joy now by rejoicing for the Geulah. It's a pure joy – "purely for the Geulah."

> *"The concept of simcha shares a connection to the Future Redemption. For it is in the Era of the Redemption that we will experience the consummate level of simcha. At that time, all undesirable influences will be negated as reflected in the verse, "And G-d will wipe away tears from every face" (Isaiah 25:8). Indeed, all the negative influences will be transformed into good.*
> *"In previous generations, the emphasis was on the service of G-d, and that service was infused with joy. The suggestion for this time is to place the emphasis on the joy itself, rather*

than on the factors which lead to the joy. The focus is on the simcha, and the goal is Geulah."[224]

25

Mitzvah-Joy

Why wait until the next world to enjoy life? Bliss is at our fingertips.

Jewish leaders of our time are calling on us to increase our sim-cha, now that we're so close to the era of Perfect Joy. But if we've had simcha shel mitzvah all along, we are not starting from zero. We're millionaires even before we add new joy on top.

So why don't we feel like millionaires? One reason is that we're subject to human nature; daily activities become routine. Even when we are spiritually in tune, what do we really know about a mitzvah? We don't even begin to plumb the profundity of mitzvah-joy. Its spiritual brilliance is hidden from us. All we know is that a mitzvah is something we got from G-d and that the joy we derive from doing it is the legitimate basis for Jewish joy throughout our history.

Let's tap into knowledgeable "insider" views on the value of a mitzvah.

Just one mitzvah one more time

The Maharam of Rothenburg[225] was imprisoned by the government. He did not allow the people to ransom him, fearing the Germans would find it a lucrative business, and he remained in prison the rest of his life. After he passed away, the Germans refused to release his body for burial. Fourteen years passed until a Jew by the name of Alexander Wimpfen offered all his money to the government in exchange for the Maharam's body. The government agreed and Alexander purchased two plots in the cemetery, with the request that when his time came, he be buried next to the Maharam.

Shortly afterward, the Maharam visited Alexander in a dream to thank him. He said that in heaven they want to repay him for the great deed he did. The Maharam offered him two options: great wealth and longevity, or to share his portion of Gan Eden. "If you choose the second option, you will have to write your will immediately, for in the morning you will be with me." Without any hesitation, Alexander chose the second. He got up, wrote the will, parted from his family and passed away the next morning.

Rabbi Hillel Paritcher, a Rabbi and famous Chassidic mentor who lived in the 1800's once related this story and asked: "What do you think of the choice Alexander Wimpfen made? The chassidim debated with one another and couldn't decide. They turned to Reb Hillel to hear what he had to say.

"He was a fool," exclaimed Reb Hillel. "Because putting on tefillin one time in this world is worth more than all of the spiritual delights of sharing in the paradise of the Maharam until the coming of Moshiach."[226]

Many people think that while mitzvahs are important, our major focus is the World to Come; that a mitzvah is a vehicle by which we merit Gan Eden, the ultimate prize. Reb Hillel understood that a mitzvah offers its own intrinsic value. The reward of a mitzvah is the mitzvah itself.[227] It not only offers us an opportunity to collect vouchers to be redeemed at a later date, but it is a powerful relationship in the present. The blessing we make when performing a mitzvah alludes to this, "He has *sanctified* us with His mitzvahs and commanded us..." When we do a mitzvah, we "take" G-d Himself, as it were.[228]

Think of it this way...

> *Someone sent a letter to the Gerrer Rebbe in which he asked, "How can I attain simcha shel mitzvah?"*
> *The Gerrer Rebbe responded: Imagine you're on your way to shul and someone stops you and says, "Come to my house, eat, drink, and I'll give you money for your needs, but there's one condition: You may not put on tefillin." Would you give up putting on tefillin for one thousand dollars? Surely not. Would you do it for larger sums? No again! You would be willing to forgo everything of this world in exchange for putting on tefillin one time. Now, think what a joy it is that you are doing a mitzvah for which you are willing to forgo all the material pleasures of this world.[229]*

The person who wrote him was struggling financially and the Rebbe's example was absolutely relatable. He could readily conjure up the delightful feeling of a financial windfall, and then apply that delight to arouse the joyous feeling associated with doing mitzvahs. Even one mitzvah is incomparably more valuable than all the material pleasures.

We thank G-d for His abundance of mitzvahs – He could have given us only a few, but He generously gave us 613! 613 channels of joyous connection. Some are easy and accessible – the order in which we get dressed, for example, right arm and foot first, or blessings for the food we eat (aren't we always eating!).

A Star and a Teenager: Meditation on a Mitzvah
A musician of international renown was about to begin his perfor-

mance. A teenager in the audience found himself, by some lucky fluke, right up in front of the audience. The musician suddenly realized that he had left something in the event-director's office. He beckoned to our young teen, one youth among a crowd of thousands, and sent him for it. That one interchange upgraded the youngster from a nonentity to an entity. The famous musician had singled him out! A simple request created a connection between them. He even thanked the teen after the event.

G-d has given us the means to connect to Him. This is an ongoing source for joy that does not fizzle out. Let's stop to delight in the concept of the great and supernal G-d connecting to His simple creations.

Now imagine the musician invited the young teenager into his room, gave him some music tips, and he became his personal protégée. Our ongoing mitzvah performance brings our relationship with G-d to a level of intimacy that should cause us to dance in ecstasy.

Bringing Heaven Down To Earth

Studying the inner dimension of Torah is like opening the palace door and getting a glimpse inside. If you would like to take that opportunity, this chapter is for you. We will discover that the incredible joy of mitzvah performance outshines the future rewards.

We're always hearing about the bliss and delight of the World to Come. We haven't experienced the full delight of it (not that we're in any rush to get there!)

> *A couple was sitting in a café in Gan Eden enjoying the ambience... the pleasant breeze, the heavenly aromas, the singing birds. They couldn't get enough of it. As they were drinking it all in, the husband turned to his wife and said: "You and your health foods! If not for your healthy diet we could have been here ten years sooner."*

The pleasure of the World to Come is great, greater than any pleasure this world has to offer. The souls bask in the radiance of the Divine Presence, the reward reaped as a result of those mitzvahs performed during its lifetime. *"One hour of bliss in the World to Come is better than the entire life of this world."*[230]

In the very same Mishnah (paragraph) we also read *"One hour of repentance and good deeds in this world is better than the entire life of the World to Come."* It's beginning to sound like a pleasure competition. It can't be both, can it? Which is the true ideal? Isn't the World to Come touted as the ultimate bliss?

But hear this, dear couple in the café – and I'm not here to rain on anyone's café time on Paradise Boulevard – but right here and right now is the time to experience the fullest measure of joy. Yes, your reward is eternal, but don't get caught up on the reward aspect. There's more to what we could get out of mitzvah performance than that. To gain fuller appreciation and reveal the inner aspect of a mitzvah, we need to probe more deeply, beyond what we initially see.

We are told that great spiritual lights are generated when we do a physical mitzvah. It's a remote concept, we see nothing. Only lofty, righteous individuals see it. We'll have to take the Kabbalists' word for it! The light is stored for us in some hidden place until G-d will unveil it. It's like groping in the dark because there's a blindfold on our eyes. The blindfold will be removed at the time of the Redemption.

Earn now, enjoy later. The bliss we enjoy later is like our retirement savings, earned through the merits we accrued in this world. Instead of cash deposits, let's imagine we deposited gems into a sealed treasure chest that will magically open at retirement. That's the World to Come, when we finally get to enjoy the dazzling gems, the profit of our toil.

And yet, much to our surprise, the G-dly delight from the Divine revelations in Gan Eden is "small" relative to the greatness of doing the actual mitzvah down here. When we actually *do* the mitzvah we unite with G-d Himself – with His Essence, which is above and beyond the comprehension of souls in Gan Eden.

It's easy to appreciate the sensory delights of fine cuisine or a piece of melt-in-your-mouth chocolate. It's harder to regard a mitzvah, whose delights cannot be seen or tasted, as spiritually delectable.

It's easy to conceive of a splendorous, far-away Gan Eden as being spiritually lofty. It's harder to consider that a physically-based mitzvah we do here and now in this mundane world is loftier than that!

These concepts are hard for us to understand because we're trapped in a world-based mentality.

True bliss can be experienced only in Gan Eden where the soul actually perceives the G-dliness.[231] There it has a clear perception of the ray of light given off by the mitzvah. Since we lack this perception in the physical world, an hour of bliss in Gan Eden has an advantage over the bliss of fulfilling the Torah and mitzvahs.

But the soul in Paradise derives its exquisite pleasure from a *mere glimmer* of the light radiated by a mitzvah. Were the souls in Gan Eden to apprehend the essence of the mitzvah instead of a mere ray of it, they would expire, dissolve out of existence.

That's why an hour of repentance and good deeds in *this* world is preferred to all the life of the World to Come – for there the soul has only a remote gleam of the Divine light, while here we have the essence of mitzvah which unites us with G-d Himself.

A Kabbalistic glimpse into the process: When we do a mitzvah there is a unification of two levels of G-d's holiness, upper and lower lights. "Upper" lights transcend and affect the world from afar. "Lower" lights refer to the Divine Presence, which *can* descend and dwell within the created worlds.

So the health-minded wife was right after all!

A Joy That is Above All

Now that we've got our priorities sorted out, let's revisit the one and only Torah source that apprises us of **the need to serve G-d with joy.** A careful look at its unique phraseology will guide us into the ultimate in authentic living.

We have clearly established that it's not enough to *serve* G-d; the service must be done with joy and a glad heart. We are ready to discover a further nuance – we should serve Him with joy **"above all."** Are you ready to move your standard up yet another notch?

"Because you did not *serve* G-d with joy *above all*... you will serve your enemies...in hunger, thirst...*in want of everything.*" (Devarim 28:47)

Two phrases in this verse that hold the key to deeper living are:

- *serve G-d*
- *above all.*

...you did not *serve* G-d...

It's not enough to *serve* Him with joy on the "decibel" level that seems reasonable to us. The joy engendered by doing a mitzvah should be *above* what seems reasonable. While joy levels are usually commensurate with our appraisal of the situation, we are here to *serve*. That means we need to invest effort. Thus, if an event would logically evoke joy-level 4 on a scale of 1-10, one who *serves* would take it to a joy-level of 5 or more.

This is not just an exercise in exaggeration. As limited creatures, we grasp only part of the power and impact of our deeds. We fathom only a minute aspect of His greatness. We discern only a modicum of the joyous wonder of being His chosen nation, recipients of His gift called Torah. So, we don't rejoice merely with the joy we perceive. We rejoice with the Divine depth, imagining it from the G-dly perspective. It's when we go beyond our human standard that we truly *serve* G-d.

...above all...

Notice that the verse ends with a comparative. "Because you did not serve G-d with joy *above all*"[232] and then the phrase seems to trail off without specifying above all *what*?

The Arizal supplies the words to complete the *"above all"* phrase. His explanation corroborates our previous discussion about the supremacy of mitzvah joy over Gan Eden joy.[233] According to the Arizal, the Jews served G d, and even served Him with joy, but their joy fell short. Apparently, more was expected of the Jews in the times of Moshe. They, who had been privy to the greatest G-dly revelations, surely knew that a mitzvah links us to the Infinite light (*bli gvul*) and that Gan Eden reward, though immensely gratifying is a limited, measured revelation.[234] (The differences in these gradations are completely beyond us, but remember, this is a peek through the open door of the Palace.)

This then is the fully developed reading of the verse according to the Arizal: Because the Jews did not utilize the **full potency** of a mitzvah-joy-opportunity, they invited chastisement and negative consequences. But why dwell on dire predictions? Now that we know better, let's do what it takes to bring about a better future.

The conclusion is clear: Simcha is so essential to our service that G-d is not compromising on it. Should we?

Section VI

The Payoffs

Advantages Of Joyous Living

Here's a little exercise:

What is your reaction to this statement from the Sages?

"When the month of Adar commences, [we] increase in joy."[235]

Are you seeing it as something to get excited about? (*Yes! We could use some spark and spice in our lives.*)

Or, are you seeing it as a chore? (*Is G-d giving me more work? I've got so much going on already. Am I going to have to laugh more, blow up balloons, and expend energy creating an Adar atmosphere?*)

What will turn one person on may turn another person off. But we can motivate people to do almost anything when we give them an irresistible payoff.

>*Tired mom: I'm not sure I want to go to that event tonight.*
>*Friend: I hear they're giving free books on How to get Rich Quick.*
>*Tired mom: I'll be ready in ten minutes.*

It's okay to entice someone into doing something good and G-dly. If we can make it tempting, why not?

It shouldn't be hard to bait you into the Adar spirit: The reason for the Adar-joy upsurge is that our mazel (fortune or Providence) is extra strong throughout the month because of the Purim miracle and because it is the birth month of our great leader, Moshe Rabbeinu.[236] It is a great month for those who are entangled in court cases or other risky affairs where our luck needs an extra boost. The more jubilance we add into the mix, the more we expand the possibility for astounding outcomes.

Oh, are you in the joy mode now? That was a quick mindset-change. Irresistible rewards have a way of turning *Shoulds* and *Wants* into *Must-haves*. Let's tempt you with some of the succulent pay-offs that joy bodes for us – Adar and all year round.

26

Benefits for the Practical-minded

Joy is a success-booster

Down-to-earth pragmatists may be dismissive about the relevance of joy. "Joy is for starry-eyed idealists. What practical use can joy have for me?" This is a misconception. Joy has so many useful benefits.

Joy's up there, and I'm down here with the broken washing machine, the tantrums, the bills, the too-tiny apartment.

The practicing Jew vs. the "cardiac" Jew

The Torah-imperative of joy can't be based only on feelings. Every aspect of Torah, including our joy, must be grounded in a real, physical experience and in tangible entities. The emotions and the joy serve as wings so the actions can soar and connect to our Source Above.

It is said in jest that the reason for the high incidence of heart attacks among Jews is because there are so many "Jews at heart" –

it's too much pressure on the one organ! Judaism – and joy – must be discharged by activities that incorporate all parts of the body.

Here are just a few of joy's practical applications:

- **Energizer and motion-motivator:** *You want to get the job done? Hire joy.* It'll get the garage organized in half the time. It gets out of bed faster. It walks faster. Watch those students tearing out to play in the yard at recess and see how they saunter and dawdle on their way back to class.
- **Healer:** Quicker recovery from health-compromising situations.
- **Competition Blowout:** You wouldn't take on a daunting opponent when you are feeling down, would you? The only way to be victorious over the "bad guy" is with simcha-spawned zeal (*zrizus*) and proactive energy – certainly not when your system is clogged with worries or sadness.
- **Success-inducer:** Try dabbing some joy onto your diet plan, exercise, studies, and enjoy the sweet taste of success.

The traditional premise was that "success is the key to happiness." Positive psychology has flipped the old success-happiness theory: it is the joy that facilitates the success.

The joy-success cycle is like a catch-22. We need joy to succeed. But how can we muster the joy if we haven't succeeded yet?

Here's another catch-22:

A chassid of Rabbi Yisroel of Vizhnitz[237] once came to see him and complained about his poor financial straits. The tzaddik advised him, "Increase in your simcha. The simcha will bring blessings for bountiful parnasa (livelihood)."

"How can I be joyful when I lack parnasa?"

"Nu," the Rebbe replied, "what won't a person do for a better parnasa!"[238]

Success is a worthy goal, but what is "success"? Wealth and other wonderful "haves" can smooth our lives and even be channeled for spiritual purposes, but let's shine the spotlight on the ultimate success – the completion of our galus assignments and the unfolding of the era of everlasting joy.

- **Goodness-locator:** When you're upbeat, you see the bright side of life and judge people favorably. The person who just asked you how your brother is – he's not nosy, he's friendly and caring.
- **A Core-exposer:** Joy puts me in touch with "the **real** me." We're always being urged to see the good in others, but how about discovering more goodness in ourselves as well?

Your neighbor, Mr. Korn, is marrying off his son. You've known the man for years, but you barely recognize him as the host at his son's wedding. Typically an irascible, brooding man who rarely smiles, now he is warm, animated and greeting his guests with enthusiasm. Which is the real Mr. Korn? The one you've known all along, right? Wrong! The nice guy is the real McCoy. Those laudable traits were always there in a state of latency and were finally unleashed from his core by the power of his joy.

We discover treasures we harbored that never saw the light of day. Not only our behavior but also our very personality traits can upgrade. The penny-pincher becomes generous and the grudge-bearer forgiving as the joy expands us from our very core.

Measure my forehead please. Suddenly I have a broader perspective of everything around me.

Everyday events will not induce that rare state of arousal. The core is revealed in special circumstances.[239] And yet, there is power in the *awareness* that there is goodness at the core of each of us. Knowing that traits such as generosity, openness and the power to forgive are already in us can spur us on to reach in and bring some out.

> *Husband: I can't find the passports.*
> *Wife: You put them in one of your pockets. I'm definite. Don't*
> *panic...reach all the way in. Those pockets are very deep.*

The good news is, we can dig into our souls and come up with passports to a truer existence.

- **Life Insurance Benefits**

If someone offered you an excellent life insurance policy – for free – would you accept? That's a no-brainer. Of course! True, some people have a hard time facing their mortality. They want to shut out the possibility that life is not going to last forever or that something could happen to them. But it's just not responsible to avoid planning ahead.

Defaulting on joy is as irresponsible as refusing a free life insurance policy. It actually *is* refusing a free life insurance policy. Here's why:

I know you're a nice guy, always striving to do the right thing. Inevitably, at some point, you and I will slip up. *"There is no man so righteous that he does only good and never sins,"*[240] said King Solomon. Here's where the insurance policy comes to the rescue. Though we slip up – we can avoid the consequences by serving G-d with joy. Really!

It works the same as with violations of law. If you were ever issued a ticket for a traffic or parking violation, you already know that it is useless to try to convince the officer to retract the ticket. Once the ticket is issued, he is powerless to void it. You must plead your case before a judge who has authority over the officer who served the summons.

Our joy in this world is like taking our case to a judge. It arouses Supernal Joy, and the Supernal Joy annuls and sweetens the judgments at their source.

A judgment can only be removed by going to its source.[241] When love and joy prevail in the world below, they cause rage and wrath to ascend upward to their origin. There, in the place of pure goodness, the anger and judgment are "sweetened." This is the unique makeup of love and joy.[242]

There's more. Life insurance policies typically cover a person for life, giving us a maximum of 120 years coverage. But this insurance covers us for the World to Come as well. Show me an insurance policy that can match that for comprehensive coverage.

The harsh consequence of "serving our enemies" can be averted by incorporating simcha into our mitzvah performance. When a Jew is happy, G-d is happy, as it were, and even the harshest decrees are annulled – analogous to an earthly king granting amnesty to his prisoners when he is in a cheerful mood.

Imagine the government announces a grand pardon, a chance to wipe clean any messy IRS issues or costly traffic violations we might have, on the condition that we dance and display great joy. For the "right price" we'd probably overcome our compunctions about making a public spectacle!

Maybe they'll come up with a joy test similar to those sobriety tests. If you pass the qualifying joy level you're off the hook, and you can go home and do a victory dance in the privacy of your living room.

Speaking of sobriety tests...
Simon is speeding along at ten miles over the speed limit, and he gets pulled over by a highway patrolman. The highway patrolman spots nine huge knives in the back seat.
"What are those for?" he asks suspiciously. Simon tells him that he is a juggler and they are for his act. The patrolman does not believe him and asks him to prove it. So Simon gets out of the car, and starts to juggle the knives.
Two fellows driving by take in the bizarre scene on the side of the road. A minute later, one of them comments, "Man, I sure am glad I quit drinking. Those sobriety tests these days are out of control!"
Now how will they ask us to prove joy?

- **A Savvy Investment**

I always imagined our relationship with G-d in simple terms. G-d gives and we receive. When it comes to joy, I discovered, it seems to follow the formula of financial investments. If we don't invest, nothing happens. The ball is in our court.

When we give, G-d returns it to us, along with many blessings. If you have any business sense, you'll recognize a great deal!

Reciprocal-joy-weather: The vapors of joy create clouds that make Divine joy drizzle down. (Expect showers.)

A powerful feature about joy – it elicits reciprocity. We give and G-d reciprocates.

The way one acts in this world is the way that he is dealt with Above. If a person is happy and acts joyously, his situation will improve. (Zohar II 184b)

When a Jewish man dons tefillin, G-d matches that action, so to speak. When we give charity, we elicit a Divine flow of mercy towards us. When we pluck a joy string on our happiness instrument below, we resonate the Divine joy and cause it to be released from Above. Joy carries more clout Above than do other activities because of its unique qualities – its expansiveness and its ability to cut through limitations and shatter barriers.

G-d wants us to break our emotional barriers and transcend our limitations. When we do, He happily overrides nature's limitations as well. All parties get a good deal.

27

The Nutshell

I promised earlier to encapsulate joy, to sum it up in a nutshell. It's got to be powerful, reliable and concise so people can carry it with them at all times. What are the magic well-phrased words that will change a person's outlook and life forever?

I freely admit, it's a challenge. Much ink has already been poured on the topic of joy, and the sheer volume of books available on the subject proves we have yet to discover the magic key! While the quest continues, I managed to reduce the entire volume into the briefest possible message – two words.

The founder of ComedyCures helped me with the first word.

> *Saranne Rothenberg, a stage IV cancer survivor, was a vibrant young lady when she was first diagnosed with cancer. She healed herself, despite the advanced state of her illness, through joy, and subsequently founded a national organization called ComedyCures. Her organization brings joy to ailing people around the United States and beyond. She is an indefatigable "joy-engine that could." I asked her, "Sara Chana (as Saranne is now known), where do you get the joy from?" Her response was quick, and short enough to fit into any nutshell: "From G-d!"*

G-d runs a free joy fund. It is immediately available to us, at any moment. He has all the joy and strength we will ever need. (Some joy-geniuses here and there have discovered this fund on their own – without reading this book!)

Want joy? Think **G-d**.

Now we are ready for the second word. It is a word that is inextricably bound with simcha, a concept that is practically synonymous with joy. (Here's a big hint: it hasn't happened yet, but it's about to.) It is – **Geulah**.

Simcha and Geulah are an inextricably bound team. When you manipulate one, you affect the other. It's like there's one light switch wired to simultaneously open two sets of lights. When we generate joy purely for Geulah, (we can use our Joy-fusion strategy, as long as we link it via our intentions), we tweak His Essential joy which tweaks the Geulah.[243]

As a bird responds to the warbling of another bird calling to it, the pure, essential joy from Above likewise responds when it recognizes its own singular tune being played in the hearts, minds and bodies of earthbound mortals. The trill has to be recognized by the bird as an authentic call and only then will the bird re-spond.

Want joy? Think **Geulah**.

Trill...la-la...
Ge-u-la-la-la...

To tap into the purity of essential joy we key in to a joy purely for Geulah.

> Meditate on the perfect future world. There will be perfect, un-marred joy. Everyone will get along. It will be free of illness, strife, worry, financial stress. We will finally have a complete Torah, complete nation, complete land. But the best part will be learning Torah with Moshiach. And it's just around the bend. What a refreshing change of thought-scenery – just the right pickup when we're down.

Cash in on this positive-feedback loop... A state of simcha helps us strengthen our trust in the imminence of Geulah. The trust and the anticipation of what's to come increases our simcha.

The source for unlimited joy: G-d.
A state of perfect joy: Geulah.

G-d and *Geulah* encapsulate all the energy we need to succeed in our commission to climb, soar, scale the mountain peaks of joy right now. (Now why did we have to fill up all those pages, when two words say it all?)

This two-word joy capsule is easier to memorize than any pithy slogan and so lightweight that we can haul it along with us wherever we go.

Don't leave home without it. I won't even stay home without it.

Section VII

Spanning History

The world is full of great people. Joy makes them greater yet.

Our colorful history has created myriad opportunities for joy-geniuses to shine, each making the world a brighter, more G-dly, place. Some unique individuals indelibly shaped history far beyond the time in which they lived. Whether their brightness was appreciated only in their immediate vicinity or they rose to greater renown, the light they beamed is cumulative and timeless and accelerates our journey to the Age of Perfect Joy.

28

Joy-Genius Gallery
of Greats

The First Joy-Genius: Our Matriarch Sarah

Who knows perfect joy? Sarah was the first to produce a form of joy that was hardy enough to outwit the ego. But it wasn't as simple to achieve as it is to report! As described in the Zohar,[244] three Biblical giants – Chava, Noach and Sarah –attempted to elevate joy and make it an ego-free experience. Finally, Sarah succeeded.

Surely Adam and Chava knew about unadulterated joy, at least for the first few hours after Creation. They enjoyed the almost perfect habitat, Gan Eden, until the serpent came along and punctured their bliss.

What does one do in a picture-perfect setting? There surely was some way even this idyllic estate could be upgraded, some Divine purpose in their having been placed there, and so Chava set forth on a mission to do some spiritual "home improvements." She would take the Divine pleasure and joy that was in the Garden and make it a useful, internal experience as her lasting legacy for all the generations to come. It would be physically expressed yet spiritually sublime. To succeed, she would have to take on the serpent, which represents Ego, the root and possibility of sin. Unfortunately, instead of conquering the serpent, the serpent won the round. What went wrong? The pleasure experience went awry.

When Chava accepted the serpent's offer and tasted the fruit, she acknowledged its sensorial pleasure. "The tree was good for eating and desirable to the eyes."[245] It became personal. Until now, existence was all about G-d's wishes. Now it was about her feelings. In that moment of personal awareness, her ego reared its head. Instead of bringing genuine joy to the world, Chava created the potential for the pursuit-of-personal-happiness, a pursuit which saddens more often than it gladdens, because the "I" can never be satisfied. The drive to satisfy the "self" can also lead to extremes, feeding power mongers, narcissists and hedonists who are entrapped – and trap others – in their lust for "having" and "being."

When we allow a sense of self to pervade an experience, it corrupts the joy. The joy loses its authentic, pure value. Even serving G-d with passion, which is good, can be tinged with personal gratification. We have to remind ourselves, even when we *shokel* (sway back and forth) during prayer with our souls bursting forth, that the purpose of passion is not that it feels good, but that it accesses G-d.

Self-awareness diminishes the authenticity of joy.

Self-directed pleasure is not necessarily bad, but it does nothing for G-d's vision to bring the world to its perfect state. Pleasure-lovers don't panic! We can "have our cake and eat it too." We can continue to enjoy the pleasures of our magnificent world. We merely need to align our pleasure-experience with Divine purpose. We won't lose out. In fact, we will gain – because in doing so we bring the world closer to its harmonious state, when perfect joy will be ours for keeps.

Ten generations later, Noach tried to repair the damage by planting a vineyard and drinking its wine. He tried to dull self-awareness by getting drunk. However, bypassing his mind was an ineffective and weak strategy. Drunken transcendence does not induce a permanent ego-transcendence. The obdurate ego, once allowed in, is always lurking, ready to rear up at the slightest provocation.

The serpent reared its head again ten generations after Noach, this time in the form of a king named Pharaoh. Avraham and Sarah had travelled down to Egypt due to a famine in Canaan, and, just as Avraham feared, the king, Pharaoh, coveted Sarah. Sarah was herself a member of royalty. Spiritually, her soul came from the level of *malchus*, authentic royalty, as is also reflected in her name which means "princess."

Sarah rejected Pharaoh's offer to share in his ego and power. Authentic royalty is totally altruistic, its joy clear of ulterior motives. We can just imagine the frivolity and ostentation that reigned in the royal palace to which she was forcibly taken. Sarah was able to rise above the egotistic temptation of power and shallowness and transcend it all because she was steadfastly "bound with Avraham and G-d." Finally, the damaged version of joy was rectified.

Joy, because it is extremely powerful and deep, is especially sensitive to misuse through externalized, uncontrolled behavior. But, thanks to Sarah's achievement, we can rise above self-indulgence to reach for true joy. We may not be successful all the time, but those successes, when they come, are magnificent.[246]

Sarah is our authentic-joy manufacturer, bequeathing her progeny with a precious gift: an externally-displayed joy that does not compromise its Divine integrity. We can connect to joy's extraordinary powers and its Divine source through demonstrative expressions such as handclapping, dancing, singing and laughing. The more physically it is expressed, the more effective the joy can be in surmounting the barriers we encounter.

Now we can appreciate the full spectrum of our historic journey that began with great joy – literally in Paradise! – and will culminate in even greater joy – Geulah! The perfect blend of joy – full-body, effervescent joy harnessed to Divine intent – was achieved on the third try, twenty generations after Chava's first attempt. Sarah's contribution was recognized and sealed in the annals of eternity when her son was named Yitzchak, meaning "he will laugh." Its future tense tells us of its futuristic import. It reminds us of the nature of our Jewish mission throughout the march of generations. Serve G-d with joy! Don't keep your simcha a secret! Be constantly and passionately in touch with your Divine simcha-supplier. At the end of the journey awaits, not only our earned reward, but also a richer degree of laughter than what we have earned – a *very* generous bonus – when we give voice to the full laughter of the Geulah.

A Kabbalistic glimpse... The name *Yitzchak* is in the future tense: "he will laugh." It foretells the future of the Jewish nation.
Sarah and Yitzchak's joy looks past the here-and-now fleeting happiness to an everlasting laughter. It alludes to the future revelation of Supernal Pleasure and laughter. Divine laughter will come when all the hard-working Jewish souls throughout the journey of Creation complete their assignments. It is the end-result, the crowning achievement of our joy throughout the galus.

Yosef the Tzaddik

Talk about misery...Yosef was sold as a slave by his brothers and brought to Egypt, where he worked his way up to an important position. But then he was wrongfully implicated in an attempted seduction charge and thrown into jail.

Here was a man who had been rejected and sold by his own family members, had finally made it up in the world and been hired manager of affairs for Pharaoh's minister, Potiphar, only to have it all dashed to the ground by being falsely framed and imprisoned. He was totally alone. There was not one relative or friend in town to pay him a visit or write him an encouraging note.

It's bad enough when disaster strikes once, but having a major crisis hit so quickly again can make a person feel totally defeated. And yet, Yosef did not wallow in self-pity. He continued to believe in a better tomorrow. Not only did he himself remain steadfastly upbeat, but he was not going to let others languish in the prison with a long face. One day he spotted two troubled, gloomy countenances. The Royal Butler and Baker were each distressed by bizarre dreams. Yosef, the consummate leader, took initiative. He set about finding out what was troubling them beyond the misery of incarceration.

His concern for them yielded results in more ways than one. Not only did he satisfactorily decipher each of their dreams, but being attuned to their needs was part of the chain of events that led to his release. The Baker was condemned to die, but the Butler was restored to his previous position in the palace, and subsequently recommended Yosef to help decipher Pharaoh's disturbing dreams. Yosef's insistence on a cheery demeanor had a meteoric outcome – his appointment as viceroy over Egypt.

Two Generations of Irrepressible Simcha

Reb Chaim Benyamin Brod, a Breslover Chassid, lived in Mezibuzh, Ukraine, post-World War I.[247] His son describes his father's remarkable, innate capability to be joyous under all circumstances in him memoirs.

Dancing in Jail

> Father was arrested on several occasions... In Moscow, he was once arrested on a Friday and thrown into jail. Immediately his friends sent a telegram to our family in Uman, conveying the news in disguised language to conceal its meaning from the secret police: "Father is sick and has been taken to the hospital."
> After a brief investigation, the police realized he was not the one they sought. On Shabbos morning the jailer brought Father a release form to sign. "Sorry," Father told him, "on the

Shabbath I don't write!" "What?" the jailer yelled angrily. "You're a religious fanatic, too?"

The jailor had never encountered anyone actually refusing to be released from jail! Assuming Father would soon change his mind, he threw him back into his cell.

But the jailer's amazement grew as Father burst into song and started dancing! Later Father explained that until then he had considered his imprisonment a punishment for his sins. But now the sole reason for his incarceration was the observance of G-d's commandment, the holy Shabbos – a thought so inspiring that he danced in joy.

The jailer tried again to get him to leave. But Father played the fool. "Why should I want to leave? Here I have a place to lie down, and bread to satisfy my hunger, I want to stay!" Seeing that Father was not his normal jailbird, the jailer asked him, "So when would you agree to leave?"

"At night, when three stars appear in the sky. Then I'll go out fast so that I can dance with the moon."

After nightfall, the jailer came to tell him that three stars had appeared. Father signed his release form and left.

Groans of Joy

My parents had little material reason to be happy. Their grinding poverty and lack of basic necessities, the constant fear of government persecution and the nagging worry about their children's future identity as Jews were enough to make anyone forget about joy and happiness.

Regardless of all this, Father was always bubbling over with irrepressible joy and enthusiasm. I remember once, Father lay ill in bed, drained of strength, and some friends came over to fulfill the Torah duty of visiting the sick. Their visit gave him new energy, and he jumped out of bed to dance with them around the room!

Father often sang, especially when he was hungry – which happened frequently – to divert his mind from the hunger. Once, when I was six or seven, I noticed that while he sang, he was swaying from side to side with strangely sharp movements. When I asked him why, he told me he had a bad toothache.

"So why are you singing?" I asked.

"When someone has a toothache," Father explained, "he groans. I am groaning, too. But my groans are groans of joy! Why make everyone else feel bad, too?"

Mother once asked him how he could be so happy when they had so many worries. Father replied, "You know how weak my body is. I don't have the strength to bear even a tenth of our worries. So let's find some gentile ruffian to carry all my worries for me..."

I didn't know Reb Chaim Benyamin, but I did know his son, Reb Chatzkel. What a freiliche yid! He was a butcher by trade and a joy-infuser by choice. His customers preferred to pick up their meat personally rather than have it delivered. It was worth it. You were sure to get a short Torah *vort*, delivered with so much relish that it perked them up for several days more than any rib steak could.

Reb Chatzkel was invited to all the weddings. The mitzvah of "bringing joy to the choson and kallah" reached new heights when Reb Chatzkel arrived. Not that it was easy for him! I discovered the inside story shortly before this book would be going to print:

He would sometimes come home from work at eight, even nine o'clock, physically exhausted. Next thing, he was pulling his Shabbos suit out of the closet. His family, knowing he needed to head out to the butcher store at five o'clock the next morning, tried to convince him to stay home and get much needed rest, but Reb Chatzkel would not hear of it. Keep Chatzkel away from the simcha? Simcha is life; it *gives* energy.

He certainly wasn't going for the food because he ate only what was made under his wife's supervision. After the wedding he couldn't go right to sleep either; he needed to unwind from all the high simcha over a cup of hot tea. Simcha is an avoda even for joyous people!

Seeing his energetic dancing at the wedding, one would think he just returned from a vacation cruise.

> I'm thinking back to my wedding. My mother was a sole survivor and my father's family had all emigrated to Israel. But picture... my grandfather stomping his joy on the table and Reb Chatzkel doing his *kazatzka* on the dance floor. We may have been scarce on family, but joy we had in abundance!

Happiness Against All Odds: Nonna

"Recently I have had some grief and turmoil in my personal life. The untimely passing of my beautiful 31-year old cousin, and the circumstances of her death, shook me to the core and "broke" my positive outlook towards life. I had fallen apart and could not put the pieces back together again. A month after this tragic event, I met a person who happened to be a rabbi."

Nonna, born in the Ukraine, emigrated to the U.S. as a little girl and grew up in Brighton Beach, Brooklyn. She knew little of her religion and was interested even less. But the shocking death of her cousin opened her to hearing the message that Torah had to offer. After resisting invitations from the Rabbi to various functions and Shabbos dinners, she finally accepted and planned to stay "for an hour." In that "hour" she finally discovered a truth she so badly needed.

She learned that in authentic Judaism, happiness is a most effective weapon in its fight against the pain in the world. "Happiness is the power that makes you do His commandments. When you are unhappy, you do not have the urge to do good for yourself, let alone anyone else."

"I learned a lot in these past six months," she concludes. "I mainly learned to keep smiling: Even when my heart still breaks about my cousin's untimely death, and I wake up and don't feel like smiling, I force myself to smile and I feel the smile inside later. First I 'do', and then I learn to feel it. I have learned to try to be happy, against all odds: like a Jew. The only way to survive! Oh, what a powerful weapon!"[248]

Senior Geniuses (You're Never Too Old to Become a Joy-Genius)

Bicky, 92, a five-time cancer survivor, was the queen of positivity. Her positivity washed over the people she engaged with. Even speaking to her by phone was refreshing, and if you didn't reach her, you would hear, "Leave a message. I'm wonderful." She lived in an independent living facility, but she was not alone – she was always in the company of her bright, positive attitude.

"I'm the luckiest lady alive," she declared with genuine enthusiasm. "I have such good friends."

"How do you do it?" the Rebbetzin of her community asked her. After all, she had lost her husband, her children lived far away, and she was sick again. "How are you so happy?"

"G-d is so good to me. He wanted everyone to think I'm dying so they'll all come to visit me. My grandson came for a week, my nephews and nieces visited. I had so many visitors this winter."

Bicky's sense of humor never deserted her. "I gotta go! My husband Lou can't find his socks." She was very sick and Lou had predeceased her, so the implication was clear. Yet, she said it humorously.[249]

> "You don't stop laughing because you grow old; you grow old because you stop laughing."[250]

Savta Senior "was the happiest person I ever met," claimed her granddaughter-by-marriage. She was always in high spirits, throughout her 95 years. She was active, and usually had a joke to share. You felt the joy radiating from within, confirmed by a twinkle in her eye. Once, wanting to crack the mystery of her never-fading smile, her granddaughter asked her, "*Savta* Senior, what's your secret? How are you always so happy?" She responded with a chuckle, "Secret? It's really no secret...

> *Just don't think about the bad things in life. Only focus on the good. That's it.*"[251]

The following anecdote gives us the words that drove Bicky's and Savta's positive verve.[252]

Mrs. Smith *moved into a nursing home when her husband of seventy years passed away. As she maneuvered her walker to the elevator, the nursing home attendant provided a visual description of her tiny room, including the eyelet curtains that had been hung on her window. "I love it," she stated with the enthusiasm of an eight-year-old having just been presented with a new bike.*

"Mrs. Smith, you haven't even seen the room yet."

"That doesn't have anything to do with it," she replied. "Happiness is something you decide on ahead of time. Whether I like my room or not doesn't depend on how the furniture is arranged, it's how I arrange my mind. I already decided to love it. As long as my eyes open I'll focus on the new day and on the all the happy memories I've stored away, just for this time in my life."

Mrs. Smith's name could be "Anyone, Anywhere." It becomes increasingly difficult to be gracious as a person loses independence. That is when people really need to be smart – smart enough to be graceful agers.

Here are Mrs. Smith's five simple rules to be happy: 1. Free your heart from hatred. 2. Free your mind from worries. 3. Live simply. 4. Give more. 5. Expect less. Now add being Jewish to that!

He Never Lost It: Rabbi Mendel

Rabbi Mendel Futerfas, a legendary chassid and mentor, lived in Russia under the oppressive regime. He endured long years of torturous exile in Siberia due to his "stubborn" adherence to Torah life, as well as daring to disseminate its teaching to others, but he never lost his good spirits and optimism. He had an irrepressible ability to rejoice and see the productive aspect in every experience. When he was finally able to leave the country, he became a spiritual mentor and guide for youth and adults alike, in England and then in Israel. He was famous for his witty anecdotes and compelling stories with relevant, useful lessons. They are often repeated, years after his passing.[253]

"It seems to me your spirits are not where they should be! Can it be! A joyless chassid?" chided Reb Mendel Futerfas on encountering a usually ebullient young colleague in a downcast mood. He told the colleague that once, when he visited a wealthy businessman in London to solicit funds for his yeshiva, he noticed the man was in a brooding mood. "What is the issue?" Reb Mendel wanted to know. The man confided that he had lost a huge sum in a bad investment. Reb Mendel scolded him, "Over matters like this you allow yourself to become sad? Let me share a little about my life with you.

"I was sent to a labor camp in Siberia due to my religious "crimes" against the Soviet regime. It was extremely difficult to keep Shabbos there. The *natchalnik* (overseer) kept a vigilant and unrelenting eye on me to make sure I produced the daily work quota. I was in exile for many years, but somehow, with G-d's help, I managed not to desecrate even one Shabbos in all that time. Nevertheless, I do not take personal credit for this.

"Kashrus presented another incredibly difficult challenge. Sometimes I had nothing to eat because the only foods available were not kosher, and despite unbearable hunger I kept strong and never once contaminated my lips with non-kosher food. Nevertheless, I do not take personal credit for this.

"There were many other challenges to fulfilling the mitzvahs and I managed to overcome each one – yet I do not believe I can rightfully take credit for any of them.

"There is only one thing for which I will take credit – that throughout all those grueling years in this most desolate of places, no matter how unrelenting the persecutions of the vicious natchalniks, I never once fell into a state of depression or succumbed to bitterness over my plight. For this I can take credit. And you are despondent over a *naar-ishkeit* (foolishness), for a few pounds that you lost?

In England they grieve over lost pounds. In the U.S. they rejoice over it.

Get yourself out of the slump and serve G-d with joy, always."

Reb Mendel spread his joy and wisdom wherever he went. On another occasion, another member of the yeshiva faculty was "caught in the act" of not sounding like his usual cheerful self. Reb Mendel had picked up on it in a phone conversation - he had eagle ears. Unacceptable! A chassid must always be joyful! The young faculty member used the opportunity to investigate Reb Mendel's "authenticity."

"Tell me Reb Mendel" the young Rabbi challenged him, "you never woke up on the wrong side?" Reb Mendel, known for his quick comebacks, was uncharacteristically thoughtful. "No," he finally responded.

"Did you receive this strength as a gift, is it a quality you inherited, or did you work on yourself to become this way?" Reb Mendel's words came slowly, as if the answer came with difficulty, "No, I did not receive this as an inheritance nor as a gift. It came to me through effort and toil."[254]

His Joy Does not Dim: Rabbi Sholom Mordechai

We have, in our own time, a remarkable Jew who was jailed for many years, victim of an imperfect justice system. (I had used the past tense in my manuscript with firm trust that he would be released before this book was published. And indeed he was (!) after serving eight years of an outrageous twenty-seven-year sentence.) His consistent, unrelenting commitment to simcha and bitachon throughout was a remarkable feat. Visitors during his difficult incarceration testified that his radiance was not marred through the long ordeal and his joy did not dim for a moment. "He exudes love of life and gratitude to G-d.

His voice brims with gregarious optimism, his voice full of energy and vigor."[255] During an average week, Reb Sholom Mordechai Rubashkin, managed to write up dvar-Torah bulletins on an antiquated computer, use part of his limited phone time for Torah classes and organize fellow prisoners' prayers, serving as an unofficial chaplain. Would we believe that the truest joy can emerge from a dismal prison cell?

It was he who brought the following insight to my attention.

Rabbi Akiva Laughed

We Jews certainly have many reasons to cry hard. We can thank Rabbi Akiva for showing us how to laugh hard. Here's a close-up on a pioneering forward-thinker.

Rabbi Akiva and three Sages were walking up the *Har Habayis*, the Temple Mount. There was only grievous desolation where glory had once issued forth. Suddenly, a fox scuttled over the very place where the Holy of Holies once stood. How shattering...what a desecration of G-d's name! The Sages broke into tears. And Rabbi Akiva laughed.

"Why do you laugh, Rabbi Akiva?" the Sages wondered. It was a valid question, on all counts. But Rabbi Akiva did not even bother to defend himself. As a matter of fact, he counter-challenged them, "Why do you cry?" "Rabbi Akiva," they could have remonstrated, "It's okay to cry at a horrific spectacle of this sort. The burden rests on you to prove that it's okay to laugh."

Rabbi Akiva said to them, "I laugh because I see the fulfillment of a prophecy of Uriah the priest: 'Because of you, Zion shall be plowed as a field.'[256] Now, this was a negative prophecy, certainly no cause for mirth, but he explained, "As long as Uriah's negative prophecy had not been fulfilled, I feared that Zechariah's positive prophecy that 'Old men and women shall yet sit in the streets of Jerusalem'[257] may not be fulfilled either. But now that Uriah's prophecy has been fulfilled, it is certain that Zechariah's prophecy will be fulfilled."

When the Sages heard his explanation, they exclaimed, "Akiva, you have consoled us! Akiva, you have consoled us!"

The Lubavitcher Rebbe explains that there was a hidden emphasis in Rabbi Akiva's counter-challenge. "Why are you crying *now*," Rabbi Akiva was asking, "and not earlier on when we first sighted the charred and destroyed remains of the Holy Temple and rent our clothing? That was the appropriate time to shed tears of sorrow."

They cried now for good reason, having seen the honor of G-d and His children even more degraded than had been forecast by the prophets. The prophets had warned that the fox would run over the area of the Holy Temple. But did the prophecy have to be carried out to its extreme? Did the fox have to scurry over the very Holy of Holies?

Present versus Future – Which Takes Precedence?

This worse-than-anticipated scenario made Rabbi Akiva laugh. When he viewed the abysmal situation on the Temple Mount, he also saw the future result. His reasoning was: If G-d made the past *worse* than promised, the future, then, will be *better* than promised, as good is always bestowed more generously. So, while the three Sages who were with him mourned the present state of affairs, joy overrode Rabbi Akiva's tears.

> **Does the Future Supersede the Present?**
> Present versus future is a dilemma that appears in halachic questions as well. For example:
> If Mr. Fisch fasts on Tzom Gedaliah[258] he will not be medically fit to fast on Yom Kippur (a week later). Does the more stringent Biblical prohibition to fast on Yom Kippur override the current (less stringent, rabbinically instituted) one?
> We look to the future to decide how to act today.

We learn from Rabbi Akiva to say, after a difficult experience, "Everything G-d does is for the good." In retrospect, all those nerve-wracking sleepless nights, the stewing, worrying, gray hairs, agonizing, were a waste of good energy. It all works out in the end.

But even this does not capture the essence of Rabbi Akiva's message. Regarding the global journey of the Jewish nation, Rabbi Akiva's positive orientation is bolder yet: Not only does the negative lead to a positive outcome *in the end*, but we are viewing the positive future *in the present.*

What shaped Rabbi Akiva's ultra-positive viewpoint?

Zion Will be Plowed like a Field

Rabbi Akiva's laughter seems to have a direct correlation to the negative forecast of Uriah the priest: "Because of you, Zion shall be plowed as a field." Why did Rabbi Akiva choose this particular prophecy as his consolation? Many verses were uttered describing the devastation of the Temple Mount if the Jews would not mend their ways. The words of our Sages are very precise. Let us study these ostensibly ominous words carefully.

"Zion shall be plowed as a field" is obviously a metaphor. There was no plowing activity on the Temple site, neither with oxen nor with machinery after the destruction of the Holy Temple. But Rabbi Akiva understood just what the prophet was saying.

Rabbi Akiva "had a field day" with the field metaphor. His deeper understanding of the plowing process broke new ground on how we could view the worst possible catastrophe to befall our people.

As we ride through the countryside we sometimes pass vast, clean stretches of rich-brown, tilled sod, pregnant with promise. Further along, we may pass fields with organized rows of golden stalks, ready for harvest. A city child might think that these are two separate, unrelated scenes. But no, the very same field that was plowed gives forth the produce. Like the plowed field, the destruction and subsequent rebuilding of our Holy Temple are not two separate, unrelated events, the first one bad, the second one good. They are *one integrated event.*

Rabbi Akiva's laughter was based on a comprehensive grasp of the process. He was able to visualize the full course of a plowed field and see the future arrayed before him in vivid glory, with all of its unfolding stages. Rabbi Akiva had an enhanced concept of the future that impacted the way he saw the present. It completely overrode the desecration that stared him in the face. As he saw it, the good had already started. Rabbi Akiva was the ultimate forward-thinker.

When we bring the future good to the current time we can be happy now. It's a powerful way to live.

> Rabbi Akiva began learning Torah at the age of forty. He would not have achieved his glory if he had projected his future based on his current status. He was able to see his future achievement and it empowered him in the present.

"You have consoled us, Akiva, you have consoled us." The Sages said it twice because they were doubly consoled. The first time, for reminding them about the extra glory and honor we'll reap in the future. The second time, for pointing out that when the negative event is worse, there is greater blessing in it, and *the positive elements and occasion for joy already exist in the present time.*[259]

> **Why did only Rabbi Akiva laugh – why did the Sages not laugh?** They, too, were great and holy individuals. The difference between them was their ancestry. Rabbi Akiva descended from converts. He lacked the distinguished ancestry of "our forefathers" but his deficiency turned into an asset: He identified directly with G-d as his Father. This helped him align more closely to the Divine way of seeing things. From the G-dly perspective the past, future and present are all equal and as accessible as the present moment, and Rabbi Akiva was able to tap into that sweeping view of time. Rabbi Akiva's compromised lineage turned into a plus and we are the beneficiaries.
>
> Joy-genius strategy: With a discerning eye we can detect redeeming positives in any situation.

The future knowledge entirely changes the current experience! Knowing we will own joy in the future alleviates the current misery and casts a brighter light on our day. We can become joyous now! No need to wait.

The darker the place we're in, the more useful it is to be aware that there are blessings in the present misfortunes. Reb Sholom Mordechai recalled the empowering image of the field of Zion as he sat in the dark shadows of his prison walls. He was, at all times, infused with the knowledge and power of the future light. The incisive insight of the Lubavitcher Rebbe into the laughter of Rabbi Akiva kept the fires of hope and joy lit for him through eight years of incarceration. These are his words, written to us (my husband was his teacher) in an email at the midpoint of those endless days:

> "To understand – and cope with – the present we need to look into the future! Awareness of the great possibilities of the future allows us to work in the present in a way that we already have those great possibilities. …This gives me the strength to be b'simcha in a place called Prison…"

Rejoicing now as part of the anticipated good future is going to stand in our credit. Here's an advance zoom-in of us at the time "when G-d will return the exiles of Zion," as rendered by King David:

The non-Jewish nations will wonder why G-d did such great things for us. We will tell them, it's because **"we were joyful."**[260]

Furthermore, G-d is doing these great things for us in the merit of the joy we exhibited **even before the Redemption came**.[261]

We were joyful – because we visualized the future.

We are joyful – because in the present we see the future positive.

We are joyful – because in the darkness we see the future light.

Epilogue

Face Forward

A tightrope walker was asked, "What is the key to your success?" He said, "I always look straight ahead – *never* down. I cannot lose focus for a moment."

When my son was learning to ride a two-wheeler, he kept looking nervously at the wheel. We urged him on, "Don't look at the wheel! Just look in the direction you want to go." As soon as he did so, he sailed forward smoothly! Driving instructors have the same advice, "Look further down the road. It helps you stay on track."

Our forward focus keeps us on track. Throughout history we have been blessed with unique individuals who kept the vision.

> *A little boy wanted an apple, but his father did not allow him to have it. The clever little boy made the blessing for apples and his father handed him the fruit as he did not want G-d's name to have been uttered in vain. The little boy grew up to be a famous Rebbe.*[262]

If you want something, do something. Keep the vision. Don't take no for an answer, and don't yield to failure.

> *Leah was engaged to be married to a young man whose name is well known today to people far beyond Jerusalem, where he lived.*[263] *One day, Leah's choson asked to see her. He told her*

that he was breaking off the engagement. "Why?" she asked, stunned at this bolt out of the blue. He explained that it was breaking his heart to see his widowed mother's distress over his two unmarried older siblings who should rightfully be getting married before him. Leah asked him, "Why go backwards? Why not storm the heavens so that they, too, will get married?" Sure enough, one of his sibling's weddings preceded their own, and the other sibling got engaged shortly before their wedding. Leah didn't take no for an answer; not only did she remain loyal to the vision of her upcoming marriage, she also created a schema of more good fortune. A vision, once conceived, can become a reality.

The Redemption, too, is a marriage of our Creator with his beloved nation.

The Chafetz Chaim[264] envisioned that marriage at all times. He was a forward-thinker. He urged people to learn the laws of the sacrifices (Kodshim).[265] If we believe the Geulah is coming – shouldn't we be preparing in advance?

We express our desire to rebuild the Mikdash (Holy Temple) by steeping ourselves in it.

- When we study the details of its construction it is as if we are rebuilding it.[266]
- When we recite the chapters about the sacrifices in our daily prayers it is regarded as if we actually bring up a sacrifice.[267]

What we *can* do now – look forward to it with joy.

"Those who are great, see the redemption amidst the gloom and turn their vision into a reality," and it makes them "laugh with joy,"[268] writes Rabbi Mordechai Kamenetzky.

Vision has been described as "a picture of the future that produces passion." We are forward-looking even when we can't see up ahead. Our simcha beaming through the darkness proclaims we are keeping the vision.

There may be challenges but there's joy in the knowing that G-d is here with us, directing it all. Just ahead of us waits a finished home. We can all become joy-geniuses, simply by facing forward.

Glossary

achdus: unity

afikomen: the "dessert," a piece of matza which is set aside earlier at the seder.

ahavas yisroel: love of a fellow Jew

avoda: service; effort and toil; used to describe ongoing efforts to grow and deepen our connection with G-d, most commonly through prayer, but also through joy, faith and trust.

baal teshuva: returnee to Judaism (by becoming a practicing Jew)

balabuste: housewife, homemaker

Beis Hamikdash: the Holy Temple

bitachon: trust in G-d.

bli gvul: unlimited, unbounded.

chassid: follower of a Rebbe; an adherent of Chassidism.

Chava: Eve

chometz: leavened bread, though any wheat product (except matzah that was made expressly for Passover, under close supervision) is classified as chometz

choson: groom

Chumash (Chumashim, plural): One or more of the five books of Moses

chupah: marriage ceremony

daven: pray

emunah: faith

erev Shabbos: the hours preceding Shabbos; generally all of Friday is considered to be erev Shabbos.

eved, or adjective: *oved*: Servant, one who serves.

frum: committed to observance of Jewish religious laws

galus: diaspora

Gemara: Talmud

Geulah: redemption

gvul: limited; also, boundary or border.

halacha: Jewish law

holelus: frivolity. Happiness devoid of meaning or purpose

kallah: bride

mashkeh: alcoholic drinks

minyan: a quorum of ten men required for public worship.

mitzvah: Divine commandment

Moshiach: the ultimate Redeemer

nachas: when children bring us true pride

neshama: soul

Purim: a festival which takes place exactly a month before Passover, celebrating salvation from Haman's plot to annihilate the Jews.

Rabbanim: Rabbis that are trained in the intricacies of halacha.

sefer, *seforim*: book(s) in Hebrew. When used in a language other than Hebrew, it usually refers to holy books.

Shechina: the Divine Presence

sheimos: holy writings are respectfully disposed of by burial in the ground.

shul: synagogue

simcha: joy; meaningful happiness

simcha shel mitzvah: joy derived from doing a mitzvah.

Sheva brochos: Seven blessings following the chupah and wedding feast. Also during the seven days of rejoicing following the wedding.

Sukkos: Tabernacles, a week-long festival, five days after Yom Kippur, to celebrate the ingathering of harvest, and commemorate G-d's miraculous "clouds of glory" which protected the Jewish people in the desert. We dwell in temporary foliage-covered huts and take Four Species which include the *esrog* and *lulav*.

Tanya: classic text of Chabad philosophy, authored by the Alter Rebbe

Tehillim: Psalms

tefila: prayer
tefillin: phylacteries
tzedaka: charity
tzores: troubles
yeshiva: school for Torah studies
Yiddishkeit: Judaism
Yomtov: Jewish festivals, lit. good days
vort: bon mot

Notes

1. The Lubavitcher Rebbe's talk on 14 Elul, published in Sefer Hasichos 5748 (1988), p. 628-632.
2. The Wave-Duality Theory states that it is possible for matter to act either as a wave or a particle. Its final state is undetermined until it is observed. Observership is a term used in relation to this: Human observers are necessary for physical phenomena to exist in any particular form. (More on this in Chapter 7.)
3. Yirmiyahu 30:17.
4. See footnote #1.
5. As seen in Olam, Jewish Press 11/21, Parsha Perspectives, courtesy of Modzitz.org.
6. See Hayom yom 18 Tammuz. Gadlus means 'greatness' and 'mochin' refers to the brain.
7. As seen in Olam Dec. 23, 2016. Article by Ann Novick.
8. Divrei HaYamim 16:27.
9. *Taanug tmidi aino taanug.*
10. https://www.psychologytoday.com/blog/imperfect-spirituality/201008/get-busy-be-happy
11. Sefer Maamarim 5657 (also known as Hemshech Samach T'samach), page 233. The Rebbe Rashab lists our greatest historic highlights, events that gave G-d the greatest pleasure, and points out their deficits: G-d derived great pleasure from our sacrifices, but the sacrificer – the person, was incomplete due to the sin of the *eitz hadaas*, Tree of Knowledge; the exodus from Egypt was not the final and complete redemption; the giving of the Torah at Mount Sinai was the betrothal, but will only be consummated at the final Geulah.
12. Initially promised to Avraham Avinu in Breishis 15:19. See Rambam Laws of Murderers 8:4.
13. Devarim 19: 8-9: When G-d will expand your borders as He promised your forefathers, you shall add three cities... See Likutei Sichos vol. 18, p. 280.
14. Yeshayahu 51:40.
15. See Sefer Hasichos parshas Lech Lecho, 5752, vol. 1, pp. 74-76.
16. Sefer Hasichos 5752, vol. 1, pp. 75-76.
17. The Lubavitcher Rebbe's talk on Shabbos parshas Lech Lecha, published in Sefer Hasichos 5741 (1980), p. 392.
18. The Lubavitcher Rebbe's talk on 15 Shvat, published in Sichos Kodesh 5739 vol. 2, p. 146.
19. As seen in *Say it with a Story* by Susha Alperowitz, p. 38.
20. Sheloh, Shabbos 97b.
21. Zohar1 117a. From Gutnick Chumash on Breishis 7:11.
22. Isaiah 11:9.

23. Mechilta on Shmos 20:7.

24. Beitzah 16a.

25. Sefer HaChhinuch, parshas Bo, mitzvah 16. Also Mesilas Yesharim, Shaar HaTaharah, end.

26. Pe'ah 8:9.

27. Koheles Rabba 1, Shir Hashirim Rabba 1.

28. Kedushas Levi, Parshas Naso.

29. 1:24.

30. Yanky Tauber in The Removable Self, chabad.org.

31. There are several versions to this story. This version was reported by Rabbi Yerachmiel Tilles.

32. The Lubavitcher Rebbe's talk on Shabbos parshas Lech Lecha, published in Sefer Hasichos 5741 (1980), p. 392.

33. Shir Hashirim Raba 1:4.

34. Igros Kodesh, Letters of the Lubavitcher Rebbe, vol. 16, p. 231.

35. Rabbi Heschel Greenberg. 'Which is Superior – the Human or the Animal?" Beis Moshiach 5 Iyar 5775 #970.

36. Yoma 75a.

37. Science can be useful on three levels. (1) It can be an illustration for Torah concepts. For example, video technology, as an example, makes "the eye that sees" more tangible. (2) Scientific technology can be harnessed for global transmission of the knowledge of G-d, evoking the Rambam's description of the future when the entire world will be filled with the knowledge of G-d. (3) The sciences and all secular concepts are a reflection and manifestation of G-d; showing how the multitude of creations are not a contradiction to the absolute unity of G-d, but in fact, actually reflect His unity.

38. The Role of the Observer in Halachah and Quantum Physics by Avi Rabinowitz and Herman Branover, from the book Fusion: Absolute Standards in a World of Relativity by Arnie Gotfryd and Herman Branover (1990) pp 92-95.

39. The Lubavitcher Rebbe's talk, 28 Sivan, published in Sefer Hasichos 5751 (1991) vol. 2, p. 646.

40. Highlights of Achdus HaB'ria (The Unity of Creation) by Ofer Gottlieb as featured in Beis Moshiach 20 Tammuz 5777, p. 22.

41. These two paragraphs were excerpted from Scientific Thought in Messianic Times: Wisdom from Above – Wisdom from Below by Prof. Shimon Silman, 2010, p. 484-495.

42. Quoted from Moshiach and Science by Dr. Aryeh Gotfyd PhD Beis Moshiach #769, 17 Teves 5771, p. 17.

43. He was the third Rebbe in a dynasty of rabbinic leaders based in Parisov, Poland in 5665. He passed away in 5672.

44. As seen in Sichat Hashavua, Vaera, 5777.

45. As heard from Dov Greenberg on Ten Talks featured by JLI National Retreat.

46. States of Matter, States of Mind by Allan F.M. Barton, p. 88.

47. Rambam, Laws of the Kings 11:1.

48. Chullin, end of p. 7b. A man does not even bruise a finger that was not decreed from Above.

49. As per a verse in Devarim 8:2. Discussed in Tanya Igeres Hakodesh, Epistle 11, English translation from Lessons in Tanya, vol. IV, p. 197.

50. Igros Kodesh of the Lubavitcher Rebbe, Vol 27, p.89.

51. Mishlei 16:15.

52. Igeres Hakodesh, Epistle 11, as translated in Lessons in Tanya vol. IV, p. 197.

53. Great, holy Tanna (Mishnaic sage) who hid in a cave for 13 years due to speaking out

against Roman tyranny.

54. 33rd day from bringing the *omer* barley offering on the second day of Passover.

55. Rabbi Isaac Halevi Luria, the Ari Hakodosh 5294-5332 (1534-1572).

56. As did the codifiers Rambam as well as the Ramah who finished his Code of Law with the advice that we should serve G-d with joy always.

57. Kesser Shem Tov, appendix 169.

58. Tzava'as Harivash sec. 110.

59. Rabbi Schneur Zalman of Liadi, founder and first Rebbe of Chabad, 1745-1812 (5505-5573).

60. Delivered by the Rebbe Rashab in honor of the marriage of his only son (eventually his successor) in 5657 (1897).

61. Lifehacker.com

62. Talmud Bavli, Taanis 22a.

63. BioHealth Diagnostics. BioHealthLab.com

64. Divrei Hayomim 16:27.

65. Igeres Hakodesh, Igeres,ch.11, as elucidated in Lessons in Tanya vol. 4, p. 194.

66. Shmos 2:6.

67. Rabbi Mordechai Chaim of Slonim. Seen in Living Torah, parshas Shmos.

68. The words are *melech poretz geder*.

69. P. Zarchi, Preparing for the Best, Beis Moshiach Issue #1032, 1 Menachem Av, 5776.

70. Likutei Sichos vol. 36, pp. 1-6. Chovos Halevovos Shaar Habitachon ch. 2, 7th cause.

71. Last chapter of Mishlei 31:25.

72. Tzvas'as Harivash 132.

73. A practice that is cherished because we are eager to occupy ourselves with mitzvahs after being cleansed of our sins.

74. Sippurei Rav Zevin on the Torah p.115.

75. Rabbi Dov Ber Shneuri, son of Rabbi Shneur Zalman of Liadi: 1773-1827.

76. See Sippurim Nora'im p. 61; R'shimas Dvarim I:94. Based on translations by Rabbis Yerachmiel Tilles, E. Lesches and Yehuda Shurpin.

77. Bava Metsia 59a.

78. The Baal Shem Tov; Rabbi Moshe Leib of Sasov in Likutei Ramal parshas Vayeitzei; the Yid haKadosh Rabbi Yaakov Yitzchak of Pshischa in Tiferes Hayehudi no. 107 p. 46.

79. From a meeting of the Tzemach Tzedek with Jewish soldiers in Petersberg. See Sand and Water for more. From MeaningfulLife. Com, available on Chabad.org. [http://www.chabad.org/library/article_cdo/aid/166403/jewish/Sand-and-Water.htm.]

80. Story appears in Okay to Laugh, p. 119.

81. The maamer "M'Ragla B'Puma D'Rabba, 17 Kislev 5746 (1986).

82. This level of joy is discussed in Tanya, ch. 33.

83. Brickman et al, (1978) "Lottery Winners and Accident Victims: Is Happiness Relative?" Journal of Personality and Social Psychology 36:8 (917-927).

84. http://www.ncbi.nlm.nih.gov/pubmed/690806.

85. Tzvi Freeman, Happiness is Not Being There. Chabad.org.

86. Divrei Hayomim 16:27.

87. The Lubavitcher Rebbe's talk on 15 Shvat, published in Sichos Kodesh 5739 vol. 2, p. 146.

88. The Lubavitcher Rebbe's talk on Shabbos parshas Lech Lecha, published in Sefer Hasichos 5741 (1980), p. 392.

89. The Lubavitcher Rebbe's talk on Shabbos Mevorchim Chodesh Kislev, published in Hisvaaduyos 5746 vol. 1, pp. 603-604.

90. Chabakuk 2:11.

91. Sukkah 51b.

92. The Ritual of the Drawing the Water. See Tiers of Joy for more.

93. Breishis 29:1.

94. Ethics of our Fathers 2:8.

95. 2:11.

96. An educator and mentor legendary for his joy in the most trying situations.

97. *Ad d'lo yada* means drinking until the mind is too foggy to add up the numerical values of the letters "blessed is Mordechai" and "cursed is Haman." See Magen Avraham in Shulchan Aruch Orach Chaim siman 695.

98. A talk by the Lubavitcher Rebbe Shabbos parshas Teruma 5752 (1992).

99. Hilchos Megila ch. 2:17.

100. Seen in Simcha u'bitachon la"Hashem, p. 7, Heichal Menachem. See also Toras Menachem vol. 11, p. 163.

101. Brochos 30b.

102. Ibid. We daven only with a feeling of gravity.

103. 29:19.

104. Ethics of our Fathers 4:1.

105. The darker the situation, the more simcha the Rebbe would demand of himself and his followers. A typical theme in our search for joy is to find it in the concealment. For example, when rearranged, the letters of *machala*, illness, also form the word *machol*, dance. The word *tzara*, constriction, also forms *tzohar*, light.

106. His message was via live satellite hookup to Acheinu's Lakewood *asifa*, 2010.

107. The writer's identity could not be established.

108. Sukka 51b.

109. Likutei Sichos vol. 26, p. 211.

110. Many communities organize joyous nightly dancing indoors or outdoors during Sukkos. They are highly energizing, and make us wish even more ardently that we could soon be privy to the real thing.

111. Questions and Answers about Torah study in Yemos Ha'Moshiach. Issue #1024.

112. Rabbi Avrohom Yeshaya Karelitz 1878-1953.

113. Jewish News by Tzvi Cohen. Highlights of a Chinuch convention in Beitar, Israel. Ami Magazine April 22, 2015.

114. There was another, larger, aperture on the altar for the *nisuch* ha'yayin (wine-libations) all year. Wine flows more slowly, and the size of each aperture was custom-designed to allow both libations to take up the same amount of time.

115. Likutei Sichos 2, p. 426.

116. Likutei Sichos 2, p. 428.

117. Kidushin 30b.

118. Mishlei (Proverbs) 12:8.

119. From Maamar Samach Tsamach 5741, elucidated by Rabbi Yossi Paltiel. Audios available at insidechassidus.org.

120. Shmuel I, ch. 15.

121. Tanya ch. 21 p. 133.

122. The Lubavitcher Rebbe to a group of students who came to explore the Chassidic way of life.

123. Chassidisher Derher #33 Tammuz 5775, page 40.

124. The full discussion can be read in *Scientific Thought in Messianic Times: Wisdom from Above*

– *Wisdom from Below* by Prof. Shimon Silman, 2010, p. 490-491.

125. Levit. 25:20-21. Every 50 years the fields lay fallow for two consecutive years. The story of an orange orchard's tripled growth is related in *Stories my Grandfather Told Me* by Libby Lazewnik, Mesora Publications.
126. Kerenhashviis.com.
127. http://www.chabad.org/library/article_cdo/aid/140658/jewish/An-Innkeeper-from-Vohlyn.htm.
128. Sichat Hashavua #1546.
129. Out of the box – even things that are somewhat silly. Likutei Maharan 2:24.
130. Igros Kodesh, vol.16, letter 6026.
131. Likutei sichos vol 2 p. 428.
132. Based on Anatomy of Joy by Rabbi Heschel Greenberg, Beis Moshiach #985, 29 Av 5775.
133. Adapted from Geula #345.
134. Tehillim 149:2 and morning prayers. See Tanya, end of ch. 33.
135. Sefer HaMaamarim 5657 p. 262-264. The Samach T'samach maamar was also published separately. See p. 86-88 in that shorter edition.
136. http://www.chabad.org/parshah/article_cdo/aid/1241533/jewish/The-Rhyme-of-No-Reason.htm.
137. Likutei Sichos vol 26, p. 218.
138. When the tzaddik Rav Gershon of Kitov was in Eretz Yisroel, his brother-in-law, the Baal Shem Tov, sent him a wondrous letter describing what he experienced when his soul ascended to Heaven on that Rosh Hashana. Delivery of the letter was entrusted to the loyal disciple, Rav Yaakov Yosef of Polnoye, who also sought to make his way to Eretz Yisroel, to visit the holy city of Yerushalayim, but due to obstacles the trip was canceled and the letter remained with him. After the passing of both the Baal Shem Tov and Rav Gershon Kitover, Rav Yaakov Yosef regretted that he had never delivered the letter and decided that for the benefit of the public the contents should be published. Source: Kesser Shev Tov. The letter was first published in 1781 as an appendix to Ben Porat Yosef (p. 128a) by Rabbi Yaakov Yosef of Polnoye.
139. From A Halacha a Day, by Rabbi Horav Yosef Yeshaya Braun. See halacha2go.com.
140. Sheloh, Shabbos 97b.
141. See Otzar Hayirah (Breslover teachings compiled by Rabbi Nachman of Tcherin) on Shabbos 119.
142. From an interview of Hadar Mizrachi, a simcha pro in Israel. As seen in Ateret Chaya Adar I, 2011.
143. Rebbe Rayatz #1056, Igros kodesh vol. 4 p. 404. Credit for translation to Sichos in English, entry of Hayom Yom 23 Menachem Av. Available at sie.org.
144. Passover, Shavuos and Sukkos. Devarim 16:14. As it says: "Celebrate your (three Divinely ordained) festivals with gladness."
145. Shulchan Aruch, Orach Chaim 529:2. "...in order to increase the vitality (*chayus*) of the family on a material level."
146. Pesachim 109a. "There is no simcha without meat." After we were exiled and sacrifices ceased, we continued to express the spiritual festival with joy by the physical drinking of wine.
147. This is according to the opinion of the Alter Rebbe, discussed in Likutei Sichos vol. 33, p. 62ff. As seen in Halachic Guide, Laws and Customs of Pesach 5777, Horav Y.Y. Braun, p. 66-67.
148. The Lubavitcher Rebbe's talk on 14 Elul, published in Sefer Hasichos 5748 (1988), p. 628-

632.

149. "You will be gathered one by one..." Yeshayahu 27:12.

150. Hayom Yom, 20 Menachem Av.

151. Shulchan Aruch Harav Hilchos Rosh Hashana *siman* 582:3 and *siman* 114:10.

152. 1:6.

153. Koheles 2:14.

154. Maaseh Avosai in Migdal Oz Ois 136, as seen in Lma'an Yisme'u, parshas Truma.

155. Corrie ten Boom. A Dutch gentile who helped many Jews escape the Nazi Holocaust.

156. Paraphrased from quote by Mignon McLaughlin.

157. Rashi and Shelah, vol. 3-4, parshas Beshalach, p. 38.

158. Toras Menachem vol. 36, p. 221. As seen in Lma'an Yishme'u parshas Tetzaveh.

159. William Arthur Ward.

160. *Al tiftach peh la'Satan.* Literally, don't open the mouth of the Satan. Kesuvos 8b.

161. Rabbi Shneur Zalman of Liadi, as seen in Lma'an Yishme'u parshas Tetzaveh.

162. Tohu and Tikkun: Kabbalistic terms which mean "chaos" and "rectification." The following articles were helpful in formulating the explanation: "18 Joyous Teachings of the Baal Shem Tov" and "Tikkun Olam: a Brief History" both by Tzvi Freeman, Chabad.org.

163. Sara Yoheved Rigler Ami-Living May 6, 2015.

164. Tehillim 22:2.

165. Rabbi Gershon Schusterman, Consider This, Nshei Chabad Newsletter Dec 2016.

166. Psalms 120-134.

167. From a talk by the Lubavitcher Rebbe, 27 Iyar 5744. As heard on an audio clip from My-Maor.org

168. Rosally Saltsman, "Why is G-d teasing me?" The Scroll. Feb 20, 2015.

169. As the Alter Rebbe writes in the conclusion of his celebrated ch. 11 in Igeres Hakodesh: "By this faith the imagined evil is truly absorbed and sublimated in the concealed Supreme Good, so that the good becomes palpably revealed." Translation is from Lessons in Tanya vol. 4, p. 199.

170. Author of *Rethinking Your Work: Getting to the Heart of What Matters.*

171. Beis.Moshiach Issue #982, Menachem Zeigelbaum 8 Av 5775.

172. Full discussion in Likutei sichos vol. 34, pp. 217-224. Rashi's refers to an active inflation of love with his seemingly redundant words *"nes'a'o libo"* – his heart "lifted" him to shore up the courage to carry out this drastic act. See last verse in Chumash Devarim.

173. The phrase seems to have been used by the Chida, possibly a translation from an Arabic expression. According to a letter of the Lubavitcher Rebbe, 10 Tammuz, 5712 (1952), he has not been able to trace this expression to any Rabbinic source. Nevertheless, he would offer it to assuage people's angst in appropriate circumstances.

174. Shabbos 88a.

175. Coercion at its finest, you say? It is called so because the truth was so in their face that it deprived them of true free choice. In that sense it was akin to coercion.

176. Megillas Esther 9:27. Megillah 7a.

177. The precise quote is, "There were only two things certain in life: death and taxes."

178. Idolatry, forbidden relations and murder.

179. Psalms 100:2.

180. Likutei Maharan part 2, Torah 24.

181. According to Rashi the Jews are liable for galus because they didn't perform the mitzvahs while they enjoyed material abundance. Therefore, the abundance will, justly, be taken away from them. According to the Rambam, they did the mitzvahs. Their liability was only in the lack of

joy which should accompany the mitzvahs. The Rambam's emphasis is on "serving" G-d, and without simcha the service is deficient. The simcha that accompanies a mitzvah makes it a true service.

182. Maimonides, 1135 or 1138 – 1204.
183. Rambam Mishneh Torah – end of the Laws on the Festival of Sukkos. Loose translation: "The joy that a person should experience in doing a mitzvah and in his love for G-d Who commanded them, is a great service…"
184. Toras Menachem vol. 19 p. 93. Also in a collection called Simcha uBitachon B'Hashem p.,20, published by Heichal Menachem.
185. Discussed in Tanya ch. 31; Sefer Hamaamarim 5657 p. 263.
186. Igros kodesh Miteler Rebbe, p. 265, as seen in Lman'an Yisme'u parshas Tetzaveh #83. The Miteler Rebbe, Rabbi Dov Ber Shneuri (1773-1827) noted to his chassidim that this has been tried and proven.
187. This idea is originally attributed to the Baal Shemtov and has been repeated in the names of other Rabbis as well. There are several variations.
188. Likutei Maharan part 2, Torah 24.
189. Shabbos 30b.
190. Quoting Rabbi Shais Taub from a lecture entitled "The Tanya's Guide to Achieving Happiness." Video of lecture available at Torahcafe.com. "Americans have rights to many things, including happiness. For a Torah Jew, happiness is not a right, it's an obligation."
191. The Lubavitcher Rebbe's talk on 14 Elul, published in Sefer Hasichos 5748 (1988), pp. 628-632.
192. Likutei Maharan part 2, Torah 24.
193. *Yeshaya* 25:12.
194. 100:2 and 126:2.
195. Tehillim 126:2-3.
196. Sefer Toras Shimon on the Torah, Festivals and Tehillim by Rabbi Shimon of Yarislav (Jaroslaw) 1758-1849. Brought also in Dvar yom B'Yomo 16 Tishrei and Toras Menachem vol.15, p. 51.
197. Mishneh Torah, end of the Laws on the Festival of Sukkos. Hilchos Lulav ch. 8, 15.
198. pp. 53-54.
199. Rabbanit Yemima Mizrachi in "Joy is Holy," Ami-Living, 11 Tishrei 5777.
200. Shmuel II, 6:16.
201. Laws of Personal Development, Hilchos De'os ch. 1:4.
202. Ch. 2 Halacha 7. Translation by Rabbi Eliyahu Touger available as a book Mishneh Torah. Also available on chabad.org.
203. Orach Chayim 697:1.
204. Proverbs 15:15.
205. The Lubavitcher Rebbe's talk on Shabbos parshas Lech Lecha, published in Sefer Hasichos 5741 (1980), p. 392.
206. Ch. 4 of Hilchos Da'os in the Rambam's Code of Law offers recommendations for healthy living.
207. Mishlei (Proverbs 3:6).
208. Ethics of the Fathers 2:13.
209. Adapted by Moshe Wisnefsky, http://www.chabad.org/dailystudy/dailywisdom_cdo/aid/2955541/jewish/Thursday-Tasting-Rewards.htm.
210. Igeres haKodesh 11th letter. Translation from Lessons in Tanya Vol. IV, p. 197.
211. Mishlei (Proverbs) 12:25.

212. Based on alternate forms of the root verb.
213. Sanhedrin 100b. See also Hayom Yom, entry of 25 Sivan. In (1) the word is *yasichenah*, spelled with the letter Samech. In (2) it is *yasichenah* spelled with the letter Sin.
214. "Happy for no reason" can constitute "pure joy" – but that is being joyous with G-d – there is a reason.
215. *Pikudei Hashem mesamchei lev.* Tehillim 19:9.
216. Tanya, Igeres haKodesh 11th letter. Translation from Lessons in Tanya vol. IV, p. 194-5.
217. My Encounter with the Rebbe, by Jem Media. "The Taskforce." Available at myencounter-blog.com.
218. Brochos 31a.
219. The content in these next few paragraphs is from the Lubavitcher Rebbe's talk on Shabbos Mevorchim Chodesh Kislev, published in Hisvaaduyos 5746 vol. 1, pp. 603-604.
220. Keter Shem Tov, appendix 169.
221. Discussed in ch. 26.
222. Tanya ch. 34; Zohar II, 225a; III, 75a.
223. Tanya, ch. 31, p. 40.
224. The Lubavitcher Rebbe's talk on 14 Elul, published in Sefer Hasichos 5748 (1988), pp. 628-632.
225. c. 1215 – 2 May 1293, author of the tosafos on Rashi's commentary on the Talmud.
226. http://beismoshiachmagazine.org/articles/sending-the-right-message-to-our-children.html.
227. Avos 4:2.
228. This is based on an expression in Midrash, *"osi heim lokchim"* – they are taking Me, as it were.
229. The Imrei Emes (1865 –1948). The question and answer is printed in Michtavei Torah, a collection of his letters.
230. Avos 4:17.
231. See Lessons in Tanya vol. II, ch. 39, p. 544. Also vol. I, ch. 4, p. 86.
232. Devarim 28:47. In Hebrew, *meirov kol.* The *mem* is a prefix to the word *rov* (abundance) and can be translated either as "from a(n)," as in our earlier discussion, or as *more and greater than* the joy you experienced when you had an abundance of everything.
233. Quoted in Shelah, Asarah Maamarot, Maamar 3:4.
234. Stemming from an aspect of G-dliness called *gvul* (limited).
235. Taanis 29a.
236. The powerful mazel of our great leader's birthday made this month propitious for the miracle of Purim.
237. Known as the baal Ahavas Yisroel.
238. Seen in Sichat Hashavua #1494 6 Elul 5775.
239. From Maamar Samach Tsamach 5657.
240. Koheles 7:20.
241. *Simcha mamtik dinim. Ein hadinim nimtakin ela b'shorshon.*
242. Tzava'as Harivash 132; *Trembling with Joy,* by Tzvi Freeman, also available at Chabad.org as 18 Joyous Teachings of the Baal Shem Tov.
243. From a talk by the Lubavitcher Rebbe, published in Sefer Hasichos 5748 (1988), p. 628-632.
244. As described in Zohar 1:122b.
245. Breishis 3:6.
246. Insidechassidus.org parshas Chayei Sarah. Also at http://www.kabbalaonline.org/kab-

balah/article_cdo/aid/379339/jewish/The-Complete-Joy-of-Sarah.htm. There are several variations of this theme. See also Sefer Maamorim Melukat II, p. 145-152.

247. Reprinted with permission from Chassidic Light in the Soviet Darkness, by Rabbi Yechezkel Brod, pp. 44-45 and 25-26.

248. Nonna was the managing director of the Russian Forwards as well as the Russian Metro Magazine at the time this was written. Excerpted from L'Chaim #1067, April '09 Slice of Life feature.

249. Bicky has since passed on, but she left a model for life down below.

250. Michael Pritchard.

251. As described by Sarah Pachter in the Jewish Press, March 3, 2017.

252. The source of this chronicle is unknown.

253. He lived from 1906-1995.

254. Many reasons to be happy, by Rabbi Chaim Levi Yitzchak Ginsberg, Beis Moshiach #920 19 Adar 5754.

255. Yated Ne'eman, 1 Av 5776.

256. Micha 3:12.

257. Zachariah 8:4.

258. A fast day that falls the day after Rosh Hashana. It marks the assassination of the Gedalia ben Achikam, governor in the land of Israel after the destruction of the first Temple, effectively ending the prospects of Jewish settlement in the Holy Land until the return of the Babylonian exiles.

259. The exchange between Rabbi Akiva and the sages is related in Makot 24b. The analysis of its nuances is elucidated in Likutei Sichos vol 19 pp 67-79.

260. Tehillim 126:2-3.

261. Rabbi Shimon of Yarislav, a student of the Chozeh of Lublin, in Toras Shimon on Torah and Festivals, quoted in Dvar Yom b'Yomo 16 Tishrei.

262. He later grew up to become a well-known Rabbi in Poland but we do not have definitive information which Rebbe exactly, as related in Likutei Sichos v. 20, p. 384.

263. Rabbi Shalom Schwadron, known as the Maggid of Jerusalem.

264. Israel Meir (HaKohen) Kagan (1839 – 1933) a halachist and ethicist of great influence.

265. See intro to Likkutei Halachos.

266. Tanchuma 96:14. One who studies the laws of the Temple is as if he occupied himself with its construction.

267. Menachos 110. Brachos 26b. Vayikra 6:2, Baal Haturim.

268. In his column Streets of Life, Ami Magazine 6 Av 5776.

✂ ---

"We've done everything we can to bring Moshiach...

There's one thing we haven't tried yet, and now is the time to try it:

A specific kind of joy - pure joy. That will bring Moshiach.

Try it and you'll see!"

- NEW JOY

About the Author

Gitty Stolik writes on Jewish thought and lore for a variety of Jewish publications. Her articles are popular for exploring content-rich topics of timeless value in an engaging style.

She is also the editor of Our Vogue, a publication with insights on the values of modesty for women and girls (archives can be viewed at ourvogue.org). Her writings are used as informational resources around the world. This is her second book. Her first book *It's Okay to Laugh Seriously* has been translated into other languages.

When she's not writing about joy and other topics, Mrs. Stolik applies the magic of joy and positivity to the field of education, in particular to the learning- and language-disabled population. She is striving to add an M.S. (Mastery of Simchah) to her academic titles.

The author coaches individuals who want more joy in their lives, and guides singles through the dating process. She also speaks on a variety of inspirational topics – especially her favorite topic – simcha!

For more information, visit okaytolaughseriously.com.